A CHRISTMAS GIFT
FROM
VIETNAM

by Sandra R. Dalton

FOUR SISTERS PRESS, LLP

© 1996 by Sandra R. Dalton

First Edition
10 9 8 7 6 5 4 3 2 1

ISBN: 0-9652191-8-6
Library of Congress Catalog Card Number: 96-85155

Cover Artwork and Design by Kathleen Petersen.

F / C

Book Production and Project Management by
Tamarack Books, Inc., PO Box 190313, Boise, ID 83719
(1-800-962-6657).

Published by:
Four Sisters Press, LLP, PO Box 1924, Boise, ID 83701,
1 (800) 448-8207, (208) 384-5233, FAX (208) 388-8006.

Printed in the United States of America.

Dedicated to my mother who taught me that we're all the same in God's eyes; my husband, Allen, who was an equal partner in sponsoring our refugee family; and, my beautiful children, Jack, Annie, and Benjamin, who were willing to share their mother and home so we could give three very special people a new life.

A Word To My Readers

This book is based on a true story. Many of the names have been changed.

I want to thank the following people for their help in sponsoring our refugees: Loc and Mai Nguyen, SOAR, the many friends and family that contributed furniture, clothes, presents, and miscellaneous items. I also want to thank Karen Bertetto, my faithful assistant who kept my office running smoothly and has helped Tong many times over the years when I was unavailable, and my former boss, Jim Steele, for his support.

I also owe a huge debt of gratitude to the many people who helped me publish this book, specifically: Kathy Gaudry of Tamarack Books for her excellent management of this book project; Win Blevins, my editor; Kathy Petersen, my illustrator; and Gail Ward, my design editor. In addition, I want to thank Rose Burnham for her many helpful suggestions, and Helen Lojek, Bob Carroll, and Luanne Harrington for their input.

I would like to thank John Thornton and Kathleen Rockney for their legal advice, and Bruce Parker for his accounting advice. Also my current boss, Guy Williams, for his support of my book project.

My heartfelt thanks goes to my parents, Jerry and Jeannette Riedel, and Jack and Marian Dalton; my sisters, Debbie, Tami, and Cindy; my children, Jack, Annie, and Ben; and my niece and nephew, Christie and Zack for their patience and encouragement. Thanks also to the Reverend Charles Spiedel who taught me that the greatest sermon we preach is the life we live, and Father Ron Wekerle for his inspiration.

This book was written for Tong. The many long hours of writing, editing, rewriting, etc. were driven by my love and respect for Tong. It is my hope that anyone touched by this story will reach out and help someone in need, for it is truly in giving that we receive.

Finally, my book would never have been completed without the many hours of reading, editing, and typing by my best friend and husband, Allen. Thank you, Sweetheart. Now that this is completed, I promise I won't wake you up in the middle of the night anymore.

DAY 1: *A Beginning*

I remember the day Tong and the woman we thought was his mother and her son arrived at the Boise airport.

"Are you ready?" my husband Allen asked, taking a deep breath.

"Yes," I nodded my head slowly. "I'm ready. Are you?"

"We'll find out," he replied with an apprehensive look.

We walked into the airport with two teddy bears, three coats, three pairs of shoes, two balloons, flowers, a banner, a video camera, a regular camera, and our three children: Jack, Annie, and Ben. As we made our way through the terminal to the gate, I looked anxiously for anyone that looked Vietnamese. It wasn't until we arrived at our gate that I saw Crista and Cindy from SOAR (Sponsors Organized to Assist Refugees) with two Vietnamese men. I sighed in relief.

"Here they come," smiled Crista. "Look at them. You came totally prepared!" she exclaimed.

"We're ready," I said excitedly.

"Allen and Sandy, have you met our Vietnamese interpreter, Loc Nguyen?" Crista asked.

"No, but we're very glad to meet you and relieved that you are here," I smiled as I shook his hand. "Let me show you the banner we made to welcome our refugees. See if you can read it." Allen and I rolled the banner out, showing the Vietnamese characters.

"Yes," he laughed. Loc's friend also smiled and chuckled as he said something to Loc in Vietnamese.

"What does it say?" quizzed my son Jack.

"It says, 'Welcome to America,'" Loc answered.

"Mom and I went to the Daos' house last night and they showed us how to write it," my daughter Annie said proudly.

"I had to write in all the symbols," Allen added. "I don't have a Vietnamese language word processor," he laughed.

"You did a very good job," Loc said enthusiastically.

I sat down and took a deep breath to calm my nerves.

"Are you excited?" Crista asked as she sat down by me.

"Excited, but nervous," I answered.

"What are you nervous about?"

"I'm worried about whether they got on the right plane in San Francisco. I'm worried about their health. I'm worried about their past and whether they'll be able to put it all behind them. I have no idea what they've been through," I rambled.

"Don't worry. You'll see—the Vietnamese are very strong people. They are survivors," she said reassuringly.

I tried to wait patiently for the plane, but was so excited to finally meet them that I fidgeted nervously. I silently prayed for them to arrive safely.

"Oh no, Mom, look what happened!" Annie cried, as the balloon she was holding slipped from her wrist and flew up to the twenty-five foot ceiling.

I looked up—it was way out of reach. Then the arrival of flight 501 from San Francisco was announced.

"It's O.K., honey," I said reassuringly. "They can share one."

"I'm sorry, Mom," Annie said, looking sadly at the balloon. "I didn't mean to."

"Way to go, Annie," Jack said sarcastically.

"It was an accident, Jack," I said.

"Mom, Jack's mean," Annie started to cry.

"It's no big deal," I scolded. "Now let's get ready, they're almost here."

I grabbed the flowers and the banner. "Can you take the movies?" I asked Allen nervously.

"Yes. I'll hold one end of the banner with my left hand and take movies with my right," he answered calmly.

"Annie and Jack, do you have the bears and the balloon?"

"Yes," they answered. "Except we should have two balloons," Jack said disgustedly.

"Mom!" complained Annie. "Tell Jack to quit it."

"Jack, please," I said anxiously.

All at once, after months of preparing it seemed we weren't ready. I looked around to make sure we had the shoes and coats. Ben, our two-year-old, squirmed in my arms as I tried to hold the banner. "Down!" he squealed.

"Here, let me hold Ben," offered Cindy.

All nine of us stood at the end of the ramp, peering anxiously at the passengers as they walked into the terminal. It seemed we waited for an eternity. Then a small dark-skinned woman with short black hair started slowly up the ramp. She was carrying a white plastic bag, with what looked like Vietnamese writing on it, and holding the hand of a little boy. An older boy peered over the woman's shoulder. Terror filled her eyes, as people crowded around the ramp. Crista walked over to her and said, "Over here. We're over here."

Khanh, the Vietnamese woman, glanced quickly at us and studied the banner. She stumbled toward us and collapsed at Crista's feet. She grabbed Crista's leg and began sobbing. She cried and moaned so wildly I thought she must be terribly sick.

"Is she O.K.?" I stuttered, tears rolling down my face.

"She's fine," answered Loc Nguyen.

Khanh continued to cry as I had never seen an adult cry before. She kept grabbing Crista and seemed to have lost all her strength. Like a thinly stuffed rag doll, she continually fell over, with Crista catching her each time. This seemed to go on for a long time, and I was getting seriously worried about her. Finally, Crista stood her up and hugged her saying, "You're O.K. now." Loc patted Khanh on the back and spoke reassuringly to her in Vietnamese. She looked desperate, but relieved.

Our focus turned to the boys, whose smiles radiated from their faces. Their wide brown eyes looked around in awe. Annie and Jack had given them the teddy bears and balloon. In contrast to their mother, the boys beamed with joy and excitement.

"Look at them!" Crista exclaimed. "They're beautiful."

We all laughed out of relief, brushing away our tears, overpowered by the range of emotions. The boys giggled and pointed to the teddy bear. The littlest boy danced his bear around.

"Look how big Tong is!" Crista cried, laying both of her hands on the older boy's shoulders. She glanced over to Jack and asked, "How old are you, Jack?"

"Nine," he replied with a proud smile.

"That's how old he is, but he's a little taller than you. He's much bigger than we thought he would be," Crista laughed.

I was in a daze. I should have been hugging each one of them, but I was so overwhelmed I just stared.

"How old are you?" Jack slowly asked the little boy.

He giggled and said something in Vietnamese very fast to his brother.

"He's five," Loc said smiling.

"What's his name?" Annie asked.

"Loc asked him in Vietnamese and the little boy replied, "Chuy."

"Chuy," everyone repeated—to the merriment of the little boy.

"What's your name?" Jack asked the older boy.

"Pham Tong," he replied proudly without any help from the interpreter.

"You're big!" Jack said admiringly.

Jack walked over to where the balloon had gone up and pointed to it. Tong and Chuy looked up and laughed. They conversed back and forth in Vietnamese, giggling.

We gathered all the coats and shoes and started down the concourse toward the baggage claim area. As we walked, I noticed Khanh's feet, sockless in thongs with thin cloth straps. She was wearing paper thin pants and a tropical top appropriate for a warm climate. Cindy had called me the previous night and told me to bring socks and shoes, but I couldn't imagine they would need socks, so I hadn't brought them. Cindy had been right. It was forty degrees outside and Khanh was practically barefoot. I glanced at the boys' feet—they both had brand new tennis shoes and socks on. Chuy was wearing a pair of little girl's overalls that were about three inches too short for him. He was quite small. Based on his size, he looked more like three, but the two missing teeth gave away his age. He looked around, mesmerized by all he saw. The huge smile never left his face, and every time anyone looked at him, he broke into laughter.

Tong was dressed like a typical American boy—a pair of jeans and a T-shirt. He also looked on in amazement, but his expression was more guarded. He watched Chuy like a mother bear watching her cub. Anytime he started to wander, Tong grabbed him and scolded him.

When we reached the baggage claim area, Loc asked Khanh if she had any bags. She indicated that she had one small bag, so we gathered around the baggage carousel and waited. I watched Khanh as she anxiously looked around. She seemed exhausted and sad, her face still wet and eyes red from crying, lack of sleep, or both. She was small, with thick black hair cropped just below the ears and dark, smooth skin. She was so thin I wondered if they had been well fed at the refugee camp.

Cindy had told us that food was often scarce in the Philippine refugee camp, and there were many reports of rape and murder. That was one of the primary reasons we had chosen to sponsor Khanh and her sons. I couldn't stop thinking of her bravery in fleeing Vietnam with two young boys. The refugee papers listed her father as an unknown American and her mother as deceased.

As we waited for Khanh's baggage, my mind wandered back to ten months earlier. My first real encounter with the plight of Vietnamese refugees came from reading the February 1991 issue of the *National Geographic*. A photograph still haunts me: a child, maybe five or six years old was peering through a fence, her hands crossed above her head, clutching the wire. Her eyes, black as midnight, were staring at each one of the millions of readers. The eyes were so hopeless and the hands so confined. How could so many readers ignore the plight of these children?

I thought of my own eight-year-old daughter, how sparkling and cheerful her eyes were, and the beautiful pictures she made with her hands—the rainbows and flowers; the teddy bears and balloons; the little square houses with windows and doors. No fences. How free her heart was.

These refugee families had risked their lives and given up any hope of continuing their family line, which extended back hundreds of generations. They felt the pangs of hunger and sickness, and watched loved ones die in agony. Locking these people in a detention center behind bars was incomprehensible. Some had been classified as political refugees and were waiting to resettle in a new country. They were waiting for a sponsor—someone who would agree to help them resettle. That's all the child in the picture needed to free those hands.

These realizations and the picture of the desperate child weighed on me for days, even weeks. I vowed never to read *National Geographic* again. The stories were heartbreaking and there was nothing I could do about all the injustice in the world. But the picture wouldn't go away. Three months later, I saw an advertisement in the local paper seeking refugee sponsors. There was a number for the local SOAR office. For several days I thought about the ad. Finally, in order to rid my mind of the desperate child in the photograph, I called the SOAR office and agreed to meet with Cindy. That was all it took. I couldn't go back.

The most difficult decision we had to make was which one of the hundreds of families from all over the world we would sponsor. Cindy warned us that Khanh and her family were by far the most difficult case because Khanh would be the only breadwinner and the boys were still too young to help. Other refugee families had several older members who could help support their families. Nobody wanted Khanh and her boys because of the absence of a father and because Khanh was unskilled. Cindy encouraged me to choose an easier family, but as I thought about the choices, I kept coming back to Khanh and her boys. She had to be brave to flee Vietnam with her sons. If I didn't pick her, she might spend the rest of her life in the Philippine refugee camp or worse.

"Here it finally comes," Allen interrupted my daydream.

Khanh's bag was the size of a large shoe bag, stuffed to the point of bursting. As Allen grabbed it off the carousel, I handed each of our refugees a coat. The boys seemed quite pleased, examining each other's coats until their mother scolded them. They immediately fell silent and put on their new coats.

When we walked outside, our breath formed clouds in the air. Khanh shivered and said, "Ooh, Ooh." The boys blew into the air and giggled. They pointed at each other's breath and laughed. They spoke quickly in Vietnamese, but again Khanh reprimanded them, and they immediately quit talking.

"Don't you wish our children minded as well?" I whispered to Allen.

When we got to our van, we loaded everything in and then pointed for Khanh and her boys to get in. Khanh looked frightened and stood frozen like a statue.

"Tell her she's going with Sandy and Allen," Crista told Loc.

Loc told her but she stood firm, her eyes beginning to fill with tears again.

"Sandy and Allen are your sponsors," Crista said gently to her. "You're going to live with them."

Loc repeated it in Vietnamese, but Khanh still looked at us distrustfully. Loc said something else and the boys climbed in the van. Khanh began to cry again, but slowly entered the van. I smiled at her, reassuring her that everything was all right. I didn't know what else to do. She must have thought Crista was her sponsor, I concluded. Crista was Hispanic with light brown skin and black hair. I had blond hair, blue eyes and light skin. I wondered if she was afraid of me. Allen and I helped her and the boys put on their seat belts, which made her even more uncomfortable. Things did not seem to be getting off to a good start.

"I'll come to your house," Loc suddenly announced. "I have to go home first and get my wife. Then I'll be up."

I sighed with relief. "Thank you," I said gratefully. Loc said something to Khanh before he left and then told us all goodbye. Khanh's face relaxed a little. As we drove out of the airport parking lot, Jack and Annie pointed out all the sights Americans are used to seeing.

"Truck, see truck," Annie said slowly, pointing to the many trucks that were passing under the freeway bridge.

Tong smiled and pointed to the truck saying, "truck."

"Gas station!" Jack said excitedly, pointing to the two gas stations on the corners of the street.

"Gas station," Tong repeated as he pointed.

Chuy just giggled, bouncing up and down pointing to all of the sights. I glanced around and looked at Khanh. She still seemed frightened as she gazed out the window with a blank stare.

"McDonalds!" Annie cried. "Look, McDonalds!"

"Do you know McDonalds?" Jack asked.

"Mac·donos," Tong repeated with a puzzled look on his face. He shook his head, "Mac donos don't know."

"You know, hamburgers and french fries," Annie said pausing, "and Coke," she laughed.

"Don't know," Tong said shaking his head.

"Boy, no McDonalds," Jack said disgustedly. "Can you imagine? Maybe they have some other kind of hamburger joints over there. I'm glad I don't live in Vietnam."

"River!" Annie exclaimed pointing to the trees lining the Boise River. Tong and Chuy looked curiously.

"River," Tong repeated, acknowledging that he

knew what they were pointing at. He said something in Vietnamese to Chuy, and Chuy laughed and pointed to the river.

"At least they have rivers in Vietnam," Jack said sarcastically.

"University," Annie said very adult-like as she showed Tong and Chuy all the buildings at Boise State University. "College," she repeated. "Do you know college?"

Tong looked confused again. He pointed and said, "Don't know."

"Basketball, football, you know college," Jack said, dumbfounded that they didn't know what a college was.

"Don't know," Tong said flustered.

"Boy, Mom, how are they supposed to be on my baseball team if they don't even know what college sports are?"

"Honey, give them some time. I'm sure he knows what a university is, he just doesn't understand the English word for it. We'll look up the Vietnamese word for college when we get home and show him. He'll understand then. Please don't use that disgusted tone of voice with him. He's been through a lot the last twenty-four hours."

Jack leaned back in his seat in dismay. "Don't they know any English?"

"I don't know, but we'll find out soon. If they don't, it's going to take a lot of patience to communicate."

We drove past the hospital and fire station, pointing them out along the way, but neither Khanh nor the boys seemed to understand what they were. As we started up the mountain to our house, Khanh became uneasy. The road leading to our house is steep and curvy, but not unusual for the western United States. I slowed down, hoping to allay her fears, but she grabbed onto the door handle and hung on tightly. There was snow about three hundred feet above us, and Tong jumped up, pointed and yelled "snow!" Chuy also pointed and laughed, "snow, snow." They giggled and talked back and forth in Vietnamese, obviously ecstatic to see snow. It occurred to me that they had probably never seen it before. We turned into our subdivision, and as we approached our driveway, Annie said slowly "our house," pointing to the large tudor-styled brick house. Khanh's eyebrows rose and her face seemed to frown in distrust again. Tong and Chuy pointed and carried on in Vietnamese, obviously amused by what probably appeared to be a mansion to them. I opened the garage door using the automatic opener, and pulled the van inside. Shortly after, Allen drove his car in. Khanh looked around totally confused, seeming to wonder how the garage doors opened.

We unloaded the van and showed Khanh and the boys the downstairs room which would serve as their home for the next three weeks. I demonstrated how the couch pulled out into a bed as Khanh watched carefully. I had put sheets and a blanket on the hide-a-bed, but noticing how cold they still were, I pulled out a few more blankets and laid them on the bed. I opened the drawers in the desk and showed her the closet for hanging her clothes. Allen brought in a clear glass vase with water to put her flowers in, and we placed them on the piano. I opened the drapes to the sliding glass door which led to a patio in the backyard.

I could hear the kids playing in the family room next to us. Chuy was laughing and chatting furiously. His mother interrupted our tour and walked sternly into the family room. Chuy was playing with Benjamin's little trucks, blocks, rocking horse, and a myriad of other toys that were by now strewn about the room. Khanh scolded Chuy and spanked him on his bottom. Chuy began to pout, but didn't say anything.

"No, please. The toys are here for them to play with," I said. Jack, Annie, and Ben were watching Khanh like she was the wicked stepmother. I glanced back at Chuy and noticed his eyes begin to fill with tears. His mother looked disgustedly at him and left the room. I sat down on the floor with the children and pulled the fire truck out. "Look," I said, smiling. I turned the knob that lowers the ladder. "See," I showed Chuy. I turned the knob the other way and the ladder lifted. Chuy giggled and waved his hand at me to do it again.

Khanh reappeared, bringing an old beat-up plastic bottle filled with dirty marbles. She shook the bottle and made the marbles rattle. Chuy laughed and grabbed it. As he shook them, Ben ran over to look. Ben also laughed, and the two of them took turns shaking the bottle, amused by the music of the marbles. After listening to the sound of the marbles for a few minutes, Chuy took off the cap and poured the many small glass balls out. They were all the same design, green, yellow, and white swirled together like food coloring that was never fully mixed.

I looked around for Tong. "Where's Tong?" I asked. Khanh also glanced around and noticed that he was missing. She called his name harshly several times.

We immediately heard footsteps running down the stairs. When Tong approached the family room, she yelled at him and hit him lightly on the side of the head. Tong became silent, folding his hands behind his back. I winked at him and he broke into a big smile, but appeared somewhat embarrassed. Khanh scolded Tong, then went back into her room. I followed her and showed her where the bathroom was. She was still guarded and just nodded her head without expression as I pointed out the shower, sink, and toilet. Allen had stayed in the family room with the children, and I suddenly realized that I was alone with Khanh. I felt so relieved that she was here. It seemed that I had known her for a long time.

I watched her closely as she inspected the bathroom. She pressed the light switch several times until she seemed satisfied that she knew how to work it. I felt close to her, yet she seemed so far away. She didn't have the same sense of attachment to me that I felt to her. As I observed her, it dawned on me that she probably didn't realize that I had waited and worried about her for months, and that I had picked her and her boys over many other families.

I expected her to feel close to me, but she had no idea how much I'd worried about her. How could I expect her to feel anything for me? I didn't go pick her out of the crowd coming off the airplane. I'm not the one that hugged her and supported her when she was so overwhelmed. All I did was sit and stare at her in a daze. I hadn't exactly been affectionate.

As I watched her walk back into the bedroom, I was so excited she was finally here that I had a strong urge to hug her. She turned around to look in the closet, and I spontaneously threw my arms around her shoulders and hugged her. She jumped back startled and stared at me with a horrified look. I stared back dumbfounded as she slowly backed away from me. Her eyes were opened wide and filled with terror. I tried to smile but only managed a wrinkled, puzzled look. I was so embarrassed and so stunned that I backed out the door, tripping on her bag. I mumbled something about going to fix dinner and stumbled down the hall to the kitchen.

"You idiot, you idiot, Sandy," I thought to myself. "Remember the book you read about Vietnamese. It said that they're very reserved, and not used to displaying emotion, particularly in public. You totally offended her." As I pulled things out of the refrigerator and started cutting up vegetables for stir-fry, my mind was whirling a hundred miles an hour. "What should I do now? She would just as soon never see me again, but she is stuck in my house. How could I blow it so fast?" I felt sick.

"Mom, why aren't you listening?" Annie demanded.

"Oh, I'm sorry honey, what did you say?" I answered meekly.

"What's the matter, Mom?"

"Nothing, Sweetheart," I tried to say normally. "What did you want?"

"Tong and Chuy love Jack's race track. They keep running the cars right off the track and laughing. Chuy can't control the levers very well, so he can only go real fast or stop. His cars keep wiping out on the corners." Annie smiled cheerfully. "I'm going back upstairs."

15

"O.K., have fun."

My thoughts returned to Khanh. "Oh Sandy, how dumb could you be? After what her life has been like, she probably thinks you're a lesbian." I felt awful. "What's she supposed to think when some strange woman throws her arms around her the first time they're all alone? What do I do now?" I pondered.

As I worked in the kitchen, Khanh came into the adjoining family room and sat down on the couch. She watched Chuy and Ben play with all the toys. Allen turned on the TV. Chuy turned around, pointed at it and giggled. Upon hearing the TV, Tong came down to see. He watched the TV as Allen changed the channels to show him the almost thirty different stations. Allen handed the channel changer to Tong, who laughed as he picked up the process of zapping quickly.

"We have enough surfers in this house already. I don't think we need anymore," I remarked unhappily.

"Let's leave it here," Allen answered as he set it on the Disney Channel.

Tong wandered into the kitchen to watch me. He looked at me with a big cheerful smile, and I gave him a hug. Unlike Khanh, Tong's face brightened and he hugged me back. I was somewhat surprised, but relieved that he seemed unafraid. It's sad that we can't all keep the light-hearted dispositions we had as children. But was it fair to expect Khanh to have the same blind trust that Tong has after all she must have been through in her life?

Tong followed me around the kitchen and closely watched everything I did. I showed him the refrigerator, freezer, pantry, and silverware drawers, carefully saying the English words for each one of them. He repeated each word twice, trying to memorize them. When I started peeling carrots, he motioned that he wanted to help.

"O.K, you can help," I answered. "First you have to wash your hands." I showed him the soap and how to turn on the faucet. As I moved the handle to the right, I said "cold," and as I moved it to the left I said "hot." He gave me a puzzled look, so I felt the water. It hadn't heated up yet. I waited a couple of minutes and then put my finger back under the faucet. "Hot," I said putting his finger in the hot water. He yanked his hand back. "Hot!" he shrieked and laughed.

We laughed for several minutes. His eyes were so full of excitement. He played with the hot and cold for a few minutes, quite amused. He repeated "hot" and "cold" each time he moved the handle back and forth. When he became bored with the water faucet, he walked over to the cutting board where I had begun to slice the carrots. He smiled at me and watched patiently. I showed him how to hold the carrot and cut with the knife. I put my finger to the blade of the knife and said "sharp!" He nodded, still with a smile, and said "sharp!" I handed him the knife and he began trying to cut the carrots. I could tell he had not cut many carrots before, because of the difficulty he had holding and cutting at the same time.

While he worked on the carrots, I cut the rest of the vegetables. He frequently looked at me and smiled. The smile covered his whole face and his bright, white teeth looked as though they belonged in a toothpaste commercial. He was a handsome boy. His hair was so black it almost had a purple shine to it. It was cut razor-straight and was the same length all around, as if a bowl had been placed on his head. He was much larger than I had thought he would be. It looked like he wore about a size seven shoe and size twelve clothing. He was around five feet tall and was filled out nicely. I wondered if his height came from his American ancestry.

I got the wok out and set it on the stove. "Tong," I said, "watch." He moved close to me and studied what I was doing carefully. As I pushed the upper right dial on the stove, I pointed to the upper right element. I stopped the dial at two and said, "Low."

Concentrating, he repeated, "Low."

As I moved the dial around to ten I tried to explain that it got hotter. He looked confused, so I went to the sink and turned the faucet on. "Hot," I exclaimed.

"Ohh . . . hot!" he repeated and laughed.

"Yes," I grinned, "very hot," I pointed to the stove as the element started turning red.

"Yes, very hot!" he exclaimed. He put his finger close to the stove and jumped back. "Hot!" he yelled.

We broke into laughter for several minutes. He was so full of joy, it was hard not to laugh with him. He followed me around the kitchen until I was done cooking. I had made quite a lot of food, thinking that they would probably be hungry. While we were waiting for the rice and breadsticks, I went into the family room. Khanh was sitting on the couch with her elbow on the armchair and her head in her hand. Her eyes were closed.

When Ben noticed I was in the room, he ran up to me and said, "Look, Mom." He pointed to a skyscraper that Chuy had made with the Duplos. Chuy laughed and jumped up and down. "Good, Chuy," I clapped. Just as I praised it, Ben knocked it down. They both giggled and jumped up and down with glee.

I found an afghan and pillow for Khanh. I slowly moved her arm to slide the pillow under her head. She jumped. I leapt back, startled, and handed her the pillow. She shook her head no and dozed back off. She looked absolutely exhausted. I nudged her again and insisted she take the pillow. She agreed and I covered her with the afghan. Her feet were still on the floor, making her look uncomfortable. I left her alone, however, afraid to disrupt her again.

"What have you gotten yourself into, Sandy?" I quietly asked myself. This wasn't the way it was supposed to be. Why was she so distant? If only she knew all that I'd done, certainly she would act differently. But how did I want her to act? To smile and be appreciative? Yes. Or was I expecting her to treat me as a saint? No. I just wanted her to be happy and trust me.

I remembered all the garage sales and thrift stores we had been to the past five months, trying to find furniture and household items for them. Allen and I hadn't been to a garage sale since college. I don't think we had ever been to a thrift store before. It was a good experience. I didn't realize how many people shopped at the Salvation Army and Saint Vincent DePaul stores. On Saturday morning there were so many families shopping for clothing, used toys, and furniture, it was hard to find a parking place. I also hadn't realized how much used furniture cost. But it was fun finding the pieces that would become our new family's home. As we gathered the beds, dressers, desks, bookcases, couch, chairs, kitchen table, lamps and kitchen items, I began to feel as though my new family were a part of us. We had furnished their entire home. Many of our friends gave us things, and we tried to match colors where we could. We had found many cute knickknacks for the kitchen, and posters and sports pennants to hang in the boys' rooms. We had accumulated so many things that we had to rent a storage unit just to house all their new belongings until they arrived.

"Are we almost ready to eat?" Allen asked, interrupting my thoughts.

I jumped. "You scared me."

"I'm sorry," he laughed. "What were you thinking about?"

"Oh, nothing," I sighed.

"Are you O.K.?"

"Yeah, I'm fine."

"Why don't you go wake Khanh up? I'll call the kids for dinner," Allen said.

I walked into the family room. Khanh was still sound asleep. I noticed that she had moved her legs up onto the couch. She was so deep in sleep, she looked like a mummy—no sound or movement. I was surprised she could sleep so soundly with all the noise.

As I watched her, I wondered what she was dreaming about. Whatever it was, it must have been something peaceful. Maybe it was the first sleep she'd had in more than twenty-four hours. Trying to take care of the boys all the way from the Philippines, and worrying about whether anyone would be there to help her when she finally arrived at her destination, probably kept her restless if not completely sleepless. She was really quite beautiful. I reminded myself that

I was going to have to have patience and understanding. It was hard to imagine what she was going through—staying with complete strangers, not understanding their language or culture.

I decided not to wake her. If she was hungry, she would wake up from the smell of the cooking. I went back in the kitchen and told Allen to get the kids around the table.

All of the children were soon seated, except Chuy. I looked around and found him trying to wake his mother. I ran in and put my finger to my lips. "Shhhh," I whispered. "Let's let your mother sleep." I said softly. Chuy gave me a dirty look and shook his head no. I picked him up and tickled him. He laughed and motioned for me to do it again. I tickled him again and we were friends. As with any other kid, however, once you start playing, there's no quitting. He didn't want to wash his hands, he just wanted to be tickled. I had a hard time getting him settled down so he could sit in his chair and eat.

After we were all seated, I showed Tong and Chuy how to put their napkins on their laps. They imitated me carefully, looking up proudly with big smiles. We passed the rice, stir-fry, and egg rolls. Neither Tong nor Chuy wanted any food. I tried to put some on Tong's plate, but he said, "No." I said, "Yes," but he squinched his face up and motioned to his stomach shaking his head.

"That's O.K., Mom. It will still be good tomorrow," assured Allen.

Before the rest of us started eating, we said the prayer we say before every meal. When we folded our hands, Tong seemed to understand. He said something sternly to Chuy, and Chuy folded his hands and bowed his head. Our refugee documents indicated that Khanh was Catholic. It seemed strange that there were Catholics in Vietnam, but Vietnam once was a French colony. It was not the dominant religion, but there were a good number of them.

Tong and Chuy sat politely while we ate, neither of them saying anything. We tried to get them to eat several times, but they refused. As I watched Chuy, it struck me how well behaved he was for a five-year-old.

When we finished, Tong helped rinse the dishes and load the dishwasher. I tried to explain that the dishwasher cleaned the dishes, but he was confused.

"Wait until we put the soap in and start it so he can hear it washing," Allen said. When we had thrown all the garbage in the trash compactor, I showed Tong how to turn it on. He hit the switch and it began its loud grinding. He stepped back with a puzzled stare. After it stopped, I opened it and showed him how it had packed everything down to about one tenth the space.

Before we left the kitchen, Allen showed him how to put the soap in the dishwasher and turn it on. Tong smiled and nodded his head, repeating "dishwasher" several times. Shortly after we finished cleaning the kitchen, the doorbell rang.

"Hello," I greeted Loc as I opened the door.

"Hello," he answered. "Sorry, my wife could not come. She had to work late."

"Oh, I'm sorry. I was looking forward to meeting her. Thank you for coming without her. Have you eaten?"

"Yes, I ate the dinner I fixed for my wife," he

chuckled. We went into the family room, where Khanh was still sleeping.

"Would you like some coffee or tea? Otherwise we have Coke or just plain water."

"I'll have some tea, thank you."

While I was getting the tea, Loc went in the family room and watched Khanh as she rested. "She's been sleeping for about an hour," I said. "She was so exhausted that as soon as she sat down she fell asleep. Do you want me to wake her?" I asked Loc.

"Yes, you better."

"O.K." I gently shook her. She didn't move. Tong walked over to her and said something in Vietnamese and shook her arm. Khanh jumped up quickly. She rubbed her eyes and glanced around the room. Loc said something to her and she nodded. He continued talking while she just stared at her lap. Tong sat in the chair and listened attentively to everything. Every now and then, Khanh responded quietly to what Loc said, but she never looked up.

"She is extremely tired," Loc told us. "She has not slept for a long time. She said they ate a lot of food on the airplane so she is not hungry now."

"Ask her if she would like some tea," I said.

Loc asked her, but she didn't want any.

"Ask her if she needs anything."

Loc talked to her for a long time. He did most of the speaking. Khanh would answer briefly without looking up. I kept wondering what they were saying. I now knew how it felt to have everyone around you speak a different language. It seemed they talked for hours, and I was becoming more and more curious.

Tong was concentrating on the conversation, but never said a word.

Finally, Loc looked at me and said, "She told me she needs many things. She did not want to ask for anything, because you have already done so much. However, after prodding her, I found that she needs toothbrushes, toothpaste, soap, towels, and toilet paper."

"Tell her we will make sure she has all of those things. Ask her if she needs anything else."

As Loc started another long conversation in Vietnamese, I felt like an idiot. Of course she needed those basic things. How stupid to ask her if she needed anything and make her feel degraded having to ask for soap and toothbrushes. I should have known she would need those things and not have made him ask.

Allen had gotten out a notepad and pen and started writing down the things she asked for. Khanh continued to stare at her hands, folded in her lap, and quietly answered Loc's questions. She looked pitiful. I felt a lump in my throat as I watched her and realized how embarrassed she must feel. I wanted to halt the entire conversation. She never looked up. She seemed like a prisoner going through an interrogation. How desperately I wanted to end this entrapment, but I didn't know how else to get the information I needed just to get through the first night. If I didn't ask her what I really needed to know while Loc was here, I would be lost.

"She says she would like some stamps if that would be possible. She also said that she and the boys need underwear and socks. She says she is very grateful to you and your husband for sponsoring them."

I should have stopped there, but I was dying to know some of the answers to the questions that had been haunting me the past few months.

"Ask her if the boys attended school in Vietnam," I told Loc.

He asked her and she said Tong did but not Chuy.

"Does she have any relatives?"

He asked her and reported that she has some cousins.

"She said she is very tired and wants to go to bed," Loc said.

"Oh, of course," I said. I took Khanh and Loc into her room.

I asked him to tell her that we were going to have Tong sleep upstairs in Jack's room if that was all right. I tried to take Khanh to show her so she would know that Tong would be close, but she didn't want to go upstairs. I took Tong up and showed him his bed.

"Is this O.K.?" I asked Tong as I shook my head up and down slowly.

"Yes, yes," he replied.

"Good, it will be fun for you to be in with Jack."

It seemed a little strange that Tong was so willing to sleep away from his mother and brother. If Jack, who is the same age, was in an identical situation, he would want to sleep in my room.

"I better go now," Loc said. "My wife will be home soon and wonder where I am." He said something to Khanh and she nodded.

"Thanks so much for all your help," I said gratefully.

"You're welcome. Call me if you need anything else."

"O.K., but you'll probably regret that offer," I laughed.

As Loc went out the door, I took a deep breath. Well, now I'm really on my own, I thought. I walked back into Khanh's room. She was looking through her papers, which she had spread out all over the floor. There were a lot of legal-type documents, some with their pictures and some without, some in English and some in Vietnamese. I wondered what they could possibly be.

I sat down and watched her for a few minutes. She just kept going over the same papers again and again. I felt helpless to try to sort things out for her. She totally ignored me, so I assumed she wanted me to stay out of her way. After watching her for fifteen or twenty minutes, I stood up and went into the kitchen. I got a cup and tea bag and took it into her room.

"Would you like some tea?" I said, smiling, showing her the cup and the bag.

She looked up and nodded yes without any expression. I went in the kitchen to make the tea. As I waited for the water to boil, I watched Ben and Chuy play basketball on the small portable basketball hoop. I wish adults could accept each other as quickly, I thought. Chuy was so wound up. I wondered for a minute if he was hyperactive, but concluded that he was just excited and needed to get some energy out after having been cooped up in an airplane for so many hours. He was such a cute little boy. Like Tong's, his hair was cut like a bowl. It was coal black and straight, but finer than Tong's. Chuy was also much shorter and more delicately built than his brother. They didn't look much alike, other than their brown-black eyes and cheery dispositions.

I took the cup of tea to Khanh along with the sugar bowl. I showed her the sugar and asked if she wanted any. She didn't look at me but nodded yes, so I put a teaspoon in. She nodded for more, so I put another teaspoon in and went back in the kitchen.

I called the kids and told them to get ready for bed. Chuy went in his room with his mother, and I took Tong upstairs to get him some pajamas. I went through Jack's drawers and found a pair of pajamas that were too big for him. I also found a pair too small for him that would fit Chuy. I gave them to Tong and showed him where the bathroom was. Tong looked at me and shook his head no. He went back in the bedroom and sat on the bed and smiled at me.

"Jack, please get your pajamas on so Tong can see," I said. Jack quickly put them on and said, "See, Tong."

I handed the pajamas back to Tong and pointed to the bathroom. He shook his head again. "O.K., it's not that big a deal. If you don't want to wear pajamas, you don't have to."

I went downstairs to give Chuy his pajamas. Their bedroom door was closed and I didn't hear anything, so I cracked the door open and peeked inside. Khanh and Chuy were sound asleep on the bed. They were both lying on their right side with Khanh's right arm under Chuy's head and her left arm draped gently over his stomach. They were lying on top of the covers with their clothes and coats on. They didn't stir when I opened the door. I stared, not knowing whether to wake them or not. They looked so peaceful. Their bodies were curled next to each other in fetal positions. Chuy's small frame was tucked neatly in his mother's protective bosom. They would be so much more comfortable in pajamas under the covers, I thought. But, I didn't want to startle Khanh again, so I let them sleep. I reached up to turn the light off and then remembered that they had left it on. I better leave it alone, I decided. I closed the door and went back upstairs to Annie's room to tuck her in.

"Mom, come here a minute," Annie said quietly. I went over and sat down on her bed. "Aren't they neat, Mom?" Annie said, smiling. "I just love Chuy. He's so cute. And Ben loves him too."

"Yes, they are neat. They're very nice boys."

"I wish one of them could sleep in my room."

"I know, Honey, but Chuy is already asleep in his mother's room and Tong will fit in Jack's extra bed better than in your trundle bed. But you'll see them first thing in the morning."

"Mom, can they come to our school tomorrow?"

"We'll see. Maybe just for five or ten minutes. Now go to sleep. I love you, Sweetheart."

"I love you too, Mommy. Goodnight."

Next, I went in to see Ben. As always, he wanted me to rock him for a few minutes. I got him out of his crib, and we rocked and sang songs for about ten minutes. Then I laid him back in his bed and kissed him goodnight.

I went back into Jack's room and told him and Tong that it was time to go to sleep.

"But Mom, Tong can't sleep in his jeans and T-shirt," Jack argued.

"It's all right, Jack. Khanh and Chuy are sleeping in their clothes too."

"But that's not fair. You never let me sleep in my clothes," Jack whined.

"Just go to sleep, Sweetheart. I love you," I said, kissing him goodnight.

"Come on Tong, it's time to go to sleep." Tong shook his head and indicated that he wanted to see what was in the room next to the bathroom. We walked down the hall, and I showed him Allen's den. He gazed slowly around the room at all the books. There were probably more books in that room than he had ever seen in his life. I showed him the computer, and he smiled and said "Yes, yes." He obviously knew what a computer was.

"Philippines," he said, and pointed to the computer.

"You had a computer in the Philippines?" I asked slowly.

"Yes."

I got the floppy disks out and loaded the word processor into the computer. "Do you want to play on the computer for a few minutes?" I asked.

"Yes," he said, grinning, and began striking the keys. He played with the keys for a few minutes, obviously enjoying himself. He would point and laugh every now and then. The letters and numbers he was typing didn't seem to say anything, but it didn't matter—he was having fun.

After fifteen minutes of his typing, I put my hand on his shoulder and said, "Tong, it's time to go to bed."

He nodded and yawned. I laughed. "You're tired now, too." I yawned to show him that I was tired also.

He laughed and went into Jack's room. I turned off the computer and went in to tell him goodnight. He was lying on top of the covers with his clothes on just like his mother and brother. He still had his tennis shoes on.

"Take your shoes off," I whispered, pointing to his feet.

He shook his head no, but I insisted, so he took his shoes off. I tried to pull the covers down so he could get under them, but he said "No" and seemed quite upset. I shrugged my shoulders and agreed to let him sleep on top of the covers. I laid the afghan that was hanging on the chair over him and kissed him on the cheek.

"Goodnight," I whispered.

"Goodnight," he whispered back.

As I wandered down the hall to my room, I realized how exhausted I was. I got ready for bed, but knew I would have a hard time sleeping if I went to bed right away, so I made myself a cup of coffee. I put on my bathrobe, got a heavy comforter, and went outside on the deck off our bedroom.

It was cold. I sat down in the lawn chair and covered myself with the blanket. It was a beautiful, clear night. The stars were bright, and the full, fluorescent-yellow moon was straight over my head, like a guardian over all the stars in the sky and all the possessions of the earth. I looked down over the city at the sparkling white and yellow lights. I wondered why the lights twinkled at night. Certainly each individual light didn't flicker off and on. Across the city, the airplanes were set up three in a row to land at the airport. They were landing to the east.

My thoughts turned to Khanh, Tong, and Chuy

arriving at the airport. I remembered Khanh's total collapse. Tears filled my eyes as I replayed the scene. My God, what her life must have been like. I didn't think I even wanted to know. I just wanted to try to make it better for her, beginning today. Thinking about the day, I was overwhelmed. I had never experienced such overpowering emotions except when my children were born.

I cupped my hands over my coffee cup and breathed into it. It temporarily warmed my hands and face. It was so cold outside that my hands were turning numb. I decided to go in and crawl under the warm covers. I went into the bathroom to brush my teeth. As I was brushing, I read the words on the plaque that was above the sink:

PRAYER FOR PEACE
Lord, make me an instrument of thy peace
Where there is hatred . . . let me sow love.
Where there is injury . . . pardon.
Where there is doubt . . . faith.
Where there is despair . . . hope.
Where there is darkness . . . light.
Where there is sadness . . . joy.
O Divine Master, grant that I may not
    so much seek
To be consoled . . . as to console,
To be understood . . . as to understand,
To be loved . . . as to love,
    for
It is in giving . . . that we receive,
It is in pardoning, that we are pardoned,
It is in dying . . . that we are born to eternal life.

I had read those simple words hundreds of times before, but that night they had new meaning. There was nothing sophisticated about the words. They were so simple to understand, yet so difficult for mankind to practice.

I prayed that night that I would have the strength to give a new life to Khanh, Tong, and Chuy without expecting anything in return. I asked forgiveness for having been so selfish as to have expected anything from Khanh after all she had been through. I vowed in the future to accept her for who she was and not to expect her to be the way I thought she should be.

DAY 2: *Getting to Know Them*

The first night I tossed and turned, listening for Tong in case he woke up scared or confused. When the alarm sounded, I dragged myself out of bed and staggered into the shower. After I got dressed, I peeked into Benjamin's, Annie's and Jack's rooms which I always did when I got up in the morning. I guess it's something mothers just do for the reassurance that they are still there. All three of them were sound asleep, as was Tong. I noticed that he had carefully refolded the afghan I laid over him and rehung it on the chair. He slept all night in his clothes with no covers on. It was chilly in the house, so I turned the heat up. I wished I had let him leave his shoes on.

After I got the children off to school and Allen had left for work, I puttered around the house, waiting for our refugees to wake up. At eleven o'clock, I still hadn't heard a sound from them. I went upstairs to check on Tong. He hadn't changed positions since I checked on him at six o'clock. I went back downstairs and paced around for another half hour. They had been sleeping for fourteen and a half hours. I had never slept that long in my life. I remembered when I was in high school, I would sometimes sleep until ten thirty or eleven o'clock, but that was when I stayed up until midnight or later. Finally at noon I went upstairs and shook Tong. "It's time to get up Tong," I whispered. There was no movement.

"Tong, wake up," I said a little louder. Still no movement. I sat and stared at him a few minutes debating what to do. I had a lot of things I wanted to get done, and if I didn't get them up, I would end up wasting an entire day. I shook him again and tried to lift his head a little. He opened his eyes and looked at me.

"Tong, it's time to get up," I said, smiling. He sat up and managed a small grin, then dropped his head back onto the pillow. It was almost as if he was drugged. He was simply too tired for me to make him get up. I went back downstairs and called my office. It had been a busy morning at work, and after I talked to Karen, my administrative assistant, I regretted ever having called. She kept me busy for twenty minutes answering questions. When I did get off the phone, I heard the water running in the downstairs bathroom.

About ten minutes later, Tong walked into the kitchen. "Good morning," I said cheerfully. "Did you sleep well?"

He looked at me puzzled, so I put my hands together in a praying position and laid my head on them. He laughed and said, "Yes."

"What would you like for breakfast?"

I showed him where the bread was and got out the toaster. Then I pointed to the eggs in the refrigerator, the oatmeal box, and several of the cold cereal boxes. He looked perplexed and shrugged his shoulders.

"Why don't you try cereal," I suggested. I got the box out and poured it in a bowl with milk. He sat down at the table and ate the whole bowl of cereal.

"Did you like them?" I pointed at the box.

"Yes."

"Do you want more?" I picked up the box and tipped it over the bowl.

"No, no," he grinned, shaking his head.

He sat down in the family room, and I turned the TV on for him. He switched the channel several times, and finally settled on *Teenage Mutant Ninja Turtles.* Kids must be the same everywhere, I concluded, shaking my head.

I waited a few more minutes but still didn't hear anything from Khanh's room. I sent Tong in to try and wake them up. A few minutes later they emerged from their room dressed in the same clothes that they had slept in. They ate breakfast, and then Khanh went back into her room and closed the door. I followed and knocked lightly on the door. She opened it without looking at me, so I went in and sat down on the bed. She had her papers strewn out all over the floor again and was browsing over them. I watched her for about ten minutes, then sat on the floor and looked through some of the papers. There were what appeared to be three passports with photographs which made them look like criminals, much like most American driver's licenses. There were several documents written in Vietnamese which I couldn't understand. There were also school records for Tong written in English, health records for all three, and copies of the airplane tickets. Khanh continued to look over the same papers again and again. It was now one o'clock. I was anxious to go shopping.

"Khanh, I want to take you to the store to get you some socks," I smiled and pointed to my socks. She looked up at me but didn't respond. She continued to look over her papers. I brought their new toothbrushes, toothpaste, shampoo, tissues, and deodorant into her room and showed her.

"These are for you," I said softly, pointing first to

the items Allen had gotten at the store and then to her. She glanced at them and nodded her head. Then she returned to her papers. Frustrated, I went and got Tong. He seemed to know more English than Khanh or Chuy, although I really wasn't sure, since Khanh had been so elusive. I explained to Tong that I wanted to take them shopping for socks, underwear, and pajamas.

He seemed to understand what I was saying and repeated it in Vietnamese to Khanh. Khanh nodded her head again, but then returned to her stack of documents. I felt like screaming, but reminded myself that it was going to take a lot of patience. I left the room and went to the closet to get Tong's and Chuy's shoes and coats. I motioned for them to come and put them on, then gave Khanh's coat to Tong and asked him to take it to her. We walked back into Khanh's room and Tong handed her the coat. She stared at it with a mystified look, then started going through her papers again. I went upstairs and got a pair of my tennis shoes and socks for her. I motioned for her to put them on. Then I gathered her papers up and put them back in her bag. She looked at me in confusion, but got her shoes, socks, and coat on. It was after one thirty when we finally got in the car.

As we started driving, I took a deep breath and said to myself, "Patience, patience, patience." I understood now why the literature that we had received from SOAR stressed how different the Vietnamese culture was from ours. Their sense of time was different. They were more relaxed and less concerned about schedules and plans. How was I ever going to get them up, dressed, fed, and off to school and work?

I decided to take them to the large shopping mall. It had lots of Christmas decorations, and I thought it would be fun for them to see all the stores. As we drove the five miles to get there, I pointed out different sights and made Tong and Chuy repeat the English words for each one of them. I was so excited to take them to the mall and show off what capitalism can accomplish.

First, we went to the lingerie area of the department store. Khanh slowly gazed around, obviously stunned by all the styles, sizes, and colors. The sales clerk wanted to know what size of bra Khanh wore and I told her I didn't have a clue. She took a stab in the dark and selected a size, hoping it would be close. It took Khanh about fifteen minutes to decide which bras, underwear, and socks she liked best, then we sent her into the dressing room to try them on. The clerk went in after about five minutes to see how everything fit. When she came out, she said that Khanh had not been wearing a bra at all and acted as though she didn't know how to put one on.

Next, I took her to look at pajamas. I showed her the short and long flannel nightgowns, thinking that they would keep her warm. She chose a short pink one, but didn't seem particularly excited about it. As we walked over to add it to our other purchases, she pulled my arm and took me to see the silk-like pajama tops with short sleeves and pant-like bottoms. She picked out a peach colored pair and handed it to me.

"You want this?"

She nodded.

"It won't keep you warm," I shook my head.

She ignored me and walked up and put it on the

pile. I wasn't sure what to do. I wasn't her mother, but I was the one paying the bill. I had never bought myself a pair of pajamas with a top and bottoms. I had always liked nightgowns. In addition, I was afraid she would freeze in such light-weight material. The winters in Idaho are not like the winters in Vietnam. But then it suddenly struck me that I didn't wear flannel. I liked pretty, feminine, pajamas too. I later learned that our pajamas were nicer than regular clothes in Vietnam. Most Vietnamese were lucky to have two sets of clothing, which they wore around the clock.

While we were looking at pajamas, the boys kept sneaking out the door which opened to the mall. I was afraid we might lose them, so I went out and made them come back and stay with us. They were fascinated by all the stores and activities. I tried to assure them that we would go and walk around the mall as soon as we were done shopping. I wasn't sure if they understood me, or whether they just couldn't resist the temptation of exploring the bustling shopping center—they kept wandering back out to look around. As they stood in wonder, entranced by all the activity, they spoke rapidly in Vietnamese, giggling and pointing at the sights.

After I had retrieved the boys for the third time, I noticed Khanh rubbing her fingers over the silk-like pajamas and staring at them like a little girl who was getting her first new dress. You are not her mother, I reminded myself. If that's what she likes, that's what you will get her. I took the flannel nightgown back and set the silk-like pajamas and all of her other clothing on the checkout counter. Then we headed for the boys department.

First we looked for socks. While I was trying to decide what size to get the boys, Tong sat down, took his shoes and socks off and started to put one of the new socks on. I was busy helping Chuy find his size and didn't notice what Tong was doing. Soon I heard a store clerk yell, "What are you doing! That is very unsanitary."

Tong jumped up with a terrified look on his face and glanced over at me. I immediately went over and said softly, "It's O.K., Tong. Let's put your shoes and socks back on." The clerk sneered and walked away. After that incident, all of my refugees were much more subdued.

We took our purchases to the checkout counter. After the clerk entered Khanh's items into the register, she raised her eyebrows and sarcastically said, "She certainly has expensive taste." I looked up and realized that each panty she had picked out was $4.00. I could have gotten an entire package with four pairs for that. I had been so caught up in finding the right size that I forgot to look at the price tag. Oh well, I decided, I could afford it, and it wasn't worth the effort to put everything back. This was not a good lesson to teach them, however. When they were on their own, they would have to watch prices closely.

As we left the store, the boys giggled and tugged at my arm, pulling me into the mall. We wandered slowly down the wide corridors, their eyes sweeping from one side to the other. None of them said anything for quite some time. Suddenly, Chuy jumped up and down and shrieked. He began furiously rambling on in Vietnamese and pointing to a stage down the hall. I laughed. He must have caught a glimpse of Santa

Claus. He kept jumping up and down, tugging at his mother's arm. Khanh seemed somewhat annoyed and scolded him, but it didn't break his enthusiasm.

"Come on, let's go see Santa Claus," I smiled. In total jubilation, Chuy started running down the mall. He obviously knew something about who Santa was, but apparently had never seen him in person. Even Khanh managed to crack a small grin as she watched her young son. Tong pointed and said "Saint Nick."

"Yes, Tong. Saint Nick," I applauded and patted his arm. "Saint Nick. Santa Claus," I said.

Tong was also pleased at seeing Santa, but didn't seem to have the same level of zeal as Chuy. Tong was nine and Chuy was five, I reminded myself. Chuy wanted to immediately run up and hug Santa. We had to restrain him, and I explained "There are several kids in front of you, so you have to wait." Khanh tapped my arm and motioned that she was going to sit down on the bench a few feet away. I nodded to her, but was somewhat concerned that she wanted to sit down in the midst of all this jubilation. Tong, Chuy, and I waited in line a few minutes until it was our turn. When Santa motioned for the boys, Chuy broke into laughter and ran up and gave him a big hug. Tong smiled at Santa, but didn't want to go up to him. I frowned at Tong and said, "You go see him too." I insisted that Tong and Chuy sit on his lap so we could get a picture taken. Tong seemed embarrassed, which puzzled me. My son, Jack, was nine and still sat on Santa's lap without hesitation. The photographer took their picture and Santa gave them a candy cane. He asked what they wanted for Christmas, but I explained that they couldn't understand English. Chuy didn't want to leave Santa, so I had to pick him up and carry him away.

We waited a couple of minutes until our picture was ready. They put it in a cardboard Christmas frame and handed it to me. I showed Tong and Chuy. We all three laughed. It was a cute picture of both of them. I gave it to Chuy who ran over and showed it to his mother. Khanh looked at it for several minutes. The sides of her lips turned up very slightly, indicating that she was pleased. They continued to look at the picture for several more minutes, talking back and forth in Vietnamese. I gave the picture to Khanh and told her that it was for her. She got a tissue out of the purse I had given her and wrapped it carefully before putting it in her bag.

As we meandered back down the mall, Khanh nudged me and pointed to the bench she had been sitting on.

"You want to sit down?" I asked.

She nodded her head and walked over to the bench and sat down. I stood there with the boys, wondering if we should leave. They were pulling my arm trying to get me to continue on our journey through this marvelous fairyland, wondering what other treasures they might find. I turned around and looked at Khanh again. She didn't look well. It was time to take her home, but first I took the boys a few stores down to the cookie shop. As we wandered down the corridor, we passed the toy store. They looked in the window and laughed, pointing and speaking rapidly in Vietnamese. Chuy pulled my arm trying to get me to go in, but I shook my head. I knew if I let them go in we would be there for a long time. Instead,

I pointed to the cookie shop. Their eyes lit up as we made our way over to the display case with all the varieties of cookies, brownies, and muffins. Chuy pointed to a sugar cookie frosted in red, and looked up at me with a big smile, saying something to me in Vietnamese.

"You want that?" I asked pointing to the Christmas cookie. Chuy nodded his head several times, apparently afraid I would not understand.

"O.K. You'll like that cookie," I agreed. "What do you want, Tong?"

"Drink," he replied.

"O.K.," I said. I got him a Coke and handed Chuy his cookie. Chuy looked at it with great anticipation. He licked the frosting and handed it to Tong to try. Tong said something in Vietnamese and refused to try it. I later learned that the traditional Vietnamese diet has very little sugar in it.

I looked at my watch and it was already two forty-five. "We have to go and pick Jack and Annie up at school now," I said.

Chuy pulled my hand, trying to get me to continue our stroll down the mall.

"No, we have to leave or we'll be late. Do you want to go see Jack and Annie?" I asked.

He nodded yes. As we drove to the school, Khanh fell asleep with her arm on the door rest and her head in her hand. It was a beautiful day, with the sun shining brightly through the car window. Tong pointed to the mountains and said, "Snow."

"Yes, snow. Cold," I shivered.

"Yes, cold," he grinned.

I swept my eyes from the majestic snow-covered

mountains north of Boise to the Owyhee Mountains south of Boise, just as brilliant with their snow blanket. I thought to myself, as I had many times before, that this is one of the most beautiful places in the world. Tong and Chuy also looked around. They seemed to appreciate the beauty of the Boise Valley too.

As we pulled in the school parking lot, I pointed to the building and said, "Jack and Annie's school."

They nodded. Tong looked at the two-story brick building in awe. Chuy bounced up and down and chattered to Tong as he pointed to the jungle gym on the playground.

"Let's go get Jack and Annie," I said as I opened the car door. Tong and Chuy nodded and jumped out of the car. Khanh didn't stir. I debated whether to wake her. I was afraid if I didn't, she might panic. I nudged her. She slowly opened her eyes as if drugged and looked at me. I pointed to the door of the school and whispered, "I'm going to take Tong and Chuy in the school with me." She nodded, then dropped her head back in her hands and closed her eyes.

First we went to Annie's room. When we opened her door and walked in, all the students looked up and stared. The room suddenly fell quiet. Annie ran up to us and smiled, "Hi, Tong and Chuy!"

Chuy threw his arms around Annie. She picked him up and gave him a big squeeze. "This is Chuy," she said proudly to the classroom. Chuy giggled and smiled at the kids. "And this is Tong," she motioned to Tong, who smiled shyly at the class. Annie put Chuy down, and he ran over to the gingerbread houses that the students had made. He slowly looked over the twenty-five brightly decorated houses and pointed to the red and white candy cane on the door of one. He glanced up at Annie, hoping she would let him take it off and eat it.

"No, Chuy. You can't eat that. It doesn't belong to you. This one is mine." She pointed to the one with the red lifesavers and multi-colored jellybeans. Chuy smiled and touched one of the candies. "No, you can't eat them. It will ruin my house," she said cheerfully. Chuy looked up at me, hoping I would override Annie's decision.

"No Chuy. You already had a candy cane and cookie today," I said smiling.

Tong stood against the closet next to the door, carefully studying all the posters on the wall, books in the bookcases, and art projects hanging from the ceiling. Unlike Chuy, he was quite reserved and seemed almost embarrassed. I walked over to him and patted his back. "Annie is in the third grade," I put up three fingers.

Tong smiled and nodded. We stayed for a couple more minutes, then said goodbye to Annie and went across the hall to Jack's room. Tong grabbed my arm and shook his head, indicating that he didn't want to go with us.

"Oh, Tong, Jack will be disappointed if you don't go to his room." I opened the door and gently guided Tong and Chuy in. When we entered the room, all the students once again turned around and stared. A silence fell over the room. Chuy spotted Jack standing in the corner of the room. He ran over and jumped on Jack, knocking him to his knees. The classroom burst into laughter. Jack introduced them, and a crowd of admirers soon gathered around Chuy. Again, Tong stood shyly in the corner and just watched. We were only in Jack's room about five minutes when the bell rang. Chuy and Tong immediately ran outside to the jungle gym and started playing. I let them stay for twenty minutes, then insisted we leave so Khanh could go to bed.

When we got home, Khanh and Chuy went into their room and slept. I tried to get Tong to lie down but he wanted to play on the computer. After I got him signed on, I rummaged through our closets to try and find pants and tops for them now that I finally knew their size. I found some pants that were too small for me that I hoped would fit Khanh. I was glad to get rid of them so I wouldn't be reminded how thin I used to be every time I opened my closet. I found lots of clothes that would fit Chuy. It was particularly difficult finding pants for Tong, however, because by the age of nine most boys have worn holes in both pant knees.

When Tong got bored with the computer, I got the world atlas out. I showed him where Boise is and where Vietnam and the Philippines are. He was interested to see how far he had come, and how much of his trip had been over water. I outlined the state of Idaho and tried to explain that Boise was just a city inside of Idaho, which was a state inside of the USA. I showed him California, hoping that he would recognize it, but it didn't seem to strike a chord with him. We looked at the map for a long time. I pointed out many of the different states, and when I mentioned New York, his head jerked up and he said,

"New York, yes, New York!"

"You know New York?"

"Yes, in Philippines," his face squirmed as he tried

to find the right English words. "Ummmmm yes, New York."

"Do you know anyone in New York?"

He gave me a puzzled look.

"Um, any Vietnamese in New York?"

"Yes, from Philippines."

After we found New York, he spotted Vermont.

"Vermont!" he excitedly said.

"You know someone in Vermont too?"

"Yes, cousin."

I was surprised but delighted that he had relatives in the United States. Next I showed him Canada and Mexico and explained that they were not part of the United States. I also showed him Europe, and asked if he had heard of Italy, Germany, England, or France. At the mention of France, he perked up.

"Yes, France."

"Do you know someone in France?"

"Yes, cousin."

"You have a cousin in France?" I asked excitedly.

"Yes!"

We looked at the rest of the atlas, but he didn't seem to be familiar with many countries until we got to China.

"China, yes, China!"

"You know China?"

"Yes," he said softly. "Yes," he said again with his voice fading out slowly. He became somber and tears soon filled his eyes.

"Tong," I put my arm around him. "Are you all right?"

"Yes," he whispered. He stood up and rushed upstairs to his room. I sat on the couch feeling disconcerted. What had I said to upset him so? I followed him upstairs and found him lying on the bed with a pillow over his head. I sat on the bed next to him and shook his arm.

"Tong, what's the matter?" I asked softly.

He shook his head under his pillow.

"Are you tired?"

He took the pillow off his face and stared at me with reddened eyes and a wet face.

"Are you O.K.?"

"Yes, tired."

"Do you want to go to sleep?"

"Yes."

"Why don't you go down with your mother and sleep," I suggested.

He looked perplexed, so I pointed downstairs and said, "Khanh, Chuy. You go down with your mother, Khanh."

"No!" he said defiantly.

I shook my head in confusion, but rubbed his beautiful head of black hair and told him to sleep. As I went downstairs, I felt bewildered and helpless. Until now, he had been such a happy boy. He was somewhat reserved at times, but mostly he had been a bundle full of joy. I wondered if looking at the map made it sink in just how far away he was from home. Maybe this was the first time he really accepted the fact that he would start a new life. As bad as Vietnam was, there were probably still things he missed: maybe his father or friends, his house, maybe his church and school, or the warm tropical climate. Perhaps the area he lived in was as beautiful as Boise, but in a different way. Ho Chi Minh City, I thought, shuddering at the name. Or, he may just be tired. It had been a long few days for him.

I went downstairs and plopped on the couch in exhaustion. As I lay there, I thought about all the things I had to do to get ready for Christmas. Instead of resting, I should have been addressing cards, wrapping presents or at least I should have gone down to my office. Instead, I lay down and the next thing I knew Ben came running up to me shouting, "Mommy, Mommy!"

"Hello, Ben," I said jumping up startled. "How are you? Did you have fun at Grandma's?" I asked, giving him a big hug.

"Yes! Grandma gave me truck," he said with excitement showing me the forty-fifth truck in his collection.

"Rrrrrrrnnnnn," he said as he drove the car along the banister.

"Hi, Sweetheart," Allen called from the kitchen. "How are you?"

"Fine," I replied with my voice hoarse from sleeping. "I fell asleep and just woke up when Ben came in."

"How long you been sleeping?"

"I don't know, what time is it?"

"It's five thirty."

"Oh jeez, I can't believe I slept that long. I don't have anything out for dinner."

"Remember, we have a Boise State basketball game tonight."

"Oh, that's right. Are you going to take Tong and Chuy?"

"I thought I would ask them if they want to go." Allen added, "What did you do today?"

I summarized our day, ending with Tong and me looking at the atlas. "I don't know what was wrong with Tong. We were having a good time when all of a sudden he started crying. I tried to find out what was the matter, but he simply wanted to go to sleep."

"Hmmm, he was probably just tired."

"Well, that's kind of what I figured. But he had been so happy up until then that I didn't know what to make of it. You know something else that seems kind of strange? When I suggested that he go lie down by his mother, he got really upset and said emphatically 'No.' It was the way he said it that bothered me. He seemed mad about something."

"Hmmm, well he's probably just exhausted from all he's been through. I'm sure he'll be fine when he wakes up. He's such a cheerful little boy."

"Yeah, I know. But, you know what else seems strange?"

"What?"

"Khanh is so strict with the boys, especially Tong. Although she's sometimes strict with Chuy, she's also loving to him. She picks him up and hugs him, and has him sit on her lap a lot, but I've never seen her hug Tong."

"Really? Well, they've only been here twenty-four hours; she's probably just not been herself. How would you feel after being awake for almost two days with little or no sleep? Then to have to move into a total stranger's home? I'm sure she's just on edge."

"Well, I hope you're right. It really hasn't been very long."

"So what are we going to have for dinner?"

"It's already almost six o'clock and I haven't even

thought about it. How about if we take them down to the Vietnamese restaurant. I think it would be good for them to meet some Vietnamese. Plus, Khanh hasn't eaten anything since she's been here except breakfast this morning. Maybe she'll eat better if she has Vietnamese food."

"O.K., that's an easy way out. Do you think we should wake them up?"

"I think so, or they might be awake all night."

I went upstairs and found Tong still sound asleep. He looked so peaceful lying on top the bed. I sat down and nudged his arm. He didn't stir.

"Tong, it's time to wake up," I said softly.

He still didn't move. I pushed him a little harder and said louder,

"Tong, it's time to get up now."

He opened his eyes and looked at me.

"Hi, did you sleep well?"

He smiled at me and replied quietly, "Yes."

"It's time to eat dinner. We're going to go to the Vietnamese Restaurant. Will you please go wake Khanh and Chuy up?"

He gave me a confused look.

"Mother, brother, get them up," I said pointing downstairs. He nodded to me then sat up. We went downstairs and he disappeared into his mother's room.

Soon they all appeared in the family room with light-weight shirts and pants on that looked more like pajamas than clothes. Tong was also wearing gray corduroy shoes that looked more like slippers than shoes and no socks. Khanh was wearing the thongs that she had worn on the airplane. Chuy was barefoot. I looked at Allen and we both shrugged our shoulders.

I tried to explain to Khanh that we were going down to the Vietnamese Restaurant for dinner, but she just looked at me with a blank stare and didn't respond.

"Tong, tell Khanh that we are going to Dong Khanh to eat."

"Yes, yes."

"Tell her."

He pointed toward her bedroom and said, "Yes."

"You already told her?"

"Yes."

"Then she and Chuy need to get shoes and socks on. Why are you wearing pajamas?"

Tong went in the room and got Chuy's shoes and socks and gave them to his brother to put on. When he was finished, they all went to the closet to get their coats.

"Tong, you can't wear your pajamas."

He looked perplexed and said, "No."

I touched the arm of his shirt and shook my head. He still was bewildered. I took him upstairs and got one of the sweatshirts and pairs of pants I had given him and motioned for him to put them on. He shook his head with indignation and put them down.

"We cannot go eat until you change your clothes," I said finally.

I handed him the sweatshirt and pants again. He reluctantly went in the bathroom to change. Then I went downstairs and did the same thing to Chuy. He gave me a big smile, but also shook his head. I nodded my head yes and helped him take his shirt off. He grinned at me and proceeded to change clothes. Khanh's outfit didn't look as much like pajamas, but was still very light-weight with short sleeves. I pointed to her thongs and said, "Too cold. Where are the shoes I gave you?" She looked at me with a straight face, but didn't say anything. I pointed to my tennis shoes and to her feet. She shook her head defiantly. I handed her the pair of socks and motioned for her to put them on. She nodded once and put the socks on followed by the thongs. It looked a little silly, but at least her feet would stay warm.

Although the van was big, it didn't have enough room for all of us, so we took the car also. When we got to the Vietnamese restaurant, they had a large table for us that we had called and reserved. Allen told them that we were bringing a new refugee family for dinner. The waitress came over and welcomed our new arrivals. While Khanh and the waitress were conversing, Chuy saw some cans of Coke on a table. Chuy pointed to them and yelled "Coca Cola!" We all burst out laughing. Allen told our waitress to bring each of the kids a Coke. When Chuy got his, he immediately took several big gulps, which caused his eyes to water.

"Coke. Philippines," Tong said cheerfully.

"Oh, you had Coke in the Philippines?" Allen asked.

"Yes, very good."

"Yes, very very good," Jack laughed.

"Coke, too," Ben chimed in, bouncing up and down in his high chair.

Khanh chuckled and grinned. I stared at her in disbelief. That was the first happy moment I had experienced with her. She had actually showed some emotion other than grief and exhaustion. I felt like jumping out of my chair and hugging her. What a relief! Things were going to be O.K. She was coming out of her shell! Maybe she wasn't as miserable as I had thought. I sat back and watched her with affection. Her face was so much more relaxed. She was really quite pretty.

While we ate, Allen had the waitress explain to Khanh that he and Jack were going to a basketball game after dinner. Tong and Chuy both wanted to go, so Khanh agreed that Allen could take them. I don't think either of them quite understood what a basketball was; whenever they had seen one at home, they had tried to kick it, thinking it was a funny-looking American soccer ball.

We had a wonderful dinner. The waitresses came back and talked to Khanh several times. Khanh told them to thank us very much for everything we had done, and that she was eternally grateful to us for sponsoring them. While Khanh was busy talking to the waitress, a young lady about twenty-five years old stopped at our table on her way out the door. "Please give this to her," she whispered, placing a $20 bill in my hand. She started to walk out the door, but I got up and asked her to please come back.

"Are you sure you want to give this to them?" I asked spontaneously. "You don't even know them."

"Yes, it's Christmas time, and I want to help them."

"They just arrived yesterday. This is their first full day in America."

"I can tell," she stammered, her voice thick with emotion.

Before she slipped out the door, I interrupted Khanh and gave her the money. "This is from the lady." I pointed to the young woman as she opened the door.

Khanh looked up to see the lady with tears in her eyes.

"Merry Christmas," the lady said faintly.

"Thank you," Khanh replied with a straight face, nodding her head with dignity.

That was the first thing I had heard her say in English. I wondered if she knew any other words. Khanh handed me the money and I put it in my pocket. I decided I would give it to her when we got home so she could put it in a safe place. After the lady left, I wished I had asked her name. She had been eating at the restaurant by herself. I should have invited her to our house so she could have gotten to know our refugee family. I vowed if anything like that happened again, I would not let a stranger get away without learning their name. When somebody gives from the heart like she did, she becomes a friend, not a stranger. It's important to know the names and addresses of friends.

Eating at the Vietnamese restaurant that night broke the ice between me and Khanh. As we got ready to leave, I felt like Khanh, Tong, and Chuy had been with us a lot longer than just a day, and that they had known the waitresses at the restaurant much longer than an hour. Everyone seemed relaxed and happy. As we walked to the door, several customers in the restaurant said goodbye and gave them their best wishes. Khanh conversed with her new friends as though she had known them forever. We promised we would come back soon.

Allen, Jack, Tong, and Chuy walked to the van and started to get in. The rest of us went to the car until suddenly Khanh ran to the van and made Chuy get out.

"No, he's going with us to the basketball game," Allen said.

Khanh shook her head no and grabbed Chuy's hand, pulling him out of the van. Chuy started to cry and argue with his mother, but she said something sternly to him and he immediately fell silent.

"Tong, explain to your mother that I promise I will bring Chuy home in two hours," Allen said desperately.

"No," Tong said abruptly. "Khanh say no."

Allen and I shook our heads in frustration. Khanh didn't say anything about Tong so he stayed in the van and left with Allen and Jack. Khanh and Chuy got in the car with us. They were shivering, so I unfolded Chuy's hat that was stuffed in his coat and put it on him. I've got to get them gloves, I reminded myself.

When we arrived home, everyone was tired from the long day. Khanh and Chuy disappeared into their room and apparently went to bed, since I never saw them again that night. I put Annie and Ben to bed early too, then went in my room and crawled in bed. It felt so good to lie in the darkness in peace and quiet. I opened the curtains so I could look at the city and watch the airplanes come and go. I took a deep breath and let it out slowly. What a day. I was both excited and relieved. Excited because I could see the enthusiasm in the eyes of our refugees as they experienced for the first time all the joys of living in America, and relieved because I could sense Khanh starting to relax and feel much more comfortable. Excited also because I liked them all so much—all three of them. Relieved because I could see light at the end of the tunnel: a time when my family would be on their own and happy in America. They were perfectly normal human beings: there didn't seem to be anything either emotionally or physically that they couldn't overcome to live a happy life. I hadn't been sure for the last few months as I waited for them whether that would be the case.

I turned on the news for a while until I heard the garage door open. I looked at the clock and it was ten o'clock. The boys came in and slammed the door. I was afraid they had awakened Khanh and Chuy, who were just a few feet away from the door. I could hear all three of them laughing and discussing the great basketball game. To them, the B.S.U. games were as important as NBA games, probably even more so. I got up and went downstairs.

"How was the game?" I asked.

"It was good, Mom. The Broncos won," Jack eagerly answered.

"Good. Tong, did you like the game?"

"Yes," he said smiling.

"The part he liked best was watching the cheerleaders," Allen laughed. "He seemed pretty confused about the basketball game and all the yelling, but he sure paid attention whenever the girls came out on the floor."

Allen, Jack, and I laughed and looked at Tong. He seemed puzzled so Allen said, "You liked the girls didn't you?"

"No understand," he shook his head.

"Girls, you know," Allen lifted one of his knees and put his hand against his face trying to pose like a girl.

"Ohhh, ohhh," Tong grinned. "Yes, girl." His face turned red as we all joined in the laughter.

"Come on guys, it's time to go to bed," I said as I escorted them upstairs.

Jack got his pajamas on, but Tong still refused to wear his. They climbed in bed, and I kissed them both goodnight. "Do you want to go tell your mother you're home?" I asked Tong.

"What?"

"Khanh," I pointed downstairs, "You go down?"

"No," he shook his head.

"O.K.," I replied. "Goodnight."

"Goodnight," they both answered.

That night I slept better than I had for several nights. I felt we had gone through the worst and the rest would be easier and less stressful. It was always more difficult dealing with the unknown than experiencing the real thing. Now that I had gotten to know our family, I felt I had a handle on what the future would bring. I enjoyed having them around. They were such simple people. They didn't expect anything and were grateful for little things that Americans take for granted. I looked forward to the remaining days they would be with us before we moved them into their own apartment.

DAY 3: *The Revelation*

It was Saturday morning and the days of sleeping in were long past. At six forty-five I heard Ben yelling at me to wake up. As I lay in bed knowing I had at most five minutes, I wondered what the day would bring. I looked forward to getting to know our family better. What I didn't know was that this day would change my life forever.

Everyone in the family was up early and headed in different directions, except Jack and me. Jack spent the morning complaining. Since Tong was still sleeping in his room, Jack couldn't play in it.

"He'll be up pretty soon," I assured Jack.

"Yeah, probably noon, so I can't play in my room all morning," Jack complained.

"I'll go get you some clothes, and you can either go outside or to Nathaniel's house to play," I said trying to calm him down.

"I don't want to play outside or at Nathaniel's. I want to play in my own room. At least it used to be my own."

"What do you want to play in your room?"

"Gameboy."

"I'll tell you what. I'll go get your Gameboy and you can play it down here with me. I haven't watched you play it for a long time and I'd like to see how good you've gotten."

"No, I want to play it in my room."

"Well, you can't right now. Tong will be up soon and then you can."

"Why can't he stay in Annie's room?"

"Jack," I laughed, "you were the one that wanted

him to stay in your room. Remember. Annie begged to have him in hers but I told her Tong was a boy and he was your age, so he should stay in your room."

"Well, I've changed my mind."

"Tong is all settled in your room now, and I want him to stay there until he leaves. Come on, let's play a game together," I said, trying to change the subject.

"I don't want to. I guess I'll just watch TV until I can get my own room back," he answered unhappily.

Tong came downstairs around ten thirty with the same clothes on that he had worn to dinner and the game last night. He still would not wear the pajamas I had bought him. I also hadn't convinced him to sleep under the covers. He had a bowl of cereal and an apple for breakfast. As usual, he didn't want milk, but I made him drink a glass anyway.

After breakfast Tong watched TV for a while. Jack had gone to his room, changed his clothes and gone outside to play. He never did play in his room. As I cleaned the kitchen, Tong followed me around helping me put things away. He put a can of pears which we never opened in the refrigerator. I explained that cans didn't go in the fridge and put the pears back in the pantry. I showed him that there were lots of cans in the pantry but none in the refrigerator. When we were finished, he sat in my chair in the family room but did not turn the TV back on.

I went around the house gathering the dirty clothes and started the laundry. When I went back into the family room, I noticed Tong sitting in my chair staring out the window crying.

"What's the matter, Tong?" I asked softly as I knelt down on my knees and held his hand. He just shook his head back and forth as if nothing was the matter, but tears continued rolling down his cheeks.

"Please tell me, Tong," I begged in a sorrowful tone.

Again he shook his head.

"I'm going to go get your mother," I said, pointing to Khanh's room. I started to stand up but Tong grabbed my arm and said, "No, no," shaking his head violently. His face was extremely serious. Somehow I felt like I had to trust him and not go get Khanh.

"I'll call Loc," I said, standing up to get the telephone.

Again Tong shook his head and said "No, please," but he continued to cry. I was really getting worried about him, but didn't know how to find out what was the matter. Something had been wrong yesterday and something was desperately wrong today. I had to get to the bottom of it. I couldn't let this nine-year-old boy bear his sorrow by himself. I called Loc, but no one answered. I decided to call the Daos. They had helped us write the banner in Vietnamese and had offered to help us interpret if we needed them. I called their number and Mr. Dao answered. I explained the situation to him and asked if he would please talk to Tong and find out why he was so upset. I handed the phone to Tong, but he refused to hold it. I held it to Tong's ear and Mr. Dao talked to him for a few minutes, but Tong refused to answer. Mr. Dao told me he thought Tong was just homesick and it was best to let him cry and get over it. I thanked him and hung up.

I sat next to Tong with my arm around him and we rocked in my chair for a few minutes. "I wish I could help you," I said softly with tears in my eyes. I laid his head on my shoulder and ran my fingers through his hair. He cried quietly but said nothing. This continued for a half an hour and he wasn't getting any better. I decided it was time to wake up his mother to see if she could help. I stood up.

"Tong, I'm going to get your mother."

I started to walk down to her room, but he jumped up and grabbed me saying, "No, no!" He took my hand and led me upstairs. I followed him into Jack's room, where he closed the door. He sat on his bed and put his finger to his mouth saying, "Shhhh." I nodded my head and sat down next to him. He started wailing desperately, and said between sobs, "Khanh, no mother."

"What?"

"Khanh," he pointed downstairs, "no Tong's mother."

"She's not your mother?" I gasped.

"No, Tong, mother, father," then he showed me three fingers while he searched for the right words, "in Vietnam."

"You have a mother and father in Vietnam?" I asked stunned.

"Yes, yes, mother, father in Vietnam," he cried with tears streaming down his face.

I grabbed him and we both cried for a few minutes. I pushed him back and forcing a smile, said, "Oh, Tong, you have a mother and father in Vietnam? Khanh not your mother?" I wanted to make sure I understood correctly.

"Yes, and three ummmm," he just couldn't think of the English words. "Jack, Annie, Ben," he said excitedly.

"You have three brothers and sisters?"

"Yes, Jack and Ben."

"Three brothers!"

"Yes, yes," he smiled and grabbed me.

"You have three brothers in Vietnam!" I repeated laughing, both out of joy because he had told me and as a release of stress from trying to deal with this incredible new information.

He grabbed me again and sobbed. "Yes," he moaned.

We held each other a few more minutes and cried.

"Oh, Tong, you poor boy," I grieved.

After we had cried for several minutes, I took Tong in the bathroom and we splashed our faces with water. Then we went back in the bedroom, shut the door, and sat down on the bed.

"Chuy, not your brother?" I asked.

"No, Chuy no brother," he said. He squinted his eyes, trying to find the English words for what he wanted to say but couldn't. He suddenly got up seeming frustrated and went downstairs into Khanh's room. A few minutes later he came back upstairs with her Vietnamese/English dictionary. He looked up the Vietnamese word he had been trying to say and showed it to me. The corresponding English word was aunt.

"Oh, Khanh is your aunt," I cried.

"Yes, yes," he said. "Chuy, cousin."

"How old are your brothers?" I asked.

He stared at me with a puzzled look, so I showed him my fingers and said, "Brothers, how many? Jack nine, Annie eight, Ben two. Your brothers? How old?"

"Oh, yes. Ummmmm, eighteen, Ummmm, seventeen, Ummmm, eleven," he smiled.

"You're the youngest."

He looked confused.

"You, like Ben, the baby!" I said, pronouncing my words precisely.

"Oh, no, no," he said. "Ummm, eleven brother, baby."

"No, you're only nine, he's eleven," I laughed thinking he was trying to trick me.

"No, Tong thirteen, not nine," he answered proudly.

"You're thirteen?" I pointed to him.

"Yes," he exclaimed with a big smile.

"You're not nine?" Again I wanted to make sure I understood correctly.

"No, I'm thirteen," he said proudly.

"Oh, Tong," I said as I shook my head. "Now everything makes sense." I sighed as I hugged him again.

We sat on the bed for a few minutes with my arm around him and his head on my shoulder. Oh my God, what am I going to do, I wondered? This poor boy. How homesick he must be. He's so far away from his family. He's been in the Philippines for six months before he arrived in Boise, so he hasn't seen them for a long time. Why would his mother send him half way across the globe? It must have been so bad in Vietnam that she was willing to risk never seeing him again, not knowing whose hands he might fall into in a strange country, and never knowing if the airplane even made it. I was sure none of them had ever flown on a plane before.

My stomach felt sick. I thought of how his mother must feel: Every night before bed she kisses her three sons goodnight but Tong isn't there. She wakes up in the middle of the night and wonders where her son is and whether he is safe, let alone happy. God, why does anyone have to go through this? How grossly unfair for some to have everything and some to be so desperate that they have to give up their sons. I wished that I could somehow talk to his mother or send her a message to let her know that we had her son and that we would not only take good care of him, but would love him and give him the best chance for a happy life that we could.

Tong suddenly stood up with a frightened look on his face. He pointed downstairs and said, "Khanh, no." He put his fingers to his lips and shook his head.

"You don't want me to tell Khanh?" I said.

"No. No Khanh."

"O.K.," I agreed. "No Khanh, at least for now."

I was so overwhelmed by the whole experience of the past few minutes that I needed a break. I took Tong into the den and turned on the computer for him. He smiled and sat down to play. I slowly sank down into the big chair and leaned back. Oh my, this was too much to absorb. What was I going to do? I was wishing that Allen was here. I had to tell him. I watched Tong type enthusiastically on the computer, as he seemed to have temporarily forgotten his grief. Everything made sense now: Khanh's lack of motherly affection for Tong, and Tong's size and maturity. I laughed to myself. No wonder he was interested in the girls at the basketball game.

I began to weep again. I just couldn't comprehend

all that Tong had said. He was only thirteen yet had gone through more turmoil than most people had to in a lifetime. I walked up to him and put my hand on his shoulder. He stopped and looked up at me.

"Tong. Have you written your mother a letter?" He looked confused. I picked up a pen and paper and pretended to write.

"You," I pointed. "Write letter to mother?"

"No," he shook his head slowly.

"No letter to your mother from Philippines?"

"No," he said, his lips quivering.

"Oh, Tong," I hugged him. He started to cry again. "You must write your mother a letter," I said firmly.

"Yes, write letter," he faintly smiled.

"We must tell Allen," I said. "Allen and me." I pointed to myself. "We will help you. Try to get your mother, father, and brothers here to America."

"Yes," Tong agreed, looking doubtful.

"Oh, Tong, you poor boy," I cried as we embraced.

"Here. You type a letter to your mother," I pointed to the computer.

"Yes," he replied.

I opened a new file for him and told him to start typing a letter. He just stared at the blank screen.

"I'll be back in a few minutes," I said as I turned to go downstairs.

"No Khanh," Tong jumped up, ran over to me and whispered.

"No Khanh," I promised, crossing my heart. As I left the room, Jack was standing outside the door.

"What's wrong, Mom?" he asked with a worried face.

"Nothing, Honey," I answered giving him a hug.

"Mom, what's wrong with Tong?"

"Nothing, Sweetheart. He's just homesick."

"Did you tell him to write a letter to his mother?"

"Oh, Honey," I looked alarmed. "Whatever you heard, you must not repeat anything."

"I won't, Mom. What's the matter?"

"I'll tell you later. Just pretend you didn't hear anything."

"But Mom, isn't Khanh his mother?"

"Oh, Jack," I cried as I hugged him. "I'll explain it all later, O.K.?"

"O.K., Mom."

I went downstairs, my mind in a whirl trying to sort out the recent events. I had to call Allen. I couldn't deal with this new revelation by myself. I called his parents' house, but he had gone to the storage unit to get some things out for the refugees.

"Do you know when he'll be home?" I asked, my voice quivering.

"Oh, probably in a half an hour or forty-five minutes," she replied. "Is everything all right?"

"Yes, everything is fine," I lied.

I went into the living room and opened the blinds. It was gray and cold outside. The mass of clouds hung drearily over the city like a big feather bed blanketing everything below it. There wasn't much shape to the clouds; they just hung listless with a few corners seeping out of the fold.

My life had seemed so simple until now. I had grown up, one of four daughters. Other than having typical workaholic parents searching for the American dream, my childhood had been pretty good. I married my teenage sweetheart at nineteen, had three beautiful children, graduated from college summa cum laude, became a CPA, currently had a great job as a stockbroker, and was destined to live happily ever after, blindly living out my life oblivious to the plight of most of the rest of the world. Sure, I cringed every time I saw an ad depicting a starving child or shuddered when I read the accounts of devastating floods in Bangladesh, but it was all so far away. There wasn't anything I could do about it except send money to the Red Cross or Lutheran World Relief. But suddenly, I found myself involved in an emotional and complicated situation. I had known Tong for less than two days, but I had grown attached to him and loved him almost as though he were one of my own. I was the only person in his life right now that he could trust, and I was the only one that showed him any affection. I found myself responsible for a young boy who spoke almost no English and was half a world away from his family. How quickly my fairy-tale existence had changed.

I decided to try and put my panic-stricken mind at ease until Allen got home by staying busy. I went up to check on Tong. I found him still staring at the blank screen. It suddenly struck me that he couldn't type a letter to his parents using an American alphabet keyboard. I told Tong to get Jack and follow me outside. Although it was cold, we put our hats and gloves on and got the bikes out. Tong was excited when he saw the bikes and immediately got on Jack's and rode around. I ran in and found my camera and took pictures of him and Jack riding the bikes. I decided if Tong's family couldn't be here, I would record his life through photographs and mail them if I could. At the very least, I would keep a scrapbook for the day when they could review all that they had missed.

The boys rode bikes for about thirty minutes until Allen drove in. I was so glad to see him. My heart felt some relief just from knowing I could now share this traumatic news with someone else. I imagined the relief that Tong must have felt when he told the story to me after keeping it inside for more than six months.

We were all cold and ready to go inside. After we took our coats and hats off, we went in the family room where Khanh and Chuy were watching TV.

"Good morning," I said smiling to Chuy.

He gave me a big grin back without saying anything. He jumped up and grabbed my hand and led me into the kitchen. He pointed to the cereal in the pantry.

"Oh," I laughed. "He's already picked up an American custom, eating cereal for breakfast." We all laughed as I poured him a bowl. Chuy giggled, knowing that we were talking about him but not sure why.

"Chuy, did you sleep well?" I asked putting my hands in a prayer position by the side of my head.

He didn't say anything; he just smiled.

"No Chuy," Tong said, shaking his head at me.

"What?" I asked.

"No Chuy. Bo."

"What do you mean?" I asked shrugging my shoulders.

"Ummmmm, Jack, Annie, Ben, Tong," he pointed to himself. "Bo," he said, pointing to Chuy.

"Bo," I repeated with a long "o" sound.

"Yes!" he said with excitement.

"His name is not Chuy. His name is Bo?" I asked confused.

"Yes, Bo," he pointed again to the boy we thought was Chuy.

"But his papers say his name is Chuy."

"Yes, but name is Bo."

I went in Khanh's room and got Chuy's birth certificate. His official name was Trinh Van Chuy . I showed it to Tong and said, "No Bo," and pointed to the name Chuy.

Tong laughed but started to get frustrated.

"Name Bo," he said sternly.

"O.K.," I agreed. "Bo," I said and pointed to Chuy. He giggled and nodded his head and repeated, "Bo!"

We all laughed. That was one of the first things Bo had said that we understood.

"We've been calling him by the wrong name ever since he arrived. No wonder he never said anything. He probably didn't know who we were talking to," I said to Allen.

"It might be a nickname, because it says Chuy on all their papers," Allen replied.

"Oh well, I'll have to remember to call him Bo," I said. "I want to get Khanh some breakfast then I need to talk to you about something upstairs," I nervously said to Allen.

"Why, is something the matter?"

"Yes," I took a deep breath.

"Khanh," Allen called. "Why don't you come in and eat some breakfast."

Khanh jumped up and came in the kitchen. I

showed her the cereal, the box of apples, and the eggs. She pointed to the eggs. "You would like an egg?" I slowly asked.

She nodded her head. I got the fry pan and the toaster out and fried her an egg. She stood and watched me. I showed her how to use the toaster and she nodded her head.

"Toaster," I said.

She never repeated what I said but always nodded in acknowledgment.

As soon as Bo was done with his cereal, he took my hand and walked me over to the counter where the apples were and pointed.

"You want an apple?" I asked.

He smiled big and nodded.

"Say apple first."

He looked at me and continued to smile.

"Say apple."

He still just smiled.

Tong interrupted and scolded him in Vietnamese. Then Bo giggled and said, "Apple."

"Good boy, Bo!" I exclaimed. "First you have to wash the apples," I said, as I ran the apple under water. Bo nodded his head once quickly.

After Khanh sat down to eat, I motioned for Tong to go upstairs with Allen and me. We went into the den and closed the door.

"Tong and I have something to tell you, but I promised him that you wouldn't tell anybody," I softly said to Allen.

"O.K.," Allen agreed looking worried.

"Khanh is not Tong's mother," I slowly said, my voice breaking.

"She's not?" Allen repeated hesitantly.

"No, she's his aunt. He has a mother, father, and three brothers back in Vietnam."

Allen looked at Tong for confirmation.

"Khanh not your mother?"

"No, no Tong's mother."

"Oh Tong," Allen's voice sank as he grabbed him and hugged him. "Bo is not your brother?"

"No brother, cousin." Tong started to cry again.

"Oh Tong," Allen repeated, continuing to hug Tong.

"I told Tong we would try to help him. I promised him we would not tell Khanh at least for now. His real mother didn't want him to tell anyone that Khanh wasn't his mother."

"Tong, we will help you and not tell anyone—at least until we figure this out," Allen said, shaking his head.

"I asked him if he had written his family and he said no. I told him he should write them, but he's afraid to because Khanh will find out."

"You should write a letter," Allen said.

"Yes, write letter," Tong repeated.

"I'm going downstairs so Khanh won't wonder what's going on," I said.

"O.K.," Allen agreed. "I'll stay up here with him for a while."

I went downstairs where Bo and Ben were involved in a game of marbles. Khanh had finished her eggs but had ignored her toast and was eating an apple by slicing pieces carefully off with a knife. All three of our refugees loved apples. Tong and Bo got excited about apples like my kids did about candy.

"Khanh, do you need anything? I'm going to the store in a few minutes," I said slowly.

She looked at me with a blank face.

"Store. Buy things like milk, eggs, soap." I pointed them out as I said them. She still didn't understand so I took her in the bathroom and showed her the toothpaste and toilet paper.

"You," I pointed to her. "Need any?" I asked, pointing to the items that Allen had bought them at the store the night they arrived. She shook her head. I'm not sure if she understood what I said or if she just wanted me to leave her alone.

"Do you want to go?" I asked.

Again she gave me a puzzled look. I had Tong ask Khanh if she wanted to go to the store, but she said no. However, she wanted Bo to go and rushed him into her room to get ready.

I made my shopping list and told Tong to get his shoes and coat on. Bo was waiting patiently next to the door with his coat on. He also had a small red beret on his head.

"Oh Bo, you look so cute!" I exclaimed as I picked him up. "I love your hat." I smiled and patted his head.

Bo giggled and looked at his mother. Khanh grinned and looked proudly back at Bo.

"Khanh, why don't you come with us?" I asked slowly. She stared at me with a confused look on her face.

"Tong, tell Khanh to come to store."

Tong must have understood, because he said something to her in Vietnamese, but Khanh shook her head and put her hand to her forehead as if she didn't feel well.

"O.K. She can come with us next time."

I was beginning to get concerned about Khanh's health. She had a dry cough and never looked like she felt well. I didn't particularly want to take five kids but they all wanted to come. Allen helped me get everyone into the van and made sure all their seatbelts were buckled.

As we drove to the grocery store, Jack and Annie pointed out the fire station, hospital, park, river, university, and Vietnamese restaurant. They remembered everything except for the park. Tong repeated "park" a few times as we pointed to it, but was confused as to what it was. Tong repeated all the words, remembering them from the last couple of days. Bo wouldn't repeat anything unless Tong became angry with him. When we got to the grocery store, we piled out of the van and held hands while crossing the parking lot. We put Ben in the shopping cart and filed in line down the aisle.

"Department store!" Tong exclaimed.

We all laughed. "Not department store, grocery store," Jack explained.

"Grosey store," Tong repeated.

"Good, Tong," Annie praised. "You say it, Bo."

Bo giggled and just looked at us with a big smile.

"Say grocery store," Jack repeated.

Bo still just smiled at us so Tong scolded him in Vietnamese and he said, "grosey store."

"Good, Bo!" we all said, clapping our hands.

Tong and Bo looked around at all the food, appearing bewildered. They seemed stunned as they gazed from one side of the aisle to the other. Simple things like potato chips, bags of cookies, or frozen TV

dinners were eyed with suspicion, then brought to me for an explanation as to what they were for. Tong liked to push the cart and arrange the items carefully in the cart. When we passed the beverage section, Bo ran up to the pop and yelled, "Coke!" excitedly, picking some up. He looked at me with pleading eyes so I agreed to let him put it in the cart. Jack and Annie disappeared to the toy section, but Tong and Bo stayed right by my side.

When we went through the checkout stand, Bo walked behind the counter and watched the checker slide the items over the scanner, with the computerized-voice stating the price. Tong and Bo both watched in amazement as she quickly moved each grocery item over the scanner, laughing when the funny voice stated the price. I walked around the counter to bring Bo back on the right side, but the checker said, "No, leave him. How long have they been here?"

I explained that they had only been in America for three days. She let Bo and Tong help her slide the groceries over the scanner. They were having fun until an older lady in line gave us a dirty look and sighed loudly. How sad it was that she was in such a hurry she was unable to enjoy watching two young boys experience American technology for the first time. The fascination on their faces made me realize how much Americans take for granted.

Tong pushed the cart out to the car and helped me load the sacks into the trunk. Once in the car, I had to argue with both Tong and Bo about putting their seat belts on. They didn't realize how important seat belts were when driving in a city. As we were heading home, Tong tapped my arm and wanted to know what all the buttons and levers on the car door were for. I showed him that if he pulled the small button toward him the window would roll down and that if he pushed the lever away the window would roll back up. Bo unlocked his seat belt and leaned forward to watch. They both thought it was great fun, but I ended their game quickly and made Bo lock himself back in—much to his dismay. I then showed Tong that the other button automatically locked and unlocked the car doors. He was astonished at everything the buttons could do. He locked and unlocked the car doors several times, laughing each time he did it.

When we got home, Khanh was in her room with the door shut. I sent Tong in to see what she was doing, and he said that she was asleep. We made what my kids call Japanese Noodles for lunch. The long thin noodles are a favorite at my house and I figured Tong and Bo would like them too. I was right. They were such a hit, I ended up having to make a second batch. I poured milk for all the kids over the objection of both Tong and Bo. Bo jumped down from his chair and ran to the refrigerator. He opened the door, searched inside, and pulled out a Coke.

"No, Bo. No Coke. Milk for lunch," I sternly said.

Bo grinned at me and shook his head no. I took the Coke from him and put it back in the fridge. Tong scolded Bo, and he quickly climbed back in his chair and drank his milk.

After lunch, I asked Tong if he wanted to go with me to the department store to get some Christmas lights. He was eager to go. Everyone else was tired of shopping, so Tong and I escaped alone.

When we arrived at the store, I asked him, "Would you like to buy a Christmas present for your mother?"

"What?"

"A Noel present. For you mother."

"Ummmm," he shook his head. "No dollars."

I laughed. "I will pay."

"Ummmm. Yes, a gift, a Noel gift," he said cheerfully. I put my arm around his shoulders and we walked into the store. Since all the women I knew loved jewelry, I took him to the jewelry counter first to look at some necklaces and earrings.

"For your mother?" I asked.

He picked up some of the jewelry and held it carefully while admiring it. He turned the display case and studied the jewelry for quite a long time.

"Does she like?" I asked, pointing to the necklaces.

"Ummmm." He thought for a few minutes and shook his head no. "Ummmm. Mother ummmm," he kept trying to find the right words. "Mother not vain," he said.

"Mother not vain?"

"Yes."

"Your mother does not like necklaces?" I asked pointing to them.

"No," he said firmly.

"O.K. Then let's go look at the candy."

"Candy?"

"Yes, candy. I'll show you."

We went to the several aisles which had been stocked with Christmas candy. As we walked slowly down one of the aisles, Tong stared intently at all the different colors, shapes, sizes, and types of candies.

"Here, does she like this kind?" I pointed to the green, red, and white ribbon candies that my grandma always used to have at Christmas time. Tong shook his head. I pointed out some candy that came in many bright colors, but again he shook his head. I tried to encourage him to select the thick, hard candies thinking that they would not melt or break in the mail. We started down the second aisle which was filled with chocolate Santas, Christmas candy, and chocolate-covered cherries. Tong wandered slowly down the aisle, carefully studying each type of candy. He seemed bewildered by all the different kinds. I supposed that he thought we were terribly spoiled by the hundreds of varieties, especially when his people were practically starving. When we got to the end of the second aisle I asked, "Doesn't your mother like candy?"

"No," he squinched his face and shook his head.

"O.K., let's go look at dolls."

"Dolls?"

"Yes, I'll show you."

I found the section of the store that had gift dolls. There were beautifully painted china dolls, cloth Raggedy-Ann type dolls, and small plastic dolls from different countries. Again Tong walked slowly down the aisle picking up some of the dolls and cautiously studying them.

"Oh, look at this one, Tong!" I exclaimed showing him the oriental china doll about six inches high dressed in a beautiful pink satin gown with a feather hat.

"Do you think your mother would like this one?"

He took it from me and held it gently in his hands, running his fingers over her painted face and softly flicking the dainty feather on her hat. Then he turned it over and carefully rubbed his fingers over the satin dress. He seemed to be enchanted by the doll.

"Ummmm. No," he said again, squinching his nose up.

"No?" I repeated with a surprised voice. "I thought you liked it!"

We had been at the store for almost an hour, and I was starting to get frustrated. I wondered what his mother was like if she didn't like jewelry, candy, or dolls. Maybe I should show him clothes, I suddenly thought. We walked over to the clothing department and looked around. This wasn't going to work, I quickly concluded. In Vietnam they wore light clothing suitable for a tropical climate, not the heavy sweaters and sweatshirts we had in Boise in December.

Just as we were leaving the apparel section, Tong grabbed my arm and pulled me over to a table with hundreds of brightly colored knitted caps.

"Sandy," he exclaimed. "Caps!"

"Yes, Tong," I said somewhat confused. "Your mother doesn't want a hat, does she?"

Tong laughed, "No, Tong want hat."

"Oh," I laughed too. "Of course, you are always shivering. Let's get you a hat." We looked over almost every cap on the table. Tong would decide on one and then throw it back in the pile and pick another one. He was having such a hard time deciding that I suggested he pick the bright red one. He agreed and took it with us. As we left the clothing department and wandered over to the Christmas ornaments, he suddenly grabbed my arm and dragged me back over to the hat table. He threw the red one on the table and picked up the gray one with a blue and white stripe.

"You want that one?"

"Yes," he said smiling proudly.

"O.K. I like that one," I said, smiling back, patting him lightly on the shoulder.

We looked through the Christmas ornaments for a while. I saw some ornaments shaped like Christmas trees that had a place for a photograph on them. I picked up three of them and put them in our basket. I wanted to put a picture of my refugees in one to hang on my Christmas tree. In another one I would put a picture of Tong and Bo for Khanh's Christmas tree some day, and in the last one I would put a picture of Tong for his mother.

We still had not found a Christmas present for Tong's mother. "Tong, can't you find any gift that your mother would like?"

"Ummmm, no," he said in despair. He looked at me for a minute and then said, "dollar."

"Dollar?" I asked. "You mean money?"

"Yes," he slowly said as his voice trailed off.

"You want to send a dollar?"

"Yes."

"Does your family need money?" I slowly asked.

"Yes."

"Well, how about five dollars?"

"Five dollar!" he yelled. "Five dollar buy five chickens and a rooster!" he exclaimed.

I stared at him in disbelief. Oh my God, five chickens and a rooster! That's what he wanted to get his mother for Christmas? My eyes started to fill with tears and then Tong started crying. No wonder he couldn't pick a present. All he was worried about was whether his family had enough to eat. Oh Lord help us, I prayed softly as I rubbed my hand over his head.

"Let's go, Tong," I whispered. I picked up the basket and we went through the checkout line. Then I put my arm around him and we walked out of the store.

Even today when I go into that store, I remember the distant look on Tong's face as he looked over the hundreds of kinds of jewelry, candies, and dolls. At the time, I couldn't understand why he wasn't excited to pick one of those wonderful gifts for his mother. As I got to know Tong better, I realized that much of the time his mind was back home with his family wondering where they would get their dinner that night.

When we got home, Tong cut the tags off his new hat and tried it on. He took my hand and led me outside to test his new hat. After walking around a few minutes he grinned and graciously said, "Thank you."

"Oh, you're welcome Tong. Does it keep your head warm?"

"Yes," he said proudly.

We walked back inside where he carefully put the hat in the arm of his coat, then went upstairs. I checked on him a few minutes later and found him sound asleep on his bed. As I watched him, I thought of how proud his family would be of him. He was very brave for only thirteen. Whatever happened in the future, I vowed to help him to see his family again. Little did I know what a frustrating vow that would turn out to be.

I went downstairs where Allen was reading a book. "We need to talk, Sweetheart," I somberly said.

"What's the matter?" he asked.

"When we were at the store, we spent almost an hour looking for a Christmas present for Tong's mother."

"What did you get her?"

"All Tong wanted to give her was money—only a dollar."

"A dollar?"

"Yes, I suggested five and you know what he said?"

"What?"

My throat felt like a ball was in it and I couldn't speak for a minute.

"What, Sweetheart?"

"Oh Allen," I sobbed, "he was so excited at the thought of sending her five dollars. You should have seen his face. He said that five dollars would buy five chickens and a rooster." I grabbed Allen and laid my head on his shoulder as tears streamed down my face. "What are we ever going to do?" I cried, hoping he had a solution to this whole mess.

"I don't know," he said softly.

"I promised him we wouldn't tell Khanh, but how can he write a letter to his family without Khanh finding out?"

"I don't know, we'll work it out. You know, he is here with his aunt and cousin. In the Vietnamese culture that's like immediate family."

"But it isn't like immediate family to Tong. He and Khanh don't seem to get along very well. And you can tell how much he misses his family."

"I know. But don't worry about it. It will work out."

That's what I loved about Allen. Things that seemed so overwhelming to me were always simple to him. He never overreacted and always approached even extremely emotional situations in a rational manner. I knew he would know what to do, so I quit worrying about it.

"Why don't we go pick out the Christmas tree when everyone gets up?" Allen cheerfully said.

"O.K. that will be fun," I said smiling as Allen wiped the tears off my face.

"Tong seems to love trees and bushes. Have you noticed how he goes up and feels all our plants?" Allen asked.

"Yeah, in fact even outside I noticed his interest in the evergreens. Come to think of it, they probably don't have evergreens in Vietnam since it's so tropical."

"Remember that Jack and I are going to the B.S.U. game tonight," Allen said. "I'll see if Tong wants to go with us again."

"That's a good idea. You know, when he told me he was thirteen, I thought about what you had said concerning him liking to watch the girls. It made sense once I found out how old he really was."

"What are we going to do about enrolling him in school?"

"I don't know. I haven't even thought about that yet."

"I looked over his school records; the math he was doing in the Philippines is way ahead of what Jack is doing. I thought maybe our schools were behind, but now it all makes sense. I would hate to put him in fourth grade if he's doing eighth grade work," Allen sighed.

"Yeah, plus I don't want him to be with nine-year-olds because they are interested in totally different things than thirteen-year-olds," I added.

"When I looked at their official birth certificates from Vietnam, I'm sure it listed Tong as born in 1982—which would make him nine."

"I wonder why his birth certificate indicates he's nine but he claims he's thirteen?" I said.

"Well, something is certainly strange. How could he be thirteen and be Khanh's son if she's only twenty-six?"

"I wonder why they didn't send Tong's younger brother?"

"Probably because they were afraid he was too immature. From the little we know about Tong, he is obviously very bright and courageous for only being thirteen."

"Yeah, I only wish we could send a fax or something to let his family know that he's O.K."

"Well, we'll worry about all that later."

"I think I'll walk up to my mother's for a few minutes and get some fresh air, O.K.?"

"That sounds like a good idea," Allen said.

I walked up the street to my mom's house less than a half mile away. There was a cold snap in the air but it felt good to shiver. Somehow it seemed to shake out the stress of the day every time my body involuntarily shook. I took long steps up the hill and watched my breath hit the cold air and dissipate just quickly enough for another cloud of fog to take its place. The rhythm that developed seemed to engulf my legs, arms, and breath in a hypnotic state. So much had happened in two days that my mind was a jumble.

The sequence of events kept going through my mind over and over again like a scratched record that couldn't advance any further. I passed my mom's house not ready to break the rhythm. I kept seeing Tong carefully studying all the fine items available for Christmas gifts but slowly rejecting each one. What a fool I was not to see the sadness in Tong's eyes as he looked over each of my suggestions. How overwhelming this all had to be for him: to be bombarded with hundreds of different things to satisfy the palate, give pleasure to the eye or softness to the skin. What don't we have in America? Our senses are so over stimulated that we only notice the things that we manufacture. We miss the smell of the pine trees in the morning, the feeling of snowflakes landing so gracefully on our faces, the sound of crackling snow under our feet, and the intricate pattern of each ice crystal on our car window. If we didn't have so much, would we notice the enchantments that nature places before us each day? When Tong learns English, I have to ask him.

My legs were beginning to itch from the cold so I turned around and headed back to mom's house. When I got there, she was crocheting an afghan with a fire crackling in the fireplace and her old Eddy Arnold Christmas album on. I recounted everything that had happened the past couple of days as she quietly listened.

"What are you going to do?" she asked.

"I don't know yet. I have to think about it. I don't want to get them in trouble, but I don't want to be dishonest either."

I stayed at my mom's house for about forty-five

minutes, and by the time I got home, everybody was up except Tong.

"Should I wake him?" Allen asked.

"What time is it?"

"Five o'clock."

"I suppose we'd better. I'll go and rouse him."

"I want to come too!" Ben yelled.

"O.K. You come help me." I picked him up and walked up the stairs. It felt good to hold Benjamin. It seemed I had been so preoccupied with our refugees that I had ignored him.

"Tong," I whispered. "It's time to get up." I shook him lightly.

"Tong, get up!" Ben yelled.

"Shhhh," I scolded Ben, but it was too late. Tong, jumped up startled and looked at us. Then he broke into a smile and laughed. We laughed too.

"You didn't have to get up so quickly," I said, grinning.

Tong poked his finger in Ben's tummy and smiled.

"Do it again," Ben giggled.

I put him down and he started playing with Tong, which gave me an excuse to go downstairs and start dinner. However, it didn't take long before Tong was in the kitchen following me around.

A few minutes later we were all sitting around the table, filling our plates. Before we ate, we bowed our heads in prayer. Khanh, Tong, and Bo politely folded their hands and lowered their heads. After we finished the prayer, Khanh gave the sign of the Cross.

It was difficult for our refugees to hold the silverware, and even Khanh struggled trying to use a knife. They used their fork to scoop everything onto their spoon and then ate from it. Khanh helped Bo learn how to hold his fork; however, when she wasn't looking, he set it down and used his fingers.

"Bo, don't use your fingers to eat your vegetables," Jack laughed.

Khanh glanced at Bo and slapped his fingers. She handed him his spoon. Jack and Annie laughed, which caused Bo to break out in a grin.

"Mom, why can't they use their silverware right?" Annie asked.

"In Vietnam they use chopsticks. Have you ever tried to use chopsticks before?"

"No, have you?"

"Yes, and they're hard to use. We would be clumsier using chopsticks than they are using silverware."

"I want to try. Do we have any?" Jack asked.

"No, but we'll get some and you can try."

"Yeah, we should get some for our refugees," Annie said.

"I want them to learn to use silverware. When Tong and Bo start school, they'll have to use silverware, and I don't want the other kids to laugh at them."

When we finished eating, everyone except Bo and Ben helped clean up. Tong started to load the dirty dishes in the dishwasher while the clean ones were still in it.

"No, Tong," Allen said. "Look, they're clean. First we have to take the clean ones out and put them in the cupboard." Tong looked at Allen with a confused expression, but helped him unload the clean dishes.

"See. Look, Tong," I patiently said. "The dishwasher cleans the dishes with soap and hot water." I showed him where the soap went. It must have been confusing why we rinsed the dishes and also put them in the dishwasher. After we finished, Allen told everyone to get coats on so we could go pick out a Christmas tree.

"Khanh, do you want to go?" I asked slowly. She shook her head and went in her room to help Bo get ready.

"Tong, tell Khanh we go get Noel tree," I said pronouncing my words slowly and distinctly. "Tell her that we want Khanh to go too."

Tong nodded his head and went in Khanh's room to tell her. When he came out, he shook his head no.

"Khanh no feel good," he said with his hand on his forehead.

"What's the matter? Where does Khanh hurt?" I asked, rubbing my stomach and then my head.

"Don't know," he replied.

"O.K. Everyone get in the van," Allen yelled.

Tong took his hat out of his coat and carefully put it on. He went in the bathroom to look at himself in the mirror on our way out. When we reached the Christmas tree lot, Bo opened the door and immediately ran across the busy parking lot over to the trees. Allen ran after him yelling, "Stop Bo. There are cars that can't see you." Bo turned around and grinned, but kept running. When Allen caught up with him, he shook his finger and sternly said, "Do not run. There are cars. You hold Tong's hand."

Tong caught up to Bo and also scolded him. Bo grabbed my hand and held it tightly while we looked at the trees. We always picked out a tall tree for the living room and a small tree for the kids to decorate in the family room. As usual, we looked at almost every tree, debating the merits of each, before we decided on the right one. The man selling the trees gave each of the kids a candy cane. When Bo unwrapped his, he threw the wrapper on the ground. I picked it up and said, "Bo, do not throw on ground." I walked him over to the garbage can and threw it in. He just looked at me with his big brown eyes and smiled.

Allen tied the trees to the top of the van and we headed for home. As we drove past the city Christmas tree, Allen pulled over and the kids oohed and aahed over it. They wanted to get out, but Allen said no.

"We have to get home and set the trees up so we can go to the basketball game. Tong, are you going to the game with us?"

"Yes," he nodded and smiled.

"You're going to go watch the girls again, huh?" Annie teased.

"Yes," Tong laughed.

When we got home, I helped Allen carry the trees in the house.

"The tree looks crooked now, but once you get the ornaments on nobody will even notice," Allen concluded. "Oh, well, we better get moving or we'll be late. Bo, are you coming with us tonight? Basketball?" Allen said, pretending to bounce a ball up and down.

"Tong, ask Khanh if Bo can go."

Tong asked her but she shook her head no. Bo argued for a couple of seconds with her, but she scolded him sharply and he immediately quieted down.

"Bo can help us make Christmas cookies." I put my arm around him. "You guys have fun at the game." I kissed Jack and Tong goodbye on the head.

After they left, Annie, Khanh, and I made dough for sugar cookies and got all the Christmas cookie cutters out. Khanh was excited when she saw the many different cutters. She called Bo, who immediately came running in with Ben. They giggled and jumped up and down when they saw all the different shapes.

After we put the dough in the refrigerator to harden, we got the gingerbread house kit out. The first step was to whip up the meringue, which acted like glue to hold the house in place. When I turned on the electric mixer, Bo ran in the other room afraid. Khanh and I laughed. She called him back in and lifted him up so he could see what the mixer was doing. They watched for about five minutes until the egg whites started to stiffen. I turned the mixer off and let Bo stick his finger in.

We put the meringue on the corners of the house and carefully propped up all four sides of the structure. Khanh held two sides together for a few minutes while the meringue hardened and Annie held the other two. When it looked like it was set, we took a deep breath and let go. It didn't collapse. We breathed a sigh of relief and put it in the fridge to harden.

I pulled out the candies we had picked out to decorate our house. Khanh laughed when she saw all of them. Bo grabbed the bag of brightly colored jelly beans that had been his choice at the store and said something to his mother.

"These are the ones Ben picked out," Annie said, handing Ben the little pieces of red licorice. "These are the ones I wanted," she added, showing Khanh the bag of pastel-colored chewy candies. "And Tong chose these," she smiled, showing Khanh the red-and-white-striped mints.

"We have to wait a while until the cookie dough and house are ready."

"Can I go and see if Shelly can play?" Annie asked.

"Sure," I agreed. "I'll call you when we're ready to make the cookies."

"O.K. Goodbye, Khanh," she cheerfully said.

Khanh waved to Annie as she ran out the door, without a coat on as usual. I got a Coke and a Diet Coke out of the refrigerator and filled two glasses with ice.

"Here, Khanh. Do you want a Coke?"

She nodded her head yes, but then stared at the two different Cokes in confusion, not sure which one to take. I laughed and handed her the regular Coke.

"I drink Diet Coke because I'm not as thin as you," I said pointing to my stomach and legs. She looked at me funny, so I filled my cheeks with air and put my arms and legs out walking like an overweight person. She laughed. "You're thin," I said, pointing to her. We both chuckled. We poured our Cokes and I motioned for her to come in the living room with me.

I got the world atlas out and sat down on the couch. "Come sit here, Khanh," I motioned to her.

She sat down by me and we opened the atlas to the map of the U.S. I showed her where Boise, Idaho is. She nodded. I showed her the same areas of the country that I had shown Tong and she also recognized New York and Vermont.

"Do you know anyone in New York?"

She nodded her head. "Is it a friend from

Vietnam?" Again she nodded her head. "Do you know anyone in Vermont?" She quickly bent her head forward once in acknowledgment. "Are you sure they're in Vermont?" She nodded her head and pointed to Vermont. Khanh looked at the U.S. map for quite a while. I had no way of telling whether she knew anything about our country.

"California," I said pointing to the long narrow state. "It's warm there. Not cold." I shivered and shook my head. Khanh looked at me and nodded. I closed the book and got the globe out. I found Vietnam and pointed to it. She nodded her head. She pointed to Saigon and said, "Ho Chi Minh."

"Yes," I said. "You lived there." I pointed to her.

"Yes," she answered.

"Your mother. In Ho Chi Minh?"

She looked at me with a blank stare.

"Do you have sisters or brothers? Like Tong and Bo?"

Again she looked at me totally confused. It was almost impossible to communicate with her. I smiled at her and she smiled back. She looked at the globe for a while. As I watched her, I kept wishing I could talk to her. I thought for a few minutes about how I could make it easier to communicate, then went and got one of our picture albums. I showed her pictures of our family at the beach.

"In Oregon," I said, showing her where Oregon was on the map. "There's the ocean." I pointed to the western coastline. She picked the globe up and ran her slender finger down the coastline of Vietnam.

"Yes!" I exclaimed. "Vietnam is on the ocean too. Did you, Tong, and Bo go to the beach?" I asked pointing to her and back to the pictures of my family at the ocean. She nodded and smiled.

"Warm. Not cold." I shivered and shook my head.

"Yes," she answered grinning.

I flipped through the pages of the picture album until I found some snapshots from last Christmas.

"My mother," I said slowly pointing first to me and then to the picture of my mom. She looked at the picture carefully then nodded her head and pointed at me with a questioning look on her face. "Yes, my mother." Then I found a picture of Allen's family and showed her Allen's mother. She nodded and pointed to Allen and his mother.

"Khanh's mother?" I asked.

She looked at me seriously for a few minutes then shook her head.

"No mother?"

She shook her head again. Next I found a picture with two of my sisters in it and showed her saying, "My sisters," pointing first to me and then to them. Khanh nodded her head in apparent understanding of what I was saying.

"Khanh. Sisters?"

Again she looked at me with a serious face and shook her head no.

"No sisters. Brothers?" I asked.

She shook her head again.

I was obviously not getting anywhere. Either she was not telling me the truth or Tong was lying. I thought about it for a minute and concluded that Tong could not have made the whole story about his family up. He couldn't possibly have been as spontaneously emotional as he was if he was lying. Plus, it made sense that she might not tell me the truth because she didn't know me well.

I checked the cookie dough and it was hard enough, so I called Annie home and we began making cookies. We set up an assembly line—with Khanh rolling the dough out, Annie pressing the cutters, and me scraping them off the cutting board and putting them on the cookie sheets. Bo and Ben had fun patting out the dough and pushing the cutters in it, but had more fun eating the dough.

Everybody helped frost and decorate the cookies with colorful sparkles, little silver balls, and multi-colored sprinkles. Some of the ones Bo and Ben decorated didn't look very appetizing but nobody cared. They tasted just as good.

After the cookies were finished, we got the gingerbread house out and carefully put the roof on. When Bo and Ben saw the house all glued together, they jumped up and down and wanted to get the candy out to decorate it.

"We can't put the candy on yet," I said. "We have to wait until tomorrow when Jack and Tong are here. Besides, it needs to set overnight so it doesn't collapse."

"No, do it now," Ben scolded.

"Come on, Mom, can't we just do a little of it?" Annie asked.

"Not tonight, honey. I want you to get your pajamas on. We'll finish the gingerbread house tomorrow. We have church in the morning so we need to get to bed at a decent hour."

"I hate church," Annie complained. "I don't want to go tomorrow since our refugees are here."

"Our refugees are going too. You and Jack can

take them to Sunday School and introduce them to all your friends."

"I still don't want to go."

"Annie, don't say that. Be thankful that you have a church you can go to."

"I wish I didn't."

"You don't mean that, and I don't want to hear you say that again. I can tell you're tired so let's get ready for bed."

"You can't tell I'm tired!" Annie yelled and stomped up to her room.

Khanh looked at me with either a smirk or grin; I wasn't sure which. I had no idea if she was thinking that this was universal child behavior or that my children were terribly disrespectful.

I took Ben upstairs, put his pajamas on and read him three books. Then I rocked him for a few minutes and laid him in his crib.

"Rub my tummy," he pleaded.

"O.K.," I whispered. Within five minutes he was fast asleep.

When I went downstairs, it was quiet and I didn't see a sign of anyone. I supposed that they had gone to bed. I sat down to read the paper when the telephone rang. It was Cindy from SOAR wanting to know how everything was going.

"It's going fine," I assured her. "I only wish we spoke the same language. It would sure make things easier."

"I know. It's frustrating to try to communicate when you speak different languages. I called to remind you that Monday you're supposed to be at our office with Khanh, Tong, and Chuy. We need to fill out Social Security applications and some other forms."

"By the way, Chuy goes by the name Bo. What time do you want us there?"

"Nine o'clock."

"Oh boy, I hope we can make it that early. So far the earliest we've had everybody up is after ten."

She laughed. "Well, they'll have to get used to it when the boys start school."

"Right. By the way, what do I have to do to get them enrolled? Do they test them or just put them in the same grade as other kids their age?"

"They usually put them in a class either one or two grades behind kids their own age. That gives them a chance to learn English and catch up with the American kids."

"So if Tong is nine, does that mean they'll probably put him in second or third grade?"

"Yeah. You probably want to encourage them to put him in second so he has a better chance."

"O.K. Allen and I will have to think about that. What about the Social Security cards? Do we have to apply for them for Tong and Bo?"

"Yes. That's the first thing we have to do. Be sure and bring all their papers."

"Like which papers?"

"Just everything they have in Khanh's bag, the birth certificates, medical and school records, etc."

"I'm not sure if they have birth certificates."

"Oh, I'm sure they do. They don't let them in the country without them."

"Oh."

"Just bring everything. O.K.?"

"O.K. Hey, Cindy, when you were at our house, you mentioned that you're active in your church. Right?"

"Yes. That's why I took this job. I wanted to help a Christian organization like SOAR give people like the Trinhs a chance."

"Have you ever encountered a refugee situation that turned out different than what the original papers indicated?"

"Well, what do you mean?"

"You know. Maybe there were more people than you thought, or maybe the relationship was different than what was on the papers."

"I'm not sure what you mean. Is everything all right with your family?"

"What would happen if you found out that things were a little different than what it showed on the papers?"

"I would try to help you as much as I could. Why? What's the matter?"

"I think there might be a minor difference in something relating to my refugee family and I'm a little afraid to fill out the Social Security application until I get it straightened out."

"What's the minor difference? I can't even try to help you if I don't know what's going on."

"But I don't want to get you involved if you are obligated to report it to someone else."

"Sandy, remember we are a Christian organization and our sole responsibility is to our sponsors and refugees."

"If I tell you, do you promise you will not tell anyone else if it's something that you're better off not knowing? I do not want to get my refugee family in trouble, but I want to do what is right."

"I promise."

"O.K. I'm only telling you so you can give me some guidance as to what I should do."

"I understand. You have my word."

"O.K. Tong told Allen and me that Khanh is his aunt not his mother. Also, Tong is thirteen, not nine."

"Oh, Sandy! How is he doing?"

"Naturally, he is very homesick."

"Boy, I don't know what to do, but I'll ask my supervisor and find out."

"Can you ask in a casual, nonspecific way? I don't want anyone to know what's going on with our family."

"I'll do some work on it and either try to call you back tonight or tomorrow."

"O.K. Khanh doesn't know what Tong told us."

"Right. I'll be really careful."

"O.K. Thanks for calling."

As I hung up the phone, my hand was shaking. I hoped I did the right thing by telling Cindy. I couldn't put Tong in second grade. He'd be humiliated. I remembered the look of pride on his face when he told me he was thirteen, not nine. He was tired of being treated like a nine-year-old. I couldn't possibly put him in with seven and eight-year-olds. But what alternative did I have? I could only hope there would be someone at SOAR that had dealt with this before. I had to trust Cindy. She had always seemed compassionate and sincere in her desire to help refugees. In any case, what was done was done. Now I only hoped that Allen wouldn't get upset because I did not consult him first.

I went in the living room and picked up a book. Before I knew it, I heard the boys coming in the back door whispering loudly.

When Jack saw me he said, "Mom, the Broncos won."

"Good, Jack. Did you have fun?"

"Yeah!"

"Tong, did you have fun?" I asked pronouncing my words distinctly.

"Yes," he smiled. "Many girls."

"Oh, many girls. How about basketball. Did you watch the game?"

"No," he laughed. "Watch girls."

We all laughed. "You're quite a Casanova. In any case, I'm glad you had fun. Now, its time for everyone to go to bed. Remember that we have church tomorrow morning."

As I walked upstairs, Tong grabbed my arm and said, "Sandy. Hat. Very warm," pointing to his new hat.

"Oh, good, Tong. I'm glad you like it," I answered, putting my arm around his shoulders. "You need to go to bed now too. Tomorrow morning we have church early."

"What?" he looked at me in confusion.

"Church."

"Church?" he asked.

"Yes," I gave the sign of the Cross.

"Oh, church. Yes," he smiled.

"Go to bed now."

"Letter," he said in a questioning voice.

"Letter? You want to write a letter?"

"Yes. Mother."

"All right. But not too late. Allen will stay up in case you need something. Goodnight, Tong," I said kissing the top of his head.

I went in our bedroom and opened the drapes. The clouds had broken up a little and there were patches of stars between the dark blotches. Although the clouds were dark and somewhat dreary, it was still a beautiful sight. In the distance I could see the tiny white lights decorating the rotunda of the Capitol Building and the twinkling lights that outlined the tall tower of the old train depot. It stood tall and majestic, as if guarding the city from any unwanted intruders. Every few minutes, an airplane would break through the clouds and streak across the sky disappearing into another dark mass.

"Are you coming to bed?" Allen asked.

"Yeah, I'll be there in a minute." I looked around the city one more time then sank into the warm soft waterbed. "So you all had fun?"

"Yeah, we had a good time. What did you do?"

"We were busy. We baked cookies, built the gingerbread house and listened to Christmas music."

"Good. Are you planning on taking everyone to Sunday School and church tomorrow?"

"Yes. I just hope we can get everyone up on time."

"We better go to sleep, then."

"You're right. Plus I'm so tired anyway."

Allen turned off the light and gave me a kiss goodnight.

We lay in bed for a couple of minutes listening to the silence.

"Cindy from SOAR called tonight."

"What did she want?"

"She just wanted to know how our new family was doing."

"Oh. That was nice of her to call. Well, goodnight."

"She also wanted to make sure I hadn't forgotten my appointment at their office Monday morning. She said the first thing we had to do was fill out Social Security applications for all three of our refugees."

"Well, that shouldn't take long."

"It shouldn't take long, but what am I going to put down for Tong's birth date? I told Cindy about Tong."

"What do you mean? What did you tell her?"

"I told her that he said Khanh was not his mother and that he was really thirteen."

"Sweetheart, we promised Tong that we wouldn't tell anyone."

"Not exactly. I promised Tong that we would do everything we could to help him and his family. We had to get some advice from somebody. I mean, what if we fill out all the Social Security cards wrong? That might permanently mess up any hope of getting his real family over here. Once information gets inside of the government's computers, there's no way we would ever get it changed. Once it gets in Social Security's computers, can you imagine where it goes from there? The IRS, Health and Welfare, the Immigration Office, the Department of Education, and that's only federal offices. Besides that, what if we have some legal responsibility not to assist in filing falsified information? I just felt like we had to trust somebody, and Cindy is the only person that is involved in this whole thing."

"What did she say?"

"She said that she would be careful not to tell

anyone. She was going to check with someone at SOAR who might have encountered a similar situation before. She said that her primary responsibility was to help our refugee family. I felt like we could trust her."

"Well, let's hope so."

"She was going to try and call us tomorrow. Otherwise we won't find out anything until Monday."

"O.K. Goodnight."

"Goodnight."

We lay in silence for a couple more minutes until I interrupted the peace again.

"Tong wasn't ready to go to bed yet. He went in your den and started writing a letter to his family."

"Did you tell him he should go to sleep?"

"No, because he really wanted to write a letter. He slept a long time this afternoon. He'll be all right."

"O.K. Goodnight."

"Goodnight. I told him you would still be up if he needed anything."

Allen let out a loud sigh. "What would you like me to do?"

"Well, do you think you could just stay awake a few minutes then make sure he gets to bed?"

"O.K.," Allen answered, somewhat annoyed.

"Goodnight. I love you."

"Goodnight. I love you, too," he sighed.

DAY 4: *You Decorated My Life*

As usual, Ben woke me up at six thirty. We went through our normal Sunday morning routine. I let the dogs out and put some coffee on. Ben went out and got the paper.

"Cold, Mommy."

"Yes, it's freezing. Close the door."

He closed the front door and ran up to Bo's door and tried to open it. When he couldn't get it open, he pounded on it.

"No, Ben!" I scolded quietly. "Don't wake Bo up yet. He's too tired."

"Yes, want Bo!" Ben started screaming.

"Ben be quiet. Everybody is asleep."

"Want Bo!" Ben continued hysterically.

"Come on, I'll make you some hot chocolate with marshmallows," I whispered, trying to keep him quiet. I had read in some parents' magazine that you should never use food as a bribe, but sometimes it was the only thing that worked. Ben settled down as I made his hot chocolate, but the damage had already been done. Within ten minutes, Bo came running into the kitchen with a big smile on his face.

"Bo!" Ben screamed in merriment.

"Ben!" Bo yelled back, giving Ben a hug in his highchair.

Bo looked at Ben's hot chocolate and pointed to it while looking up at me with big hopeful eyes.

"You want some?"

Bo nodded his head.

"O.K.," I agreed. I made Bo's hot chocolate and got the cereal out. Ben wanted Rice Krispies with bananas on it. When Bo saw what Ben was having, he wanted the same thing. Although they couldn't communicate in spoken language, they were the best of friends. Bo couldn't speak English and Ben didn't know much of any language, but it didn't matter. If two little kids could get along so well without any formal communication, there had to be hope that adults could get along better.

After we finished breakfast, I read the paper while the boys played until about eight o'clock, when we woke up Jack, Tong, and Annie. As expected, none of them wanted to get out of bed. I heard a myriad of excuses from Jack and Annie, the same ones I listened to every Sunday morning. Even Tong hid his head under the pillow and ignored me.

"Come on guys. We're going to Sunday School. It's time to get up."

I went downstairs but after ten minutes still hadn't heard anything from the older kids. So I went upstairs and found them all still in bed. I resorted to a bribe again, telling them I would take them to the donut shop for breakfast if they would hurry and get dressed. It was only the fourth day our refugees had been with us and already I had resorted to using food to bribe my kids twice just this morning. I hoped this wasn't the start of rapid deterioration in my parenting skills. It worked again—Jack and Annie were dressed and ready in less than ten minutes.

"Mom, Tong won't get out of the bathroom," Jack whined.

"Well, Honey, maybe he's busy getting ready."

"No Mom, all his clothes and toothbrush are downstairs," Jack answered rhetorically. "He just locks himself in there so he won't have to go to Sunday School."

I laughed. "Jack, he probably wants to go. I'll go upstairs and check on him."

I went to the bathroom and knocked lightly on the door, "Tong are you in there?"

"Yes, Sandy," Tong moaned.

"Are you O.K.?"

I didn't hear anything so I went and woke Allen up. He got out of bed and knocked on the bathroom door. There was no answer. He tried to open the door but it was locked, so he went around to the door entering from his den, which was open. I could hear Allen and Tong talking but couldn't make out the conversation. When Allen came out, he said that Tong had diarrhea and a terrible stomach ache.

"Is he O.K.?" I asked worried.

"Yeah, he's all right. He must have a touch of the flu."

"Should I get him some antacid or anything?"

"I don't think so. He probably just wants to stay in there for a while and be left alone."

"Well, does he need a pillow or blanket?"

"No, Mom," Allen said sarcastically. "He's sitting on the toilet."

"Oh," I answered. "I guess I'll just take Jack and Annie to Sunday School and then come right back. I'm not going to take Bo if Tong can't go. I don't think he would like it if I left him alone in the kindergarten class."

"You're probably right. I'll keep checking on Tong, so don't worry about him."

Jack, Annie, and I got ready and left for the donut shop. They weren't happy about Tong and Bo not going to Sunday School. I went back home after dropping them off, instead of staying as I usually did, because I was worried about Tong. When I got home, he was lying in bed with his eyes closed. I sat on his bed and put my hand on his forehead, but it didn't feel hot. I was relieved.

"Are you all right?"

He frowned and rubbed his stomach.

"I'm sorry you don't feel well. Do you hurt anywhere other than your stomach?" I asked, pointing to my head and acting like I was shivering. He looked at me with a blank stare as if saying, "just leave me alone."

"I'm going downstairs. Do you want Coke or anything?"

He shook his head and closed his eyes. I went to the kitchen where Allen was reading the paper.

"Maybe I should wake Khanh up and have her check on Tong," I said.

"I'm sure he's all right, Sweetheart. I don't think you need to wake her up," Allen answered.

I decided to wait a while and sat down to read a book to Ben and Bo. We just got started when the phone rang. It was Cindy from SOAR. She had talked to one of the other women in her office who had a little experience with unusual cases like ours. She recommended that we not fill out any papers until we had everything straightened out.

"What does she mean, straightened out?" I asked Cindy.

"I'm not sure, but I think she means until you decide whether Tong wants to go back to his family or stay here."

"Oh. How are we supposed to figure that out when they don't even speak English?"

"I don't know."

"Maybe I should tell Loc Nguyen what's going on. Do you know much about him?"

"He's worked with Vietnamese refugees for a long time and seems to be very dedicated to helping them. He spends a lot of time counseling Vietnamese for free. I think it would be a good idea to see if he can help you."

"O.K. I'll talk to Allen and we'll try to figure out what to do. Is there anyone in your national organization that might be able to help?"

"I don't know, but I'll try calling around tomorrow. I still want you to bring your refugee family to the office in the morning so we can at least start part of the paperwork. We can't get Khanh enrolled in any of the refugee programs or the boys enrolled in school until we have applied for Social Security cards."

"All right. We'll see you tomorrow."

Allen and I talked about our plight and decided the only thing we could do was ask Loc to help us. Our biggest problem was communication. We didn't know any other Vietnamese, and Loc seemed trustworthy. In any case, I wanted him to talk to Tong and make sure he wasn't seriously ill. I called Loc and caught him just as they were leaving for breakfast. He said they would come over after breakfast, about noon.

"If we're going to talk to Loc about Tong's dilemma, we need to tell Tong what we're doing first," I told Allen.

"I know. Let's let him sleep for a while and then we'll wake him and talk to him."

Khanh came out of her room about ten o'clock. I immediately took her up to see Tong. She talked to him for a few minutes and indicated she thought he was fine. I felt somewhat relieved. I tried to make her some breakfast but she put her hand to her forehead and shook her head.

"You don't feel well either?" I asked skeptically.

She shook her head and rubbed her stomach.

"Would you like some tea?" I pointed to the tea bags and she nodded her head yes. Great, I thought. Everybody's sick. Khanh hadn't acted like she felt well since she arrived. Plus, she had a dry cough that worried me. I was anxious to get her a checkup at the health clinic. Our refugees were supposedly checked by a doctor and certified as healthy before they left the Philippines.

I skipped church, which was something I rarely did. I had been excited to take our refugees with me, and all my friends were anxious to meet them, but I thought I should stay at home with them under the circumstances.

I picked Jack and Annie up from Sunday School. When I returned home, Allen and I woke Tong. He was feeling a little better but still had diarrhea. We explained that we wanted to tell Loc about Tong's family, and Tong agreed. He seemed eager to get Loc involved.

It was about noon when the doorbell rang. Loc was accompanied by an older boy of around sixteen or seventeen, a little girl about six, and three beautiful women.

"Hello," I welcomed them. "Please come in."

They smiled and shook our hands as Loc

introduced them as his wife, Mai, his two children and his wife's sister and her daughter.

They came in and sat down in the living room. I offered them drinks and snacks, but nobody took any. I went in the family room where Khanh was sitting in the chair looking somewhat anxious and frightened.

"Khanh, please come in and meet Loc's family."

She looked suspiciously at me and shook her head no.

"Please come, Khanh. Remember Loc from the airport? They're just here to see how you're doing." I took Khanh's arm lightly and led her into the living room. Allen went upstairs and got Tong.

Bo and Ben also came running in to exchange greetings. Annie took the little girl up to her room to play and Ben and Bo ran off to play ball. Loc talked to Khanh for a while and then repeated their conversation in English. Khanh wanted us to know how grateful she was for everything we had done.

"Loc, please ask her if she needs anything."

He asked her, then told us, "She does not need anything. She is very happy."

"Will you please ask Tong how he is feeling? He has been sick this morning."

Loc asked Tong and then repeated his response in English. "He has a stomach ache and diarrhea, which are the result of drinking too much milk. He had the same problem in the Philippines when they first got there, and when he quit drinking milk, he was fine."

I felt awful. Tong had resisted drinking milk, but Allen and I had made him. Loc explained that the digestive systems of Vietnamese people are not accustomed to a lot of dairy products. Many of them get sick when they first arrive in America because they suddenly start drinking a lot of milk and eating too much cheese and ice cream. Although I felt guilty because Tong's illness was my fault, I was also relieved that it was nothing more serious.

"Loc, will you please also ask Khanh if she feels well?"

Loc asked her and she said she felt fine. I told him that she acted as though she didn't feel well most of the time, and he said it was probably just the change in diet and climate. He also admitted, however, that she would never complain even if she did not feel well because she didn't want to be a burden to us.

"Loc, we have something else we need to talk to you about," Allen solemnly said. He proceeded to recount what Tong had told us about his purported age and family.

"I see," Loc slowly said. "This is a problem. We must discuss it with Khanh and find out if Tong wants to return to his family in Vietnam."

Allen and I gave Loc permission to talk to them about it. He conversed with them for quite a while, but we had no idea what they were saying. We could only try to interpret the conversation through Tong's and Khanh's emotions. Tong was standing by himself. He began crying so hard that I had him come and sit by me. As he sobbed, he laid his head on my shoulder and I gently rubbed the top of his head. Khanh placed her face in her hands and silently cried. It was frustrating to watch what was going on but not be able to understand what they were saying. After what seemed an eternity, Loc interpreted their conversation for us.

"Tong said that his mother is Khanh's sister. Tong has three brothers but there is not enough food for all of them because Tong's father has no job. He used to be a cook for a wealthy family, but all the wealthy families have left Vietnam. Tong's mother worked for an American defense company until the war ended. Then she was unable to get a job because the government prohibited the hiring of people who had worked for American companies. They tried to flee Vietnam but were caught and tortured. Tong said when Khanh was granted refugee status, Tong's mother begged Khanh to take him with her so he would not starve. Tong said that he came here voluntarily and does not want to go back to Vietnam. He loves his family in Vietnam very much, though, and misses them terribly. However, he believes it is his duty to stay in America and work so he can send money to his family. Khanh said Tong is lying, and that she is Tong's mother."

"Did you ask Khanh if she has any brothers or sisters?"

Loc asked her and she said no.

"Tell Khanh that Tong told me he is really thirteen, not nine."

Loc talked to her, then interpreted their conversation. "Khanh said that Tong is nine. She will not answer any more questions."

"Ask Tong if he believes he is only nine," I said.

Loc asked and reported that Tong knows he is older but that his mother told him it would be better for him to be nine in America because he would do better in school. "Tong wants to follow his family's wishes, so he will be nine."

"Tell him that if he is nine, he will have to go into the third or fourth grade," I said.

Loc told him and said that Tong understood.

"What are we going to do?" I asked Loc.

"I do not know, Sandy," Loc sadly replied.

Tong was still upset, so Loc and his wife asked him to go with them for the day to the mall. Allen and I agreed that it would be good for Tong. When they got ready to leave, Tong looked confused. Loc told him that he was going with them for the day, but he shook his head and backed away.

"Go with them, Tong. It's O.K.," I reassured him.

Loc and his wife talked to him for a few more minutes.

"He thought we were going to take him back to Vietnam," they laughed. I laughed lightly too, although with guilt for making fun of such a thing.

"Tong, you will come back here in a few minutes," I said. "You go with them. It will be fun."

He reluctantly agreed and they left. Khanh took Bo and disappeared in her room. I thought about our predicament for an hour then went to Khanh's door and lightly knocked. Bo cracked the door and peeked out. When he saw it was me, he opened the door wide and giggled. Khanh was sitting on the floor going through her papers. She glanced up at me then back down at her papers.

"Can I come in?" I asked.

She looked up at me again. I indicated that I wanted to sit on the bed. She looked back down without any emotion so I sat on the bed. She had put on her light yellow pants and top. The material was so thin it almost looked like paper.

"Would you like a Coke?" I asked.

She looked at me for a minute then nodded yes.

"Coke, Coke!" Bo exclaimed.

"O.K., you can have a Coke too."

I went in the kitchen and got two Cokes and took them back in the bedroom. I saw Khanh pull a small book out of her bag. As she started looking at it she began to cry.

"Can I see?" I asked softly.

She showed me the book—an old picture album that was falling apart. She showed me a picture of her, Tong, Bo, and a Vietnamese man standing in front of a small room that looked as though it was made out of cardboard boxes. There was a cushion on the floor and clothes were hanging on a wire running across the room. The whole area was only about ten feet by eight feet.

"Is this the Philippines?"

She nodded yes.

"Who is this?" I pointed to the Vietnamese man.

She pointed to herself in the picture and then to the man.

"Your friend?"

She nodded. "Bo's father?" I asked. She shook her head no. I wasn't sure who it was, but it was someone obviously important to Khanh.

"Can I look at the other pictures?"

She turned the page and showed me a picture of her, Tong, Bo, and about ten other people. She pointed to Tong and then to a lady.

"Is that your sister?"

She nodded yes then pointed to a man and three other boys that looked about the age of the boys that Tong said were his brothers.

"That must be his father and brothers."

She nodded yes. Tears came to my eyes as I looked at the picture. It looked like a photograph that I would have in my album. A nice happy family getting their picture taken at a family outing. In the picture the kids were smiling and the adults had their arms around each other.

"Who are they?" I asked pointing to two other ladies and a man.

"Ummm," she said. She made a circle with her finger around all the people. "Are they all in your family?" She nodded yes. Then she turned the page to a picture of her at the beach in a bikini. She was beautiful. She looked like a model in an advertisement for a beach resort. I laughed. "Look at you. Very pretty. In Vietnam?"

She grinned and nodded yes. There was one more picture of the Vietnamese man from the Philippines, and that was all the photographs. Because the plastic pages were badly torn, we taped the book back together. The album looked like it was decades old. The plastic film that covered the pictures was yellowed and scratched. It made it hard to see the photographs. She carefully put a rubber band around the book and put it back in her small bag. I was dying to know what else was in that bag but I didn't want to be nosy. There couldn't be that much more in it—it was quite small and she had already taken out some clothes and shoes.

"Let's go eat some lunch," I said patting her leg. As we got up, I pointed to her outfit and said, "That's cute." She smiled and lifted her shirt up a little so I could see the pants better. She pulled the elastic around the waist and rubbed the soft material. It looked like her stomach was bloated. Maybe she was just slightly bulging around the middle like most mothers, but it didn't look normal. We went in the kitchen and made Oriental noodles. She did not eat much.

After we cleaned the kitchen, I asked Khanh if she wanted to go to the store with me, but she declined. I wondered why she never wanted to go anywhere. If I had just arrived in a new country, I'd be excited to get out and see my new home. I hoped after she got used to being here, she'd be more eager to investigate her surroundings.

At the store, I bought a few things for Khanh, including an alarm clock, some thin writing paper and airmail envelopes, and some fingernail polish. I also picked out two small pocket date books for Khanh and Tong so they could record phone numbers and addresses for us and Loc Nguyen in case they got lost.

When we got home, Khanh and Bo were sleeping. My kids were at the neighbor's playing.

Since I had a few minutes to myself, I decided to take a walk along the Greenbelt. The Greenbelt stretches about ten miles along the Boise River and is a peaceful place to walk and view wildlife, particularly in the winter when few people venture out into the cold. There was a light scattering of clouds, and the sun streamed through every now and then as the breeze blew the clouds slowly across the sky. The trees were bare except for an occasional pine tree. The squirrels were scurrying around looking for food, periodically taking a break to chase up a tree. The busy squirrels were in contrast to the late-season ducks floating lazily down the river.

Although the Greenbelt was beautiful in winter, I missed the smell and sound of the cottonwood trees in summer. I closed my eyes and pictured summer along the river. I could hear the leaves on the trees gently hitting each other as the breeze blew softly and the chorus of birds chirping. I could smell the river and the trees as they blended together to create such a distinct aroma. I opened my eyes just in time to avoid a bicyclist who swore at me as he whizzed by. I noticed I was on the wrong side of the path, but why did he have to be so grouchy? I walked about forty-five minutes until my nose and legs were starting to get numb, then headed home.

Loc and his family had brought Tong back home and left already. He was watching a basketball game on TV with Allen and Jack.

"Tong, did you have fun?" I cheerfully asked.

"Yes," he smiled.

"Good. Did you go to the mall again?"

"Yes."

"They said that he had fun," Allen reported. "Loc's wife said that he was a very mature boy and will adjust just fine. She said he will get over the homesickness, but it will take a long time."

"When everyone wakes up, I thought we'd decorate the gingerbread house and then decorate the kids' Christmas tree," I said.

"All right. After we decorate the tree, I need to take my grandparents' presents to mom's house. She wants to mail them tomorrow," Allen answered.

"O.K. I'm making beef stew for dinner. I'll make it now and heat it up when everybody's hungry."

"Good idea. When are you going to decorate the big tree?"

"I thought I'd do it after we finished the little tree. If you're going to your mom's, maybe you could take a couple of the kids so I won't have quite as much help while I'm trying to get the lights and expensive glass balls on. They can all help after I have that done."

When Khanh and Bo awoke about a half an hour later, I let the kids have one of the cookies we had made the night before. Then I asked, "Are you ready to decorate the Christmas tree?"

"Yeah!" I heard Jack and Ben yell.

"Jack, will you go and get Annie, please? Tong and Bo, do you want to help decorate the tree?" I asked slowly, pointing to the tree. Tong said something to Bo in Vietnamese and they both nodded yes. Allen got the movie camera, and I dug out the box with all the ornaments for the kids' tree. I also unwrapped the two boxes of multi-colored candy canes which I had bought to hang on their tree. Bo pointed at one and smiled at me with a questioning look on his face.

"No, you can't eat them now. Let me show you what we're going to do with them." When everyone was in the room, I gave them each one candy cane. Jack and Annie showed Tong, Bo, and Ben how to hang them on the tree. They hung all the candy canes, and then we began unpacking ornaments. As we pulled the ornaments out of the box—first a snowman, then Santa Claus, and next Big Bird—Bo and Ben would scream with excitement. Most of the ornaments for the children's tree were handmade by the kids over the years. One year we made some bread dough ornaments shaped like ducks and geese. Another year, we decorated white Styrofoam balls with glitter and sequins. There were also sophisticated ornaments that had been made during art class at school with the children's pictures on them, and simple ornaments cut out from coloring books

It took them about fifteen minutes to decorate the tree. When there were no ornaments left, they were all disappointed. Allen rewound the videotape he had taken of them decorating the tree and played it. They couldn't believe they were on TV. Khanh, Tong, and Bo laughed and pointed at themselves, speaking furiously in Vietnamese. When the tape ended, they wanted to watch it again. We replayed it several times for them to watch. They never tired of it.

In order to get everyone away from the TV, I reminded them that we had the gingerbread house to decorate. It worked. The kids jumped up and ran to find the candy. Unlike decorating the tree, however, we had too many little hands and too small an item to decorate. Everybody wanted to decorate at the same time, and everybody wanted to place the candies on the same part of the house—the roof. After a few minor skirmishes, we compromised by letting two decorate at a time. The job was so tedious that Ben and Bo tired of it quickly. Jack put a few candies on and was ready to go play outside. Annie and Tong had a tremendous amount of patience and worked on it for quite a long time. When it was done, it looked like a house that five little kids had built. One side was decorated with red and white hard candies and the other with green and red M & Ms. One side of the roof was covered with jelly beans and the other part with licorice. It looked precious. However, it didn't last long in its original state. We left it on the center of the counter in the kitchen, and each time I went out of the room, I could tell some little fingers had snatched something off the house.

After we finished the gingerbread house, Allen called Tong and asked if he wanted to go with him to his mother's. I'm not sure Tong knew where he was going, but he had grown accustomed to having fun when he went with Allen and Jack, so he agreed to go. Bo wanted to go too, but once again Khanh said no.

"We'll be back in an hour or so," Allen said as he kissed me goodbye.

"All right. We're going to decorate the big tree while you're gone. Is that O.K.?"

"Sure. Annie said she'd help watch Bo and Ben," Allen said.

"Have fun, Jack and Tong," I said, giving them a hug as they left.

I dug the several boxes of Christmas decorations out from the closet under the stairs, then got the ladder out and climbed up to put the angel on top of the tree. Annie helped me string the small, colored lights around the branches. Khanh sat on the couch watching us, jumping up periodically to pull the little boys off the ladder. They couldn't understand how we could have such a fun-looking contraption that they couldn't play on. Once we had the lights on the tree, Khanh helped me string the beads gently along the branches. She looked like a ballerina as she gracefully circled the tree laying the beads softly on the needles. She wouldn't leave them until she had them just perfect.

Once the beads were on, I opened the box of dated ornaments. They were organized by year, so I took the oldest out first. "Look, 1977. Two birds and a heart," I pointed to the painted glass ball. "Allen and me. We were married in 1977."

Khanh smiled and nodded, then took the ball from me and ran her petite light brown finger over the birds. She slowly turned the ball around and tapped her finger lightly on it, listening attentively to the soft tingle. She handed it back to me carefully. I put it high up on the tree where I knew none of the kids could reach it. Next I took out the 1978 ball with three little angels playing trumpets on it. I handed it to Khanh. Again she smiled and delicately brushed her fingers over it. She was like a little china doll just being brought to life. She turned the ball over and studied each part of it, then gave it back to me. I hung it high up on the tree.

"Oh, Mommy, look at this one!" Annie exclaimed as she showed me the little boy in the sled.

"Yes. That's one of my favorites. I bought it the Christmas of 1981, three months before Jack was born. We knew he was going to be a boy. When I saw that ornament, I just imagined my little boy sledding down the hill. We were so anxious for him to be born. We hung it on our tree, and every time I looked at it I got a tingle just thinking of having my own little boy. Go ahead and hang it, but put it up high enough so Ben and Bo can't reach it."

Next I pulled out the 1979 ball and handed it to Khanh. Again she looked at it with adoration.

"You hang it," I told her as I pointed to the tree. She smiled at me and placed the ornament high upon the tree. We hung the 1980 and 1981 balls and then pulled out the ornament for 1982, which was a plastic

Christmas stocking with Jack's picture in it that said "Baby's First Christmas." Khanh showed it to Bo and they both laughed. Bo and Ben were dying to hang some ornaments so I let Bo hang that one. We found some other plastic decorations and let Ben and Bo put them on the tree.

I had a memory associated with each of my dated ornaments. One year we had gone to Disneyland right before Christmas, so I picked out a Mickey Mouse ball. Another year we had spent many days after school sledding, so I picked out a glass ball with little kids sledding down a hill. I let Annie and Ben hang their picture ornaments. Ben laughed when he saw his. He didn't believe it was him in the picture. I always put the kids' picture ornaments in the front on the lower part of the tree so they could see and touch them easily.

It took us about an hour and a half to decorate the big tree. Khanh seemed to really enjoy it. I felt close to her as I shared with her all my beautiful ornaments that I had collected over the years. At the same time, I felt sad watching her admire the fine glass balls because I knew she had nothing. It started to sink in that no matter how much I helped her begin a new life in this country, she would never have all that I had. She didn't appear to feel sad, however. She seemed peaceful as she looked over each of the decorations, placing them on the tree.

That night drew us closer together. I began to feel affectionate and protective toward Khanh. Although there were many times I questioned her treatment of Tong, I grew to love and respect Khanh for whom she was.

DAY 5: *The Interrogation*

Allen and I woke up at our usual weekday time, six o'clock, and got our kids ready and off to school. I was supposed to have Khanh and the boys at the Refugee Center at nine o'clock, so at seven thirty I woke Tong up against his wishes. He moaned and tried to get rid of me, as though he had learned a lesson from my own kids. At least I knew he was starting to feel comfortable in our house.

I went down to Khanh's room and tapped my knuckles lightly on the door. I waited a couple of minutes but nobody came to the door, so I carefully cracked it open and peeked in. Khanh and Bo were sound asleep in the fetal position that had become their trademark. They were in their clothes and shoes lying on top of the covers. The bedroom and bathroom lights were on. I inhaled the familiar smell that I had grown accustomed to since our family had arrived. Although they had washed their clothes a couple of times, the odor still permeated their room. It was not a bad smell, just different from what we were used to. Since many Oriental restaurants had a similar aroma, I supposed it was from eating a lot of fish and rice.

I tiptoed quietly up to the bed and gently tapped Khanh's shoulder. She jumped up startled and stared at me with terrified eyes. "I'm sorry I scared you," I said softly. "It's time to get up," I said smiling. She nodded her head and shook Bo, saying something to him in Vietnamese. Like Tong, Bo was not interested in being awakened.

I was glad I had gotten them up early, because it took them quite a while to get dressed. Tong and Bo had a bowl of cereal for breakfast, but Khanh wouldn't eat anything. She didn't even want any tea. Before we left, I collected all of Khanh's papers in her room and put them in a bag.

Tong put his new hat on. When Khanh noticed Tong putting his hat on, she got Bo's cute red beret and put it on him. Khanh still refused to wear the tennis shoes I had given her, opting instead for her more familiar sandals. She did put socks on under them, however. We pulled out of the driveway at eight forty-five. The sky was gray. The sun had only been up about forty-five minutes, but was partially hidden by thin clouds blanketing the city. There were patches of fog floating listlessly in the pockets between the hills that looked like loosely spun cotton candy. It was a beautiful sight. The air was warmer than it had been for several days, and it felt like it might rain. I pointed to the thin layers of clouds floating over the landscape and said, "Fog."

"Yes, fog," Tong answered. "Fog in Vietnam, too," he added. Then Tong said something to Khanh and Bo in Vietnamese, and they talked for about five minutes. I presumed it was a discourse about the weather, maybe reminiscing about the climate of their homeland.

I stopped at the muffin shop to get a cup of coffee. I asked Khanh if she would like some coffee, tea, or a muffin, but she shook her head no. When I opened the car door, Bo yelled "Coke!" I turned around to look at him and he greeted my eyes with a big smile and a look of anticipation.

"No Coke," I smiled back.

The Refugee Center was about seven miles across

town. I couldn't get there on the freeway, so it took about twenty minutes of meandering through heavy traffic. I pointed out schools, buses, the river, and other points of interest as we drove along. Tong always concentrated on what I said, and repeated after me at least once for each new word. Khanh and Bo just looked and nodded their heads.

About a mile before we reached the Refugee Center, Khanh rolled her window down and laid her head on her arms, which were folded on the window sill.

"Are you O.K.?" I asked Khanh. I suspected something was wrong because although it was warmer than the past few days, it was still cold. She didn't answer me so I asked, "Do you want me to stop?" She continued to ignore me. We were only a short distance from the Center, so I kept driving until we reached the Refugee Center. I parked the car and walked around and opened Khanh's door. She stepped out and immediately vomited. She staggered over to the bushes along the side of the building and continued to throw up.

"Stay in the car," I said sternly to Tong and Bo, as I shut the door. I ran over to Khanh and asked, "Are you all right?" She continued to have dry heaves so I just rubbed her back and whispered, "You poor thing. It's all right. We'll go in and find you a place to lie down."

We stayed out by the bushes for about ten more minutes until Khanh stood up. It had started to drizzle, which along with the chilly air, caused me to shiver. Khanh looked pale and weak and was shaking uncontrollably.

"Come on. I'll help you," I said softly, putting my

arm around her and draping her arm over my shoulder. I practically carried her inside the building and sat her down in the lobby. Then I went back out to get Tong and Bo. They were waiting patiently in the van. I grabbed the bag of papers and told them to follow me in. After I got them seated next to Khanh, I looked around for a rest room. There was one down the hall, so I went back and slowly helped Khanh walk to the bathroom. She started to lie down on the cold tile floor of the restroom, but I said, "No, Khanh. Let's clean up and go find a more comfortable place for you to rest." I helped her wipe off her face, and she rinsed her mouth with soap. It was amazing that she hadn't gotten anything on her clothes.

We went back into the office. I asked the receptionist if they had a place for Khanh to lie down. She led us to a room with a couch where she immediately collapsed into the soft brown cushions. The interpreter came in a few minutes later and talked to Khanh. Then she reported to me that Khanh had been having trouble keeping food down since she left the Philippines. She also was not used to driving in an automobile. After Khanh had rested for fifteen minutes, she sat up and wanted to go ahead with the scheduled interview, but I told the interpreter that I would rather take the papers with me and fill them out at home. Khanh still looked weak and pale, and we still needed to go to the SOAR office. The interpreter left the room and went to discuss the situation with the caseworker. They agreed that it would be better for me to take the papers and come back when Khanh felt better. They gave me a stack of papers an inch thick and we left.

It was only about one and a half miles to the SOAR office, but when we arrived, Khanh got out of the car and vomited again. I stood outside in the cold damp air with her for about ten minutes, rubbing her hunched over back until she slowly straightened up and went in. We went to the bathroom and cleaned up again. Although Khanh barely had strength enough to stand up, she insisted on staying and conducting the interview at the SOAR office.

When Crista and Cindy entered the room they greeted our family warmly. Khanh seemed to enjoy seeing someone she knew again. There was also a Vietnamese boy about eighteen who was going to act as our interpreter. He spoke perfect English without any trace of an accent, so I guessed he had been one of the lucky ones who had fled Vietnam before the fall of Saigon.

I didn't want to discuss our conversation with Loc Nguyen concerning Tong's family situation with Cindy because Crista and the interpreter were there. I decided to wait until we were done with the interview and I could talk to Cindy in private.

We sat down at a long metal table with folding chairs. The walls were whitewashed with no hanging pictures or windows, and there weren't any plants on the table or desk. There was one box of tissues sitting on the long table. The room was cluttered with papers and reminded me of an interrogation room inside a prison.

Crista and the interpreter sat down at the table with us. After Crista introduced the interpreter, named Quong, she looked at Khanh and said, "We need to ask you some questions today so we can start filling out your papers. It is very important that you answer all questions truthfully. Do you understand?"

I glanced quickly over at Crista and stared at her, wondering why she said "truthfully." Quong repeated everything Crista said quickly and smoothly in Vietnamese. Crista didn't slow down to allow Quong to catch up, they just both spoke normally at the same time without any apparent disruption. I was amazed at how skillfully Quong kept up with what Crista was saying. He indicated that Khanh understood, so Crista began the interview.

First she gathered all the papers together and sifted through some of them. Then she asked Khanh what her and Bo's full names, birth dates, birth places, parents' names, etc., were. Crista carefully wrote all of the answers down. Then she asked, "Where is Bo's father?"

The interpreter asked Khanh, who answered quietly as she stared into her lap, her nervous, fumbling hands damp with sweat. Quong explained that Bo's father lived in Vietnam but that Bo had not seen him for two years.

Next Crista asked, "Are you divorced?"

Again Quong asked her. She answered hunched over in her chair like a shackled prisoner. The interpreter reported that "Yes, she was divorced from Bo's father and she remarried a Vietnamese man while she was in the Philippines." I stared at Quong stunned, not sure at first that I had heard him correctly. That must have been the man she showed me in her picture book. I looked over at Khanh and slowly cracked a weak smile. She looked back at me and grinned sheepishly, obviously noticing the shocked look on my face.

"Do you have an official divorce decree from Vietnam showing that you are divorced from Bo's father and a marriage certificate from your spontaneous fling in the Philippines?" Crista asked sarcastically. I glanced at Crista, shocked by her comment. How could she have said such a mean, judgmental thing?

Quong asked Khanh, then reported that she and Bo's father tore up their marriage certificate and she had no papers proving her marriage to her husband in the Philippines. Crista threw her head back and sighed, "Oh, I see, whenever you want a husband, you just pick a name, and whenever you want a divorce, you just tear up a paper."

My eyes filled with tears. I was concentrating so hard on the conversation that my hands began falling asleep from folding them so tight in front of me. I was afraid to say anything or make a scene because I didn't want Khanh to know that Crista was making fun of her. Fortunately Quong did not repeat Crista's last comment.

The room suddenly felt hot and stuffy. I wanted to take my refugees and leave. How could anyone who worked full-time with refugees have her attitude? I was both furious and scared. I felt like someone was attacking my own family, but I was also afraid of the power Crista might have if we didn't fully cooperate. I wondered where Cindy was. I had only met Crista at the airport and had never heard her name before that. Why was Cindy abandoning me now, I wondered? My face was hot and I supposed it looked red. Khanh, Tong, Bo and I were sitting at one side of the table facing Crista and Quong. As I shifted my eyes toward Crista's face, I became horrified. It seemed as if she was three times her normal size, hovering over the table and staring at us as if casting a spell. It seemed as though we were all in a trance in a room that was dead silent for what seemed like hours. My throat was dry and I was afraid to say anything for fear that nothing would come out. Why was I so upset about this? They were not interviewing me, I reminded myself. I had only known my refugees five days. What was the big deal?

Suddenly Bo fell off his chair. Startled, I jumped up and rushed over to him. He looked at me with a huge smile and giggled. I laughed and picked him up and hugged him.

"You are being such a good boy. Would you like to get a drink?" I asked.

I don't think he knew what I said, but I took his hand and led him out of the room to find a drinking fountain. The air outside the interrogation room smelled fresh and felt cool. There were a couple of ladies cheerfully talking in one room. One of them came out in the hall and smiled at Bo, saying "How are you?" Bo nodded his head and answered, "Fine, thank you." The lady and I both laughed. He said it like a typical American child who had been drilled on what to say when spoken to by adults. Bo spotted a box of candy in what appeared to be a break room. He ran into the room, where there were also a pop machine and a water fountain. He looked around, then reached in the box and grabbed a package of cookies and licorice. He then went up to the pop machine and yelled, "Coke!"

"You can pick one treat, Bo," I said with authority. He looked at me with pleading eyes and a big grin.

"You pick either cookies, or licorice, or Coke. Not all three." I shook my head. He nodded his head up and down then pulled the cookies and candy close to his chest. "Just one, Bo," I said putting up one finger. He wouldn't voluntarily let anything go, so I took the cookies from him and put them back.

He looked up at me and said, "Coke," pointing to the pop machine.

"No," I said firmly. I got a drink of water and also lifted Bo up for a drink. Then I held one hand while he clung tightly to the licorice in his other, and we went back in the room with Khanh and Tong.

Everyone glanced up when we entered. Khanh still looked pale and Tong seemed tense. "Let's continue with our interview, shall we?" Crista suggested in a pleasant voice.

"First I need to go put fifty cents in the candy box," I answered. "Tong and Khanh, would you like a Coke or a drink of water?" They both shook their heads, so I left with Bo tagging behind me to pay for the licorice. I showed Bo the money I put in the box so he understood that the candy was not free. When we went back in the room, Quong was talking to Khanh who was listening attentively. Tong's head was resting in his cupped hands with his elbows on the table supporting them. He was deep in concentration listening to the interpreter.

When Quong finished his conversation with Khanh, he said, "In Vietnam it is the custom that when a married couple wants a divorce, they just rip up their marriage certificate. There are no official marriage papers like in the United States. Everything is more private and much simpler."

"I didn't ask for your personal commentary," Crista snapped. "Please keep your remarks to repeating only what Khanh says."

"O.K.," shrugged Quong. "I was only trying to help you understand the customs of the Vietnamese."

"I am already familiar with most of their ways, thank you. Now please refrain from any editorial comments."

Quong rolled his eyes and answered, "All right."

"So why didn't your new husband come with you to the United States?" Crista asked suspiciously.

Khanh and Quong talked back and forth for several minutes. Tong was listening carefully to Khanh while she was speaking and then quickly turned his attention to Quong while he was talking. Soon I noticed Khanh's eyes starting to fill with tears. Her voice never faltered, and her nose never dripped, but soon tears began streaming down her face. As I watched her, water also began to swell in my eyes.

Oh God, why does she have to go through this? I wanted to scream out. I wondered how many times in her life she had been interrogated and by how many different parties. Why again in America? She's supposed to finally be free here! I wondered why the SOAR people needed to know about her husband. In America when applying for jobs, employers are forbidden to ask questions about a woman's husband. When applying for a credit card, there are many laws prohibiting discrimination against women. I didn't understand why she had to sit through this humiliation.

Quong interrupted my thoughts saying, "Khanh's husband broke up a fight between two Philippine guards. When the police came, they arrested him because he was Vietnamese. The guards claimed that they weren't doing anything and that Khanh's husband had started the fight. That happened seven years ago. He was sentenced to ten years of work in the Philippine refugee camp. He still has three more years, and then he's scheduled to go to Australia." Quong paused for about five seconds and then softly added, "Khanh misses him very much."

"That story is preposterous," Crista said sarcastically under her breath but loud enough so everyone could hear. "He sounds like a troublemaker."

I put my arm around Khanh and hugged her. She wiped her eyes with a tissue and looked at me as if begging for help.

"I think we should go," I said abruptly. "Khanh has had enough for today. She doesn't feel well, and I don't think this has helped much." I stood up to leave but Crista interrupted, "I really need to ask Tong some questions first. If we don't get further than this, it will take us forever to get anything done. We need to get the Social Security applications filled out so they can get their medical cards and school admittances."

"O.K.," I reluctantly agreed. "Go ahead and ask Tong some questions but I think Khanh has had enough. Khanh, do you want to go lie down?" Quong repeated what I said, but she shook her head. "Ask her if she wants anything to eat or drink." Again he asked her but she shook her head no.

"All right, let's get started," Crista urgently said. "Tong, what is your full name, age, birth date, and parents' names?" Tong slowly gave his complete name, recited his age and birth date according to his birth certificate, and said that Khanh was his mother and

Bo's father was his father. I thought it was strange that she would ask Tong these questions. Why didn't she cover Tong when she asked Khanh about her and Bo? I began to feel defensive.

"You're a big boy for nine," Crista said, staring at his eyes.

"Yes," Tong said, smiling. I knew it was hard for Tong to crack that smile. The stress showed in his face. Khanh also looked worried.

"Did you go to school in the Philippines?"

"Yes, and he was a very good student," Quong interpreted Tong's answer.

"Did you go to school in Vietnam?"

"Yes, he was also a good student in Vietnam," Quong said.

"Did you take math in the Philippines and in Vietnam?"

"Yes, math is one of his favorite subjects. He always gets good grades in math."

"What kind of math problems were you doing in Vietnam?"

"He was doing geometry and division," Quong responded.

"Oh, that's interesting. Most nine-year-olds in the U.S. are only studying multiplication and maybe a little division but certainly not geometry," Crista said, raising her eyebrows and acting impressed.

Tong's face drooped and he smiled faintly as Quong repeated what Crista had just said. My face began to feel hot again. Did Cindy tell her? Why else would she ask any of these questions?

"Did you meet lots of friends in the Philippines?"

"Yes," Tong answered. "Many friends."

"Did Bo have lots of friends?"

"Yes, Bo many friends too," Tong smiled.

"Do you miss your friends in Vietnam?" Crista asked in a very friendly, chit-chatty voice.

"Yes," Tong nodded.

"What kind of things do kids play in Vietnam?"

Quong answered, "They play soccer and running. There are not many toys in Vietnam like in the United States."

"What grade were you in, in Vietnam?" Crista asked nonchalantly.

"Eighth grade," Tong answered proudly. Suddenly his face lost its smile and his eyes were full of fear. Khanh looked down at the table and stared at her sweaty hands.

"Oh really? Eighth grade and you're only nine?"

I stared at Crista in horror. How could she do this to him—to be so cruel to a young boy who has been through so much?

"Apparently Cindy talked to you about Tong's family in Vietnam," I interrupted.

"Not necessarily," Crista said evasively.

"Look, let's not play games. We're dealing with a nine-year-old's life. I told Cindy about Tong's family in confidence because we needed help, but since then I have resolved the problem. Loc Nguyen came over last night, and we discussed the situation with Khanh and Tong. Everything is fine."

Khanh's hands were shaking, and Tong's eyes were filled with tears. Quong was also visibly upset. "Let's continue the interview," Crista said nonchalantly. "Now Tong, tell me all about your other family in Vietnam."

"Wait," I demanded. "It's not fair to put Tong through this. Yesterday we hashed everything out with Loc Nguyen in an emotional meeting. Since SOAR apparently cannot help us as a co-sponsor of our refugees, we will not discuss this situation further until I have consulted an attorney. I will take the Social Security applications with me and fill them out after I have seen an immigration attorney."

I stood up to leave and motioned for Khanh, Tong, and Bo to get their coats on.

"We already checked with a lady in our Seattle office who said that we as members of SOAR should not get involved in family problems. There is nothing we can do," Crista apologetically said.

"Well, then I won't need your help any further. I will handle everything with the Refugee Center. Now we have to leave," I said firmly, putting my coat on, getting my purse and leaving the room.

As we walked to the car, I felt like screaming in anger and bawling in frustration. I wanted to hug all three of my refugees and tell them everything went well, but I couldn't lie to them. I also couldn't break down because then they would know something was wrong. So I smiled at them and put my arm around Khanh.

We were just getting in the car when Quong ran up and breathlessly asked, "Is everyone all right?"

"Yes, please tell them that everything will be fine. And thank you very much, Quong. I trust that everything which took place is confidential?"

Quong looked me straight in the eye and said, "You have my word. When a Vietnamese man gives his word, it is always honored."

"Thank you. You were a great help."

As we started to drive home, I noticed that Khanh was shivering. I turned the heat on high and took my coat off and laid it over her. She smiled at me but looked embarrassed. About two miles before home, Khanh opened her window again. "Do you want me to pull over?" I asked pointing to the side of the road. She didn't say anything; in fact she didn't even look at me. I drove a couple more blocks and pulled into a parking lot. Then I walked around and opened her door. She quickly jumped out and ran over to the grass and vomited. I stayed by her, rubbing her back for about five minutes until she walked back to the car.

When we got home, Khanh immediately went in her room and closed the door. I told Tong to go and get her clothes so I could wash them. He brought out a handful of clothes, so I took him in the laundry room and showed him how to work the washer and dryer. After we started the washer, I said slowly, "Tong, please go to Khanh and ask her if she would like some tea or Coke, and tell Bo to come out and play with me so his mother can sleep."

Tong nodded and disappeared into Khanh's room. Pretty soon, Bo came running out in his pajamas. Tong also went upstairs and changed into what looked like pajamas that he had brought from Vietnam. I debated whether to say anything about wearing pajamas during the day and decided that I should teach them the American way, so I said, "Tong, in America we don't wear our pajamas during the day, only to sleep." I laid my head against my folded hands to illustrate. Tong gave me a disgusted stare and said sharply, "In Vietnam, not pajamas." I looked at him in confusion.

He appeared hurt, but maintained his proud stature. He turned and walked away.

I sighed in frustration. Just when I thought I had a handle on what was going on, something like this happened. I went in the living room and sank into the couch. It struck me that I had been insensitive. There was obviously a reason they kept changing into their pajamas. I was trying to help them learn American customs because I wanted them to fit in and not be ostracized by neighbors or teased by kids at school. Why was I so determined to make them Americans? My mind debated the merits of letting them live according to their culture or encouraging them to adapt to American traditions. If we lived in New York, their ways would be more acceptable, but there was little cultural diversity in Boise. I stood up and sighed again, rubbing my hands through my hair in frustration. I reminded myself that I was not their mother and they would find their own way.

I called Allen to find out if he was coming home for lunch, but he said, "I can't come, Sweetheart. I've got a meeting. Sorry."

I explained what happened at our SOAR interview and we agreed that our best course was to consult our friend Bob, an attorney. I called Bob's office and as expected, he wasn't available, so I left a message.

"Bo, Tong," I called upstairs. "Come down and eat some lunch, please." As soon as I finished the sentence, they were running into the kitchen with big smiles on their faces. "What would you like for lunch?" They looked at me funny. "You know, to eat." I pretended to put food in my mouth. Tong shook his head, "Nothing."

"You're not hungry?"

"No," he shook his head again.

"You really should eat something. It is lunch time. Bo, are you hungry?"

Bo nodded yes, so we made some Oriental noodles.

While Bo and I were eating, the phone rang. It was Bob. I explained our situation, and he said it was beyond his area of expertise. He recommended that we call Evan Schoonover, who was an immigration attorney. I called his office, but he was unavailable. His secretary wanted to know why I was calling. I told her I wanted to see Mr. Schoonover regarding an immigration situation. She tried to schedule me in three weeks, but I told her that I really needed to see him today. She said that wouldn't be possible because he was totally booked.

I responded by asking, "Will you please leave him a message and tell him that Bob Littlemeister assured me he would see me today since it was an emergency."

"Oh, Bob Littlemeister referred you?"

"Yes. He told me that Mr. Schoonover would surely see me if he knew how important it was."

"Oh. Can you tell me why you need to see him today?"

"I really can't. If you don't think he can see me, please tell me right away so I can call Mr. Littlemeister back and get his second choice."

"Well, if Mr. Littlemeister thought it was urgent, Mr. Schoonover can probably see you this afternoon at four thirty. Let me get your number and I'll call you back if that won't work. Otherwise, just plan on coming at four thirty."

"All right. Thank you very much. I'll see you at four thirty."

"What's your . . . " I heard her say as I hung up.

"Attorneys," I said in disgust, shaking my head.

Just as I hung up, the phone rang. It was Karen from my office. She said many of my clients had called and wondered when I'd be back. There were also a number of things she needed to discuss with me. I told her I would try to come in for a few minutes tomorrow. I cleaned up the house, did some laundry, and made another grocery list. Khanh wandered into the kitchen about two o'clock and got an apple. I made her some tea. She refused to eat anything else. I was starting to get worried about her. She hadn't eaten much since they arrived in America. I didn't know if she had a touch of the flu or if she had something more serious. The dry cough concerned me because of all the press reports on the resurgence of tuberculosis, particularly among refugees.

After she finished her apple, she got out the only book she had and started reading it. It was a 1960 edition of a Vietnamese/English dictionary. She studied it quite often, although I wondered how much good it did since it didn't teach her to sound out the words. I tried to learn a few Vietnamese words, and even though I learned how the words were spelled, I never did learn to pronounce them. The Vietnamese and English languages are very different. Her dictionary, like her photo album, was falling apart.

The afternoon went quickly. Before I knew it, Jack and Annie were running in with stories about their day. They wanted to play with Tong and Bo, but I made them do their homework first.

Allen and Ben came home a few minutes later. As always, Ben came running up with a big smile yelling, "Mommy!" I picked him up and hugged him tightly.

"Tong, do you want to help me cook?" I called. Tong ran quickly into the kitchen. I understood his interest in cooking now that I knew his father was a cook. We put a chicken with potatoes, carrots, and onions in a baking pan and placed it in the oven. "Allen, do you want to come to the attorney's office with me?"

"I think I should stay home," he answered apologetically.

"All right, but keep an eye on dinner."

I went in the family room where Khanh was watching TV and motioned for her to come with me. We went in her room and I explained that I needed to take her sack of papers with me. She distrustfully looked at me, so I tried to reassure her that everything was fine. She nodded that it was O.K. for me to take them. I breathed a sigh of relief, kissed all the kids and Allen goodbye and left.

The attorney's office was plush like most lawyers' offices. The receptionist greeted me, and I told her my name, mentioning I had called earlier. She told me to have a seat for a few minutes. I waited twenty minutes before she showed me into Mr. Schoonover's office.

"Hello, Mrs. Dalton," he greeted me cheerfully.

"Hello. Thank you very much for seeing me this afternoon. I realize it was short notice."

He asked me the standard billing questions: name, address, place and length of employment, spouse's name and place of employment, etc.

"Now, what's the emergency?"

"First, I need to ask if everything I tell you is in confidence."

"I can assure you that everything you say is absolutely confidential and I have no responsibility whatsoever to report it to anyone."

"Good," I answered in relief. I recounted the events starting with the arrival of our refugee family and ending with the questioned relationship between Khanh and Tong. "The reason I wanted to see you is that I need to apply for a Social Security card tomorrow for Tong. I hope you can tell me two things: what information to put on the application and how to get his family over here. He misses them very much and my husband and I promised to try to reunite them."

"Boy, this has turned out to be a little more than you bargained for, huh? Did you sign any forms when you agreed to be a co-sponsor?"

I had to think for a minute and then remembered. "Yes, we signed a form. I can't remember for sure what was on it. I think it indicated we were responsible for helping our family find an apartment, getting the boys in school, and after that we were supposed to keep in touch with them for the next six months in case they needed any help."

"I would like to read that form. I want to make sure that you fulfill all of your responsibilities and there is nothing that addresses situations like the one you're in."

"All right, I'll bring you a copy. What about Tong? How should I fill out his Social Security application?"

"First, let me explain that I almost exclusively represent large corporations who hire highly skilled employees from foreign countries. I usually try to figure out a way to keep them in this country while the companies need them here. I deal with a completely different section of the immigration law than what you're dealing with. Do your refugees have birth certificates?"

"Yes. Tong's shows that Khanh is his mother and that he was born in 1982."

"Without researching this too deeply, what I would do is fill out the papers with the information you have on the birth certificate. That is the only official information you have. To use anything else is pure speculation. There may be other things you don't know. The only legal document you have is the birth certificate. You don't know for sure that anything else they tell you is true. You simply have no proof. In addition I can assure you that there are many similar situations with Vietnamese refugees. They faced such terrible conditions that they did anything to survive."

"All right. That makes sense. Now, how do I get Tong's family over here?"

"That's a much more difficult problem. There are many people that have been trying to get family members over here for seventeen years. Since you are filing Tong's papers showing he is Khanh's son, you will have to file showing Tong's father and mother in Vietnam as his aunt and uncle. Since aunts and uncles do not have a high priority, it could take many years. I am aware of a Laotian that had a similar family situation to Tong's. When he reported his story fifteen years after he originally entered this country, it was totally up to the immigration official handling the case whether he would allow the man's family to come over. But you really have no choice, because if you report that Tong entered this country as Khanh's nephew, they will probably send him back to his family in Vietnam. What you're telling me is that you do not want that to happen."

"It doesn't matter what I want. It's what Tong and his family want."

"I understand. It will be difficult if not impossible to obtain refugee status for Tong's family. Your best bet is that the U.S. will normalize relations with Vietnam within a few years and then Tong can fly back to Vietnam to visit."

I wanted to cry but maintained my composure. I wondered how I could break the news to Tong. Everything was so nebulous. Maybe in a few years the U.S. would normalize relations, but a lot of things could happen by then. His mother or father in Vietnam could die. In any case Tong would have grown up.

"If you would please send me a copy of any forms you signed, I will review them so we make sure you and Allen fulfill your responsibilities. Is there anything else?"

"No, thank you very much."

I left feeling numb. What were we going to do? I didn't want to tell the truth to Tong—that it would be years before he saw his family again. But I had to be honest so he could decide whether he should return to Vietnam.

When I got home, I could smell the chicken cooking. The kids ran up to me and gave me a hug, glad that I was home. I looked at all their faces with such bright eyes and happy faces. At least Tong was here safely and had enough to eat. His parents had made the ultimate sacrifice. It was now my responsibility to follow though and help raise him.

That night after we put the kids to bed, Jack came into my room complaining, "Mom, Tong's singing in my room and I can't sleep. Will you please come tell him to stop?"

"All right," I agreed, getting out of bed and putting my bathrobe on. I went into Jack's room and heard a deep wailing sound coming from Tong whose head was under his pillow. I listened for a minute in confusion— not sure what he was doing. It sounded like he was singing an old Negro Spiritual. He kept repeating the same words over and over again in a low mournful wail. I sat down on his bed and removed the pillow.

"Tong, are you all right?"

He looked up at me with tears falling down the sides of his face. He shook his arm at me to leave and put the pillow back over his head. He continued his lamenting cry.

"See, Mom, he sings terrible and I can't sleep."

"Honey, he's not singing. He's mourning. He's terribly homesick for part of his family in Vietnam. This is his way of trying to expel the sadness from his body. Please try to understand and just let him cry until he falls asleep."

"O.K. But I know I won't be able to go to sleep."

"Why don't you put your pillow over your ears and then maybe you can."

"I'll try," he sighed. "Goodnight, Mom."

"Goodnight, Sweetheart. I love you." I kissed Jack goodnight and bent down and patted Tong on the back. "Goodnight, Tong. I love you, too."

He continued mourning.

DAY 6: *The Rabbit Died*

I had hoped things would settle down by the sixth day and we could start getting into a routine. Unfortunately, it didn't turn out that way. It ended up being one of the most frustrating days we had while our refugees were with us.

The day started out being a repeat of the day before. We had another appointment at the Refugee Center at nine o'clock for orientation. Once again, Khanh vomited, but this time she did it in the car. To my pleasant surprise, however, she had brought an air sick bag with her from the airplane. When we reached the Center, she laid down for a few minutes, and then we were led to a room by our appointed caseworker and an interpreter.

The first thing the caseworker asked was if I had filed for their Social Security numbers. I explained that I had the applications filled out and was going to drop them off at the Social Security Office after our meeting. She acted perturbed that it hadn't been done yet and explained that she couldn't file for any benefits until the Social Security applications had been turned in.

The caseworker proceeded to interview Khanh, asking most of the same questions that Crista had asked the day before. My first recommendation to SOAR was going to be that one of their representatives sit in on the meeting with the case worker so everything didn't have to be repeated. This time when the caseworker asked Tong his age and grade in school, I jumped in and answered for him before the interpreter had a chance to repeat it in Vietnamese. When she asked Khanh where her husband was,

Khanh repeated the story of her divorce, but this time she didn't explain her remarriage in the Philippines.

After the social worker finished the interview and filled all of her papers out, she explained what we could expect: "All refugees are expected to work. They must actively seek a job, and if we call them for a job interview, they must show up for it. They will be provided with medical cards for six months which will cover most of their medical expenses. A benefits coordinator will review Khanh's application for welfare assistance and determine how much she will be eligible for. The maximum will be about $300 a month, which will be reduced for every dollar over $500 she earns in a month. She is expected to attend English classes every Monday, Wednesday, and Friday mornings at nine o'clock for the first three months. Many employers will not even consider her for a job until she can speak some English. Do you have any questions?"

The interpreter had carefully repeated everything she had said in Vietnamese. Khanh shook her head no.

"Very well then, you may go."

"When will they receive their medical cards?" I asked as she rose to leave the room.

"In about a week."

"Is there any way I can get her into a doctor sooner?"

"No, she will have to wait. Why, is there something the matter?"

"I don't know. She has a dry cough. In addition, she keeps vomiting every time we drive anywhere, and she hasn't been eating well."

"I'm sorry but unless it's an emergency, she'll have to wait."

On our way home there was an Oriental grocery store that I decided to stop at. Khanh, Tong, and Bo were excited when they saw the selection of Vietnamese food. There was a young man who spoke Vietnamese and walked around the store with Khanh, pointing out the most popular items. He tried to convince me to buy them a set of painted glass rice bowls, a rice-cooker, and a twenty-five-pound bag of rice. I went over and looked at the prices. The bowls were $25 for a set of four and the rice-cooker was $65. The man started to get a box of the bowls down, but I told him I wasn't going to buy them.

"But they will need them very much," he pressured me.

"They'll have to do without them for now."

"But they must at least have a rice-cooker. That's what they use in Vietnam every day."

"Well, I use a pan and they'll have to learn how to cook rice in a pan."

"But this is a different kind of rice. They can't eat American rice."

"They'll have to learn. I've never owned a rice-cooker in my life."

Just then, Tong ran up to me with a can of yellow fruit that I had never seen before. He spoke furiously to me in Vietnamese, but I couldn't understand him.

"He want that," the young man smiled at me.

"O.K. You can get it. Go set it on the counter." I pointed toward the checkout stand. Bo, who was standing next to Tong, ran off and came back a few seconds later with another can of what looked like pickled beans. He didn't say anything but looked up at me with his big brown eyes and smiled.

"You want that, Bo?" I asked. He nodded his head. "All right," I agreed. "Go put it by Tong's."

Khanh wandered up to the checkout counter empty-handed. "Khanh, do you want something?" I asked. She shook her head no. I thought of how upset she would be if she knew how much the young man had pressured me to buy something for them. They had never asked for anything other than necessities.

Our trip home was uneventful. As soon as we arrived, Khanh immediately went in her room and fell asleep. Tong and Bo begged to play outside on the bikes. Although it was cold, I agreed, bundled them up, and sent them out.

Allen came home at noon and we fixed lunch. Khanh was still sleeping, so she skipped lunch again. After we cleaned up, I went to work and Allen stayed home.

When I got to my office and looked at the desk stacked with messages and papers, my first inclination was to turn around and go back home.

"Are there any emergencies that need to be taken care of first?" I asked Karen.

"Well. You might want to call Ron and Beatrice. They've called several times and seemed upset that you hadn't been in for several days."

I rang Ron's number and he immediately answered, as if he had been waiting for me. He was upset because his two million dollars in bonds had fallen $400. He was even more upset when he found out I had sponsored a Vietnamese refugee family. He was an Army officer during the Vietnam War and thought there should be a law prohibiting Vietnamese from entering the country. I mentioned that Khanh's father was an American soldier, but it didn't matter. Ron still thought she should have remained in Vietnam.

After we completed our conversation, I said to Karen, "Ohhhh, I could scream!"

"What's the matter?"

"Of all the nerve. Ron is going to drive me nuts. He's worried about his bonds losing $400. In addition, you should have heard his response when I told him about our refugees. He acted like I was on drugs. I've seen his income tax return every year for the last eight years. He has income of $250,000 a year and has never made a charitable contribution."

"He can be frustrating, all right. Sometimes I wonder why we put up with him."

I read some more of the material that had piled up in my mailbox while I worked up enough energy to call Beatrice.

"Hello, Beatrice, how are you today?"

"Oh, Sandy, I've been waiting for your call. Are you all right?"

"Yes, I'm doing fine. Why?"

"Well you haven't been in for a few days and I was starting to get worried about you."

"Oh, well, I've been very busy."

"What have you been doing?"

"We are sponsoring a refugee family and they just arrived last Thursday."

"Your church?"

"No. Just my husband and I."

"Oh. Where are they from?"

"Vietnam."

"Vietnam! Why'd you do something like that?"

"It's a long story, but we basically just wanted to help this family."

"With all the starving people in this country?"

"Beatrice, if there are starving people here it's because they're either not aware of the programs or choose not to participate in them. I know there are a lot of people that need help in America and we do many things to help domestically, but we just felt that our family from Vietnam needed help more than many of the low-income Americans."

"Well, I believe that charity starts at home. I don't think we should be out feeding the whole world when our own people are starving."

"I understand, Beatrice, and I'm glad that you help people in this country, but this is something that we wanted to do. It's not something we think the U.S. Government should do. It just seems like our taxes go up and up, but poverty in America keeps going up, too. No matter how much money we give to help the poor in this country, the poor just keep ballooning. I don't know what the answer is. We give money to the Salvation Army and offer our home for kids that need help. We debated being foster parents, but have heard such horror stories about how Health and Welfare handles the cases that we were afraid to do that."

"Do they speak English?"

"The older boy knows a little bit."

"I don't think anyone should be allowed in this country unless they speak English. My folks only spoke a little English when they came over from Germany ninety-five years ago, but they learned it quick.

Nowadays, people come from all over and expect us to speak their language. It's a disgrace that everywhere you go in the cities they have all the bus schedules and signs at the airport in two or three languages. I say that if they can't speak English, then it's their problem to figure out what it says."

"Well, anyway, Beatrice, why did you call me last week?"

"I've got a CD due at the bank. You know, I was reading the paper Friday and the man in there recommended that I buy some Pepsi. What do you think?"

I chuckled, "Beatrice, you've never owned a stock in your life except a couple of utility stocks. I suppose it's never too late, even at age ninety-four."

"You know they own Pizza Hut?"

"Yes."

"Well, I order from them every week. I love Meatlover's pizza, and the delivery boys are always so nice. I just thought maybe I should buy their stock."

"I think if you want to own some Pepsi stock, it would be fine for you to buy one hundred shares."

"Well, then, buy me some. Maybe they'll give me a discount on my pizza."

"I wouldn't count on it. But you can think of it this way: by paying full price you're helping the bottom line. That's what will make your stock go up."

"That's right. You won't be gone too much anymore, will you?"

"I'll be in and out for a few days, but if you really need me just tell Karen and she'll get ahold of me."

"All right. Thank you, goodbye."

Hanging up the phone, I turned to Karen, "It's time to get out of the market, Karen. Sell quick."

"Why?"

"Beatrice is buying her first stock in ninety-four years."

Karen laughed. "Did she give you a hard time about your refugees?"

"You know Beatrice. Somehow when people live beyond sixty-five, they think this omniscience has descended upon them. Nothing is gray: It's all black and white."

"What do you mean over sixty-five? We should include all males regardless of age and all females over sixty-five."

"Right," I laughed.

I spent the next two hours solving similar emergencies. By the time I was ready to go home about four o'clock, my desk was a little cleaner.

I went home and when I opened the door, Ben came running up to me with his arms wide open. "Mommy!" he yelled.

I grabbed him and gave him a kiss. "How are you?" He gave me a big hug that assured me he was fine.

"Hi, Mom!" Annie ran up and also gave me a hug.

"Hi, Sweetheart! How are you?"

"I'm fine. Mommy, do you know what Mark did today?"

"What did Mark do?"

"He kept pulling my pony tail and saying, 'Giddyup.'"

"Did you tell him not to touch your hair?"

"Yes, but he kept doing it."

"Well, that probably means he has a crush on you."

"Oh, yuck! I hate Mark."

"Please don't say hate. You don't hate anyone, you just dislike them."

"See you later, Mom," Annie cried as she ran off.

"How did work go?" Allen asked as I walked into the kitchen.

"Frustrating," I sighed.

"Why?"

"When the cat's away, the mice think they need a baby sitter."

"Oh," he laughed, "do you have to go in tomorrow?"

"I don't know. Let's see how it goes. I really should if I can. Where are the other kids?"

"They're all up in Jack's room playing race cars."

"I thought I'd cook that frozen fish and some rice for dinner. Since they're used to eating lots of fish, Khanh might eat better."

"That sounds fine."

I went upstairs and opened Jack's bedroom door. "Hello, everybody."

"Hello," I heard back from a harmony of voices. Nobody looked up. "Where's my hug?" I asked.

"Just a minute, Mom," Jack said, concentrating on the race with his tongue hanging out of his mouth. Bo looked up, grinning. "Bo, come give me a big hug," I said with my arms open. He jumped up and threw his arms around me.

"How about you, Tong?" Tong smiled and stood up and put his arms around me too. "How was school, Jack?"

"Good."

"Is that all?"

"Yeah. It was pretty boring."

"Oh well, you guys can play for a few more minutes and then it's time for dinner. Do you have any homework?"

"I already did it with dad. I had spelling, science, and math. I can't believe how much homework Mrs. Black gives us."

I went downstairs and asked Allen where Khanh was. He said that she had spent most of the afternoon in her room. He wasn't sure whether she was sleeping. I walked up to her room and put my ear to the door. I didn't hear anything so I knocked quietly. When she didn't come to the door, I cracked it just a little and peeked in. She was lying down on the bed. I opened the door a little wider, and she opened her eyes and looked at me. She smiled.

"How are you, Khanh?"

She nodded her head and sat up. She was wearing a sweat suit I had given her. As she sat on the edge of the bed, her stomach seemed to have a slight bulge. That was about the fifth time I had noticed it. "Do you feel all right?" I asked her. She just smiled at me, not knowing what I said. I felt her forehead which was slightly warm. "Do you want to come help me fix dinner?" I asked. She followed me. She peeled carrots, and Tong came down and helped make salad. Whenever he saw a new vegetable, whether it was lettuce, onions, or tomatoes, he always remarked about how big they were compared to those in Vietnam.

While we were cooking, I casually commented to Allen, "Sweetheart, I think Khanh's pregnant."

"You, what?!" he answered in a stunned voice.

"I think she's pregnant."

"What in the world makes you think that?"

"She just looks and acts like it. Have you noticed the little bulge she has around her middle."

"No," he said quickly glancing over at Khanh.

"Look more carefully sometime and you'll see it."

"Sandy, she could just be a little overweight."

"No, not just in one place. She's tiny everywhere else."

He kept looking over at Khanh.

"Please don't stare at her or she'll know we're talking about her."

"How could she be pregnant? Her husband was in Vietnam the whole time she was in the Philippines."

"I haven't had a chance to tell you yet that she got married again in the Philippines."

"You're kidding!" he exclaimed.

"No, please settle down or they're going to think something is wrong. Besides, she never feels well, she won't eat anything, or take aspirin."

"I think you're crazy."

"I hope you're right. In any case, I think we should call Loc and see if he can come over tonight or tomorrow night. I need to find out what's the matter with her. The lady at the Refugee Center said I couldn't take her to a doctor until I get the medical card, and that could be a week or so."

"Well, then call Loc."

I went over to the phone and called him. Fortunately, he and his wife said they would gladly come over tonight.

We ate dinner and cleaned up. I sent Annie over to

play with Shelly and Jack over to Nathaniel's. I explained to Tong that Loc and his family were coming over, and he seemed pleased that he would get to see them again. Soon after we had cleaned up, the doorbell rang. This time only Loc and his wife had come. We invited them in and got tea for the adults and Coke for the kids. Once again Khanh didn't want to come in the living room. Although I explained that Loc and his wife had just come to visit, she didn't seem to want to have anything to do with them. I had to coax her out of the chair and lead her lightly by the arm into the living room.

Loc talked back and forth with Khanh and Tong about how they were doing and whether they needed anything. Tong commented about having too much food to eat. He said that in Vietnam, they ate at most one meal a day. As usual, they said they didn't need anything and wanted us to know how much they appreciated everything we had done.

"Loc, ask Khanh how she feels," I said.

He talked to her for quite a while and then reported back that she felt fine.

"Tell her I'm worried about her because she vomits often and doesn't eat well."

Again, Loc talked to her for several minutes and then reported, "She said that she doesn't like to drive in the car because it makes her sick. She also said that she doesn't get hungry. She likes your food very much but just doesn't feel like eating."

"Ask her if she feels pain anywhere."

Loc asked her and reported that she felt fine and was very grateful for all we had done.

I sighed. "Loc, I think she might be pregnant. Will you please ask her?"

Loc and his wife both looked startled. "What makes you think so?" his wife asked.

"She has a bulge around the middle and just acts like she is pregnant."

"We don't want to offend her if she's not," said Loc's wife with apprehension.

"I don't know how else to find out. If she's not pregnant, then something else is wrong. She's been with us long enough that I know she does not feel well. I have to find out if she's sick and needs medical treatment."

This time Loc's wife talked to Khanh. Every now and then, Loc would interrupt the conversation. I studied Khanh and Tong carefully. There was nothing in their faces or voices that would give me a hint what they were saying. Khanh was rubbing her hands together slowly and picking the polish off her nails. Tong's head moved back and forth from speaker to speaker, his eyes concentrating on what each one said. They talked for about ten minutes and I wondered if Mai was ever going to translate their conversation into English.

Suddenly, I noticed Khanh's eyes fill with tears. Mai was talking softly to her in a kind voice. Khanh buried her head in her hands and began to wail. Mai went over to the couch and sat by Khanh, gently putting her arm around Khanh's shoulder. Tong was also visibly upset. Finally, Loc broke the ice and said, "You are very observant, Sandy. She is pregnant."

I stared at him in disbelief. How could she be pregnant?! Although I had wondered if she was pregnant, I thought there would be another explanation. Supposedly they had medical checkups in the refugee camp that would have detected it. I glanced over at Khanh conspicuously. How could this have happened?

"She is about three and a half months along. The baby is due toward the end of May," Mai said graciously.

"Who is the father?" I asked, half in a daze.

"Her husband that she married in the Philippines."

I was completely astounded. How could she be so stupid as to get pregnant? All of her dreams of peace and hopes for prosperity for her family could be ruined. I stared at Khanh. She was still crying. I wanted to go over and comfort her, but at the same time I wanted to scream at her.

"She said that she misses her husband very much. She knows he cannot come to America for a long time."

Suddenly, I felt empathetic toward her. My eyes started filling with tears. "Tell her that she can write to him. When the baby is born, we'll send pictures."

That made Khanh cry even harder. The tension in the room was broken when Tong got up and left. "Tell her that I'll take her to see a doctor as soon as possible. In the meantime, she must start eating better or the baby will not be healthy."

When Loc told her, she nodded her head in agreement.

"Ask her if she needs anything," I said.

Loc asked her then repeated back that she needed some pants with an elastic waist.

"Tell her that I will get her some. Is there anything else?"

"She wanted me to tell you that if you have a sewing machine and material she can make some pants. She also thanks you very much for everything you have done. My wife and I must go now. We will try to come on the week end."

"Thank you so much for coming on such short notice. Loc, can you go see if Tong's all right? When he left the room, he seemed upset."

"Yes. I will see." He went in and talked to Tong for a few minutes. When he came back in the living room he said, "Tong is angry at Khanh's husband for getting her pregnant. He did not know she was with child until tonight. He is worried that they will be sent back to Vietnam if the government finds out. I assured him that they will not be sent back."

"Thank you Loc. I'll call Cindy tomorrow and ask her what to do. They really won't send them back, will they?"

"No, I'm sure they won't. This happens sometimes. She will have more difficulty finding a job, though."

"I haven't even thought about that," I rolled my eyes and sighed. "Let's just hope there are no more surprises. Thanks again for coming. Goodnight."

After Loc and his wife left, Khanh and Bo went to their room. I went in the family room and sat by Tong. He was staring off into the distance with a somber face.

"It will be all right, Tong," I assured him. His trance was not broken. I put my arm around him and added, "Everything will work out fine." He got up and without looking at me went upstairs.

I called Annie and Jack home, then got Benjamin in bed. As usual, nobody wanted to go to sleep. I went in to check on Tong and found him lying on his bed with the pillow over his head. I sat down on the bed and said softly, "Tong, why don't you get your pajamas on." He didn't move. I rubbed his back and took the pillow off his head. He had been crying. "Oh Tong," I sighed, "everything will be fine. You have been through so much. We will get you into a routine soon and things will settle down. What you really need is to start school and meet some friends. I'm going to call SOAR tomorrow and insist that you start school." Tong just gazed at me with glassy eyes. I stared at him for a while then whispered, "Where are you?" He just looked at me like I wasn't there. "Are you with your brothers in Vietnam?" He squinted his eyes. "Oh Tong," I cried, lifting his upper body and rocking him back and forth. Tong cried hard and said many things in Vietnamese. "I only wish I could understand what you're saying. Even though I don't understand the words, I can feel your heartache." We sat in silence for about ten minutes until Tong settled down. "Go to sleep now. You're tired," I whispered. I kissed his forehead and went to my room.

I got my pajamas on and crawled in bed, waiting for Allen. The next thing I knew, I opened my eyes and glanced at the clock. It was ten minutes after two. I sat up and looked at Allen, who was sound asleep. I had dozed off. I lay in bed, suddenly wide awake.

I thought about Khanh and all that had happened during the day. I recounted in my mind our trip to the refugee office and the Vietnamese store. Then I rehearsed the events that had taken place with Loc and his wife. Never had I gone through so many emotional ups and downs in six days. I hoped we were through with major surprises. I kept thinking about Khanh being pregnant, and although I tried to put it out of my mind, I just couldn't. I tossed and turned, trying to get back to sleep. I was too anxious to sleep. One minute I was mad at Khanh and the next I was sympathetic. "Allen," I shook him gently, "can you wake up?" I whispered. There was no movement or sound. "Allen," I said a little louder, "please wake up." He moaned. "Allen," I said sternly, "please wake up right now." He immediately sat up.

"What's the matter?" he said in a worried voice.

"Will you talk to me for a little while? I can't sleep."

"What about?" He lay back down and turned over.

"Don't go back to sleep. Please wake up."

"All right, what's wrong?"

"I am so upset about Khanh. I can't believe she got pregnant. She could have blown everything. How could she do such a stupid thing? She was so level-headed and downright crafty in her quest to leave Vietnam. She managed to survive a very hostile environment as an Amerasian and eventually get out of Vietnam. Somehow, she was able to get out of the Philippines without them knowing she was pregnant. She obviously had to use her head to do all those things, but how stupid could she be to get pregnant? Just when I had developed admiration and respect for her, I find out she's pregnant! Not only that, I've grown fond of her. I've felt so sorry for her because she's sick all the time. And then, I find out it's all self-imposed. How stupid could she be?" I rambled.

"Wait a minute, Sweetheart. Let's start over. First of all, what else did you expect her to do? I'm sure they don't have any means of birth control in the refugee camp."

"Well, she never should have gotten herself in that situation in the first place!"

"Sandy, have you forgotten that she got married?"

"But that was mistake number one. Why in the world would she do something so stupid when it probably took her years to get out of Vietnam and she finally had a chance for a decent life for her and her sons?"

"Did you ever think that maybe she fell in love?"

"Allen, don't be ridiculous. You don't get yourself in a position to fall in love when you're fleeing for your life."

"Oh, I see. In other words, love is something that you plan ahead and only do if it's the right time and place."

"You know what I mean, Allen. A person in such a crucial situation isn't in the frame of mind to be thinking of love. Please be realistic."

"Sweetheart. You're the one being unrealistic. Love is a feeling, not a situation. She's a human being. Maybe she didn't want to fall in love. Maybe it just happened."

"Well, by letting it just happen, she could have been sent back to Vietnam and given up any hope of a better life for Bo and Tong, and now the new baby. That seems like a pretty stupid thing to do."

"No one ever said that human beings aren't stupid. Just give her a break. She's been such a heroine in your mind—let her be a woman, too."

"Well, so much for worrying about what she could have done to herself and her boys. Now look what she's done to us. What are we supposed to do now? She's not going to be able to get a job, at least not for long. How is she supposed to support two boys and a new baby under the circumstances?"

"I don't know. We'll just have to talk to Cindy and see what to do. It will all work out so don't worry about it."

"Don't worry about it! Who's going to pay for all the doctors and hospital? We're probably responsible for adding another lifetime member to welfare. It's not fair to the American taxpayer. That's what we've really done—brought somebody over from Vietnam and added them to the welfare rolls. That's not the way it's supposed to work."

"Sweetheart, please don't worry about it. We'll take care of it in the morning. There's nothing we can do about it tonight, so let's get some sleep. Now, goodnight."

"Goodnight," I sighed. "I'll try to go back to sleep. I'm just so disgusted." I gave him a kiss, and he started snoring about two minutes later. I lay in bed and stared at the ceiling trying to calm down for a long time. The next thing I knew, the alarm clock was going off.

DAY 7: *A Trip to the Health Clinic*

The seventh day was not quite as eventful as the first six. It came at the right time. Allen and I needed a break. I was not normally an overly emotional person, but since our refugees arrived, I felt like I was the leading actress in a soap opera, except it wasn't make-believe. My two priorities were to get Khanh to a doctor and to enroll the boys in school.

I called the Refugee Center and left several messages, but nobody returned my call. Then I called Cindy and told her the latest news. She was shocked. She had handled many refugee cases in her career, but had never run into a family with as many unexpected events as ours. I asked Cindy how to enroll the boys in school. She told me I had to wait until they had an apartment. That was frustrating because I had hoped to start them before Christmas break. Allen and I wanted to send them to St. Joseph's Catholic School, the same school our children attended, but it was too expensive. Cindy encouraged me to start looking for an apartment, but I wasn't sure she understood the gravity of the situation. I asked her how Khanh was going to pay for an apartment. She assured me that since Khanh was pregnant, she would qualify for more benefits.

I waited all morning and part of the afternoon for the caseworker from the Refugee Center to call me back, but she never did. I decided to call Loc to get his advice as to what to do next. He agreed that it was important to get the boys in school, but thought it was just as critical to get them in an apartment of their own. Like Cindy, he assured me that she would get plenty of welfare to pay rent for a nice three-bedroom apartment, so I should start looking. I was bewildered. I couldn't imagine sending them out on their own yet.

After I talked to Loc, I called the Central District Health Department. I asked the receptionist if I could speak to the Director of the Department. She wanted to know why and I explained that it was confidential. She took my number and said she would try to have him call back. I figured I would be waiting the rest of my life for that call, so I changed strategies. I called back and tried to schedule an appointment, but once again the receptionist said it would have to wait until after the holidays. I explained that it was an emergency, but when I told her what kind of emergency, she said she couldn't do anything until after New Years. I asked for the name of her supervisor. She gave me that name so I called back and asked for her. I repeated my story and got the same answer. I asked for her supervisor and got the name of Mary Locke. When I finally got through to Mary, I told her that I was the niece of one of the local Congressmen and that he had told me to call and ask for her. I explained that Khanh needed an immediate appointment because she was pregnant and was not well. I couldn't believe my luck. Mary responded that she was so glad the Congressman remembered her from the campaign six years ago. She wanted to know if I could bring Khanh in that afternoon. Once Mary agreed to schedule Khanh, I explained that she didn't have a medical card yet but that the Congressman was sure that wouldn't be a problem. I told her I would bring it in as soon as I received it which would be any day. She said that would be fine.

I finally felt like I was making progress. Since luck

seemed to be on my side, I decided to go to the Refugee Center and park myself in the reception area for a while. No one would return my call, and I had to find out how much assistance Khanh could expect for rent.

We made it to the Refugee Center without Khanh getting sick. I had my refugees sit down and then explained to the receptionist that I needed to talk to a caseworker about Khanh's situation. She told me I would have to come back later when the caseworker was there, but I told her that we would just wait. I had already taken almost a week off from work and didn't feel like I had accomplished much. I needed to get them an apartment, get their health checked and get the boys in school so they could start a routine. We waited for about fifteen minutes and didn't seem to be getting anywhere, so I went out to the car and got a basketball out of the trunk. I brought it in and sat Tong on the chair directly across the small room from me and Bo on the floor by the door.

"O.K., Tong, catch!" I yelled. Tong looked at me shocked that I would be playing ball in an office. I winked at him and shifted my eyes toward the receptionist. I threw the ball to him and he threw it back to me. Bo stretched out his arms and yelled something in Vietnamese, so I bounced the ball to him. We continued to play for a few minutes, but didn't seem to be getting anyone's attention. I told Tong and Bo to keep playing while I went to get three Cokes, potato chips and a package of cookies. I went back to the office and gave Tong and Bo each a Coke and opened the packages making as much noise and spilling as many crumbs as possible without being too obvious. Soon the receptionist came out and announced that our caseworker was out for the day but that Mrs. Roberts might be able to help us. She led us back to her office.

We were in luck again. Mrs. Roberts seemed much kinder than our own caseworker. She even said hello to Tong and Bo in Vietnamese and got some color crayons and books out for them to play with while we talked.

"So what can I help you with, Mrs. Dalton?" she asked after we sat down in front of her desk.

"I met our caseworker yesterday and filled out a bunch of paperwork in order to start receiving benefits for Khanh. Last night, I learned that she is pregnant, so Cindy from SOAR said that I should reapply for everything since she would now fall under different programs."

"Oh, I see. Well, that sounds right. She will now qualify for the WIC Program which means she will receive extra food stamps for baby formula, milk and things like that."

"What about rent?"

"It won't affect the amount she receives for rent."

"Do you have any idea what that might be? I would like to get the boys enrolled in school but can't until I know where they're going to live."

"I really am not in a position to tell you, because that's up to Mrs. Smith. There are very strict guidelines she has to adhere to."

"Cindy thought that because Khanh was pregnant, she would receive enough for a three-bedroom apartment."

"I don't believe that is correct. Mrs. Smith will

come up with a specific dollar amount that they will be allotted for rent."

"Do you know approximately how much that might be?"

"Again, Honey, I just don't know. I would suggest you start looking for low-income apartments now so that when you receive the benefits statement, you're ready to move in."

"But I just don't have any idea how much they can spend. Will it be $400 or $700 a month?"

"Probably somewhere in between. She is still expected to work, even though she is pregnant."

"I agree. Most American mothers have to work while they're pregnant, so I expect Khanh to also."

"Do you have any more questions?"

"How long will it be until we know how much they'll have for rent?"

"I'll have to tell Mrs. Smith tomorrow that Khanh is pregnant, which will slow things down a little. You probably won't get anything until after the holidays."

"After the holidays! That's still three weeks away. They're supposed to move into their own place within a week."

"Can't they stay with you?"

"Well, yes they can, but everyone thinks they should be out on their own right away. And besides, I don't want to wait until after New Year's to get the boys in school."

"Honey, you shouldn't have to wait to get those boys in school."

"I shouldn't?"

"Why, no. They'll be going to the refugee program at Franklin School regardless."

"They will?"

"Yes. It's a terrific program and a wonderful school! They started it a few years ago when they consolidated all of the language and culture classes that refugees attend in one school. I think they have around one hundred kids there from about twenty-four different countries. I know there are a number of Vietnamese kids."

"I haven't ever heard of it before. Cindy and Loc Nguyen must not be aware of it. They said I had to wait until they moved so I could enroll the boys in the school closest to where they lived."

"Oh, no. They'll go to Franklin School for at least a couple of years until their language, history, and math skills are up to the same level as other kids their age. The lady who is in charge of the program is Mrs. Carhill. You can probably call her this afternoon. You'll really like her. She loves kids and is always thrilled to have new refugees."

"Thank you so much. You've been a great help to me. If I can enroll the boys in school, my only other problem is getting the benefits information from Mrs. Smith."

"I'll tell you what. I'll talk to her and see if I can help her so we can get it to you sooner."

"Oh thanks. That would be wonderful. You've been so much help already."

"I think it's wonderful that you've sponsored this family. The boys are so well behaved."

As we left, I let out a big sigh of relief. I finally felt like we were getting somewhere. It was five minutes before Khanh's doctor's appointment, so we had to rush to Central District Health.

When we arrived, there was a bunch of medical forms I had to fill out for Khanh. The only sections I could complete were name, address, and phone number. I had no idea whether she had ever had heart problems, cancer, etc. When I explained the circumstances to the receptionist, she responded coolly, "I'm sorry, but we will not be able to see her today then. You will have to reschedule when there is a Vietnamese interpreter here."

"But Mary Locke said she would make sure and get us in today since Khanh has been sick."

"What's wrong with her?"

"For one thing, she's pregnant. She hasn't been eating well and keeps vomiting when she does eat. In addition, she has a dry cough that has me a little concerned. I have three children at home. I want to make sure she doesn't have tuberculosis."

"It sounds like she's just pregnant to me. That's not an emergency. I'm sure she was tested for TB at the refugee camp. They wouldn't have let her leave if she tested positive. Besides, there's not a doctor on staff anyway. She could only see a nurse."

"Then I would like her to see the nurse. I've seen reports of immigrants entering the U.S. with TB."

"I'm sorry, that's against our policy. We cannot see a patient without those forms filled out."

"All right. I'll fill them out."

"But you don't have an interpreter."

"Yes I do—Tong. He speaks English. We'll have the forms completed shortly."

I began the arduous task of trying to explain the questions to Tong (difficult in itself). To try and get Tong's response back in English was almost impossible.

Some of the questions we managed to get answered. For most of them, an interpreter couldn't have helped, since Khanh wouldn't have the slightest idea what things like AIDS, heart bypass surgery, etc., are. I answered no to anything that Tong couldn't answer. I figured that nothing would be prescribed today anyway, and I would have Loc help me ask Khanh the questions later.

I had Khanh sign the forms, then gave them back to the receptionist. While we were waiting, Bo picked up a package with what looked like a balloon in it from a bowl on the magazine table. He brought it to me with a big smile. I looked at it and realized it was a condom. I shook my head in disgust, and put it back in the bowl. We waited for forty minutes until a pleasant-looking, rather chubby lady in her fifties called, "Khanh Trinh."

"That's us," I said. She led us into a small room with an old bed against one wall, a chair next to the bed and some cupboards against the other wall. There wasn't enough room for all of us, so I took the boys back to the waiting room and told them to stay there. I went back to the small room and explained Khanh's circumstances to the nurse. She was friendly and seemed sympathetic. She agreed to do a complete exam on Khanh, including blood tests, a check of her teeth, and a gynecological exam. She thought it would take about an hour, so I told her we would leave and come back.

Franklin School was only about a mile away, so I decided to go and see if I could meet Mrs. Carhill. She wasn't there, but the office secretary told me that if I came at seven thirty the next morning, Mrs. Carhill could talk to me.

I took the boys to McDonalds and got them some french fries. They marveled at all the characters on the walls and the big statue of Ronald McDonald outside on the playground. Although it was cold, Bo played on the slides for a few minutes before we went back to the Health Clinic.

We waited at the Clinic for almost an hour before the nurse came out. It was closing time and everybody else had left. "You have a very sick lady on your hands. She doesn't have anything that a lot of medical work and healthy eating won't cure, but it's going to take some time."

"Why, what's the matter?" I asked, worried.

"To start with, she's malnourished. She is slightly dehydrated too. She needs to eat more vegetables and iron-rich foods, but she also must start drinking more. In her condition she should particularly drink milk. Her body is using muscle to keep going, which isn't a good situation. The second major problem is her teeth. She has thirty-nine cavities and many of them have decayed clear down to the roots. Her whole mouth is infected. You must get her into see a dentist right away."

"She'll be O.K., won't she?"

"She'll be fine. I have a little concern for the baby, but babies are amazingly strong. Many of them in third world countries end up all right even though their mothers were malnutritioned during pregnancy. However, now that she is here, it's critically important that she eat better. She has to give the baby the best possible chance to be healthy."

"How far along is she?"

"I think about four months. It's awfully hard to

tell, though, because it could be smaller than a normal American baby because of the lack of good prenatal care."

"I have a real hard time getting any of them to drink milk. Tong even got sick from too much of it. The interpreter told me that their bodies aren't used to it and that it makes them ill."

"If she won't drink milk, give her ice cream, yogurt, or cottage cheese. She has to get more calcium both for her own bones and teeth and the baby's. I'm going to send this bottle of vitamins home with you, which will help. Make sure she takes one every day. Then see if you can get her in to see a dentist tomorrow. I think the infection in her mouth might be what's making her sick. She has a slight temperature, which is probably being caused by the infection. I did a TB test but we won't know the results for a while. Her lungs sound fine, though."

"Do you have a dentist here?"

"No. You'll have to call around. Some of them will take medical cards and some won't. Tell them it's an emergency and have them call me if they want. I would also like to reschedule Khanh for an appointment with the doctor after the holidays."

"Can't you schedule her sooner?"

"I really can't. The doctor is leaving on a vacation tomorrow and won't be back until after Christmas. She'll be all right until then. I want you to take these kits home and get a stool and urine sample from each of them." She handed me a brown bag. "If you can bring them back tomorrow or Friday, I'll run some more tests and make sure there's nothing else wrong."

"O.K. I want to thank you so much for all your help. I realize it's late and we've probably kept you."

"Well, I was supposed to pick my granddaughter up at day care at four o'clock, but I called and told them I'd be late. We were just going to get shoes, but we can do it tonight."

"I'm sorry. I hope she won't be upset with you."

"If she is, I'm used to it. She lives with me so I'm just like a mother. It seems like kids are always mad at their moms."

"Isn't that the truth?" I laughed. "We'd better let you run, but thanks again for all you've done."

When we got home, Jack, Annie, and Ben were there. They were glad to see me but upset that I wasn't home earlier. They each had Christmas pictures they had made at school, and were excited about the parties and activities being planned for Christmas. I couldn't believe it was only two weeks away. I still had so much to do. I didn't know when I was going to get all the Christmas cards addressed and presents bought.

That night after dinner I sat down in the living room to read the paper. Khanh came and sat by me and read her English book while we listened to Christmas music and enjoyed the beautiful tree. After I had read the paper, Jack came in and asked "Mom, when are our refugees going to leave?"

"I don't know yet Honey, why?"

"Because, I'm tired of them. They've been here long enough."

"Well, we can't just kick them out. Khanh isn't in very good health right now, and I have to get her feeling better before they leave."

"Why can't they just move into their own apartment and you can take her to the doctor then?"

"They're not ready to be on their own yet. We have to get the boys enrolled in school and through orientation classes first."

"How long is that going to take?"

"I don't know. Why are you so anxious for them to leave?"

"Because you don't even care about us anymore. You never do anything with us. You're always with the refugees," he said bitterly.

"Come here, Sweetheart," I reached my arm out and put it around him. "I know I've spent more time with them lately, but it's because they need a lot of help. It won't be much longer and they'll be on their own. Then you'll have me all to yourselves again."

"But you love them more than us," he pouted.

"Oh Jack, don't be silly. There's nobody I love more than you and Annie and Ben," I laughed.

"We haven't gotten to do any of the things we usually do during Christmas time."

"Like what?"

"Like go shopping and pick presents out for everybody. And then wrap them. And then make fancy ribbons with our bow-maker. And make Christmas ornaments. And we've only gotten to make cookies once. Usually we get to do it a lot of times."

"I'm sorry, Jack. You're right, we haven't been able to do as many things. But I want you to remember that what we are doing is much more important than shopping or baking. I know that's fun and we'll have lots of other Christmases to do that, but what we're doing this year is providing a family with the chance for a new life. Remember that Christmas celebrates the greatest gift of all. It's about giving, and what we're giving is much greater than gifts we can buy at a store."

"I know, Mom, it's just that I wish they didn't have to be here forever."

"They won't be. Now, what would you like to do tonight? I'll play with you. Other things can wait."

"Let's play war."

"All right, you go get the cards."

We played for about an hour, until it was time to get everyone ready for bed. I tried to explain to Khanh that we had to get up early so we could take the boys to school. I wasn't sure if she understood or not.

As soon as I got everyone in bed, I went in my own room exhausted. Although I hadn't done much physical activity since our refugees had arrived, it seemed that the emotional stress wore me out each day. I went to sleep wondering what tomorrow could possibly bring.

DAY 8: *The First Day of School*

When the alarm went off, I hit the reset button and fell back to sleep. The second time it rang, I jumped up and glanced at the clock. It was six fifteen. I knew I would have to hustle to get everyone dressed, fed and the refugees in the car by seven fifteen.

Allen woke our three up, and I worked on our refugees. When I tried to get Tong up, he put the pillow over his head and waved me away. "You have to get up Tong. I'm going to take you to school today. School, Tong. Wake up." I shook him several times but got no reaction.

I went downstairs and knocked lightly on Khanh's door. I didn't hear anything, so I opened the door slowly and peeked in. The light was on and she and Bo were cuddled together in their fetal position, which I had grown to adore. Her chin hugged Bo's head, and her arm held him tight against her, as if protecting him from some unknown intruder. Usually when I opened the door, Khanh woke up. This time, however, they both stayed fast asleep. They looked so peaceful, I hated to wake them up.

"Khanh," I whispered. No response.

"Khanh. It's time to wake up," I said a little louder. Still no movement. I shook her lightly. Suddenly, she jumped up and started to scream. Her face looked terrified and she grabbed Bo to protect him.

"It's O.K., Khanh. It's only me," I said apologetically. "I'm sorry. I didn't mean to scare you." She sighed in relief and collapsed back on the bed.

"It's time to get up. We're going to take the boys to school today." She took a deep breath, probably trying to slow her heart rate down, then shook Bo and said several things in Vietnamese. Bo moaned and mumbled something back. She scolded him and sat him up involuntarily. He started to cry.

"Bo, if you get up I'll get you an apple," I said cheerfully. He didn't even look at me. Apparently apples didn't work anymore. I thought about offering a Coke, but decided that would start a bad habit. I left their room and went back upstairs to find Tong still asleep with the pillow over his head. "All right, Tong. You have to get up now." I said sternly, pulling the pillow off of his head and shaking him.

"No," he replied firmly.

"Yes," I repeated, sitting on the bed and pulling him up. "You have to get up now." I insisted. He opened his eyes and looked at me for a minute and then broke into a smile.

"Sandy, good morning," he said sweetly.

I laughed, "Good morning, Tong. Did you sleep well?"

"Yes, thank you."

"You must hurry," I pointed to my watch. "We have to leave soon."

He gave me a questioning look and asked, "Go?"

"Yes. Go to school."

"Oh, yes, school," he smiled. He jumped out of bed, got his clothes and went downstairs to the bathroom.

It was a struggle, but we managed to get everybody dressed and fed on time. Jack, Annie, and Ben were upset that I was leaving so early with the refugees. I promised I would try to be home when they got home from school so I could do something with them.

We arrived at Franklin School right on time at seven thirty. There was only one light on in the school, and the parking lot was still dark. There was a light skiff of frost on the grass and the ground was frozen solid. I told the boys to get out of the car and walk carefully. I went around and opened Khanh's door and helped her out. The ground was slick, so I grabbed her arm tightly and started walking slowly with her. "Slick," I pointed to the ground. She nodded. I hadn't planned very well and had on smooth-soled dress shoes, which made it more treacherous. When we reached the grass, Khanh shook her arm free from my grasp. I insisted on at least holding her jacket lightly because I was still afraid she could fall. I felt a motherly bond now that I knew she was with child.

We finally reached the door but when I tried to open it, it was locked. "Great," I sighed. We were all shivering from the cold. Tong and Bo looked slowly up at the two-story school. It was one of the oldest and largest school buildings in Boise. It had a basement that could be seen through window wells, a main story and an upstairs. It took up the equivalent of two big blocks. They gazed around at the building and the school grounds. It must have been much bigger than their school in Vietnam or the Philippines. I knocked on the door. "Ouch," I shook my hand, as the cold vibrated through my fingers. Nobody came, so Tong and I walked to the other end of the school, where we found an open door. I sent Tong down the hall to the door Khanh and Bo were at to let them in.

We waited about twenty minutes for Mrs. Carhill. When she finally came in, she apologized profusely for being late. She was a tall gray-haired lady with an enthusiastic air about her. Upon seeing Tong and Bo she exclaimed, "Oh, what do we have here?" stretching out her arms. "What beautiful boys!"

"This is Tong and Bo," I introduced them.

"And this must be their mother," she reached out her hands and clasped Khanh's. "How old are you, Tong?" she asked.

"Nine," Tong smiled.

"Oh you're a big boy for nine!" she exclaimed. "And how old are you Bo?"

Tong repeated what she said in Vietnamese and Bo showed her five fingers.

"What charming boys! How long have they been here?"

"Since last Thursday."

"Brand new! Did they come from the Philippines?"

"Yes. They were there six months."

"Good. They have an excellent introductory program there. We find that if they were in the Philippine Refugee Camp, they usually know at least some English and understand a few of our customs."

"Tong speaks some English. Khanh speaks almost none, and it's hard to tell with Bo. He never says any English words, but I don't know if that's because he doesn't understand any or he just doesn't want to say them."

"Well, let's go in the refugee classroom and sit down and fill out all the necessary paperwork."

She led us into a large room with round tables, some which were low with little chairs and some which were larger with bigger chairs. There were small hand-painted flags from about thirty different countries hanging from the ceiling. Along one side of the room were bookcases with books written in different languages. Along the other side were books written in English along with a tape recorder and headsets. The walls were brightly decorated with pictures the children had made depicting Christmas. Most of them had either a Santa Claus or Christmas tree on them, although some had Crosses and Nativity scenes. Almost all of them had snowflakes.

We went through many of the same questions we had gone through before. I gave her the school and medical records that they had brought with them from the Philippines. Without looking at them, Mrs. Carhill said, "I think it would be best to start Tong in second grade and Bo in kindergarten. They will spend part of the day in a regular classroom with American kids and part of the day in the refugee classroom. As they learn more English and understand our customs better, we will slowly increase the time spent in the regular classrooms."

"Tong's school records show that he is well ahead of most second graders, and I think it would be better to put him in fourth grade," I said.

"Yes, but we usually start them out a year or two behind so they have a chance to catch up with the other kids in English and History. If he's nine going on ten, he would normally be in the fourth grade."

"Yes, but he's a big nine-year-old and he'll be ten soon."

"When is your birthday, Tong?"

Tong looked at me but didn't say anything. "He must not understand you. I believe it is in March," I answered.

She looked at the records and said, "Yes, it is March. Well, O.K. We can try him in fourth, but it's better to move them up than to have to move them down."

"I know, but I'm sure he'll do fine in fourth grade. I have a fourth-grader at home, and I think Tong is ahead of him in some areas such as math."

We finished the paperwork and Mrs. Carhill said the school nurse would look over the records and tell me if they needed anything else. "Why don't you let the boys stay a little while this morning and then you can start them full-time tomorrow."

"Oh that's wonderful! They can start tomorrow?"

"Sure. School begins at eight fifteen and ends at three o'clock. There's a bus that will pick them up. I'll call the bus driver and have her call you this afternoon. Will you be home?"

"There's a bus that will pick them up? We live clear across town."

"Yes, in fact there's another little girl that lives close to you that takes the bus. There is only one bus for all the refugees and it starts on your side of town. It will probably pick them up very early."

"That's great. I thought I was going to have to drive them every day."

"Breakfast is served in the lunchroom at seven fifty. They can also participate in the hot lunch program."

"Great. How long should we leave them this morning?"

"Maybe two hours. I'll leave them in my room with the other refugees so they can meet some of the children. We have several other Vietnamese. In fact, I think there's one in Tong's class."

"Did you hear that Tong! There are several other Vietnamese refugees in this school."

"Yes," he smiled.

"In fact, let me go see if I can find one of them so she can explain to Khanh what we're doing."

She left the room and came back a few minutes later with a beautiful Vietnamese girl about nine or ten. Mrs. Carhill told her to explain to Khanh in Vietnamese that Tong and Bo were going to stay a couple of hours this morning. She told Khanh and Khanh nodded her head. Soon after, the bell rang.

The children filed into the classroom immediately. There were many different ages and colors, and they were in various states of physical condition. There was a little boy without a leg and a young girl with a glass eye. Like any other kids, they were giggling and teasing the opposite sex. Tong stepped back into the corner as the children enveloped the room. Bo laughed and jumped up and down, pointing at some of the older boys that looked Vietnamese. In an orderly manner the children took their seats and quieted down.

"I want to introduce two new students to you this morning," Mrs. Carhill said pleasantly. "This is Tong," she motioned to him, trying to get him to stand next to her. Tong blushed and smiled sheepishly. "And this is Bo." Bo giggled, causing the classroom to break out in laughter. "They are from Vietnam. They just arrived here last Thursday. Can you welcome them?"

The children responded in several languages, saying hello. The teacher assigned Tong a spot at the big table and Bo a seat at the small table. She started the older kids on their early morning tasks and then had Bo's group form a circle on the floor in the corner.

Khanh sat down next to Bo. The teacher pulled out some large flash cards with pictures of things commonly encountered in America. She had each child take turns identifying an object in English. When it was Bo's turn, he giggled and pointed to the card. It was a dog. He began speaking furiously in Vietnamese, but the teacher calmly told him to say the English word. He didn't seem to understand, so she called one of the older Vietnamese students over to interpret. He still giggled and started jumping up and down. He was so excited to be in a room full of children. The teacher was patient with him, but Khanh scolded him several times and slapped him on the bottom. I motioned to Khanh that it was time for us to leave, but she shook her head.

We stayed for another half an hour during which Khanh became increasingly critical of Bo and his antics. Mrs. Carhill had the interpreter tell her that Bo was doing fine, and that it might take him several days to settle down. She asked Khanh if he had ever been in a classroom before. Khanh said no.

We stayed a few more minutes, and then I told Khanh we had to leave. She shook her head again, but this time Mrs. Carhill had the Vietnamese girl tell her that we should leave for a little while so Bo could get used to being away from Khanh for short periods of time. I took her arm and led her toward the door. She turned around and looked at Bo, who immediately started crying. Khanh tried to go back, but I held her arm firmly and led her out the door. She glanced back at Bo screaming, his arms reaching for her. As I closed the door, she began crying too. I put my arm around her and said, "It's O.K. Bo will be fine. Every mother feels sad when she first leaves her son. I know it's difficult." Khanh continued to sob as we walked slowly down the stairs.

"When Jack and Annie started school, I cried too. It's not easy watching them grow up and become independent." She suddenly grabbed my hand and stopped me. She started to turn around and walk back to the classroom. "No, Khanh. Bo will be fine. Why don't we sit here for a few minutes?" I sat down on the step and she followed me. We sat there for ten minutes as teachers and students occasionally wandered up the stairs staring at us with puzzled looks.

"Why don't we go outside for a little while?" I said, standing up. I started to walk down the stairs but Khanh didn't follow. I turned and saw her pathetic, pale face yearning for her son.

"Oh, Khanh," I sighed sympathetically. "Let's go upstairs and peek in the window of Bo's room. But we are not going back in." A look of relief fell over her face. We walked to his room and peeked in the window. Bo was sitting at the small table with a big smile on his face. It looked like they were coloring. Before he had a chance to notice his mother, I grabbed Khanh's arm and pulled her away from the door. "See, he's having fun. Now let's leave for a while." She followed more confidently this time.

We went to my office for a little while. Khanh sat at my desk while I returned some phone calls and solved minor emergencies. I had been working about an hour, when Khanh interrupted me saying, "Bo?" softly.

"Yes, we will go get Tong and Bo soon," I smiled reassuringly. I really needed to get back to work full-time. I was getting behind and some clients were starting to get anxious. I promised Karen I would come in tomorrow.

We went back to school to get Tong and Bo, but they didn't want to leave. I promised them they could go all day tomorrow, so they reluctantly said goodbye to their new friends. It was almost lunchtime, and Bo asked Tong to ask me if they could go to McDonalds. I agreed, and as soon as we pulled into the parking lot, Tong said "McDonalds! French fries, Coke!" Bo repeated it in Vietnamese. As we were getting out of the car, Bo suddenly jumped out and ran across the parking lot right in front of a car. The driver of the car slammed on the brakes and honked the horn. Bo stopped in front of the car and looked at it quite amused. Khanh ran after him, grabbing his arm and leading him to the sidewalk. My heart was racing. The car had just missed him by an inch. Tong walked over to Bo and scolded him harshly. Bo started to cry. I knelt down and put my arm around him. "Cars go very fast. You must always look," I tried to explain to him.

Bo played outside on the playground for a few minutes after lunch, until Khanh put her hand on her forehead and asked Tong to tell me she wanted to leave.

As soon as we got home, Khanh and Bo went in their room to lie down. Tong went up to Jack's room to play with the race cars. I sat down by the phone and opened the yellow pages to dentists.

I called our own dentist first, but he was out of town until after the holidays. So, I decided to start with the F's in the yellow pages. I called ten dentists and explained the urgency of the situation, but every receptionist responded that they weren't taking new patients or they didn't accept medical cards. I decided to call Central District Health to get a list of dentists that accepted medical cards. I talked to four different people, but none of them knew of such a list. I also called the Refugee Center and SOAR, but again nobody knew of a list, so I returned to the yellow pages and continued calling the Gs. I called several more and finally responded to a receptionist's refusal to accept medical cards with, "It is the Christmas season so I thought maybe you would make an exception." No exceptions.

I continued to make my story more extreme each time, but to no avail. I called a total of twenty-three dentists, then quit for the day in frustration, concluding that dentistry must be the most selfish profession there is.

I sat down to read the newspaper. When I was halfway through, Jack and Annie came running in the door waving papers and yelling, "Hi, Mom!" They had lots of stories to tell about spelling tests, plans for the Christmas program and what their friends wanted for Christmas.

That night, the kids and I made hot apple cider, started a fire and read a couple of stories from our *Treasury of Christmas Stories.* Tong and Bo listened attentively, studying the pictures carefully. I made everyone get in bed early, since the bus driver had called and said she would be outside our gate at seven o'clock in the morning. I called Loc and had him explain to Tong and Khanh the plans for the next day. Tong and Bo were excited to ride the bus and attend school all day.

After I finally got everyone to sleep, I addressed Christmas cards for awhile and made a list of the things I still had to do to get ready for Christmas. It was overwhelming. I was coming to the stark realization that some of the things simply wouldn't get done—I just didn't know which ones yet.

I fell asleep exhausted.

DAY 9: *We'll Take Your Tired and Weary*

Five forty-five in the morning came early. This time when I woke Tong up, he jumped out of bed quickly with a smile radiating from his face. "You go wake up Khanh and Bo," I whispered to him. He nodded his head and went downstairs.

As I stood in the shower, I remembered it was Friday. I felt like screaming, 'It's Friday!' Then I remembered it was Friday the thirteenth. What more could possibly go wrong? In some respects I couldn't believe a week had already passed; in others, it had seemed like a month. I got out of the shower and woke Allen up, then went downstairs to make sure my refugees were up. I could hear the shower going downstairs, so I assumed they were getting ready.

I went in the kitchen and washed two apples to send with Tong and Bo on the bus since they would be on it for an hour.

I decided to go to work in the morning and leave Khanh home alone. She would probably relish the peace and quiet.

"Are they ready?" Allen asked at six forty-five.

"I don't know. I sent Tong down at six o'clock and I haven't seen him since. I can hear them so I know they're up."

"Why don't you knock on the door?"

"All right," I agreed. I went and knocked lightly on the bedroom door. Khanh peeked out. "It's almost time to go," I told her. She nodded. I went out and got the newspaper and put some coffee on. Allen and I sat down and read the paper for ten minutes. Then he jumped up and demanded, "What are they doing? It's time to go." He marched down to their room and knocked firmly on the bedroom door. We heard a lot of chatter coming from the bathroom but nobody opened the door. "Tong," Allen said sternly.

"Yes," he replied.

"It's time to go. You're going to miss the bus." We waited a couple more minutes until Tong finally opened the door. He came out ready to go, but Bo was crying in the bathroom.

"What is going on?" Allen asked him.

"Oh," Tong said looking confused as he tried to find the right words. Unable to communicate, he went in the bedroom and came out with the sack that the nurse at Central District Health had given us.

I couldn't help but grin. "They're trying to get stool samples," I said as my cheeks blushed in embarrassment.

"Oh. Did they have to do it this morning? We have one minute to be out front, or the bus will leave without them."

"Tong, go tell Khanh that Bo has to leave right now. They can get that later." I pointed to the sack.

Tong disappeared into the bathroom while Allen went and got their coats and hats out of the closet. We stood in front of the bathroom door, Allen tapping his foot impatiently. We could still hear Bo crying. Allen knocked loudly on the door again. "I'm leaving," he announced. "Come on Tong." Allen helped him put his coat on, gave him his hat and he and Tong went out the door.

"I'll bring Bo in just a second," I yelled running back to the bathroom. Bo was still sitting on the toilet with Khanh scolding him.

"Khanh, Bo has to leave right now." I went over, got Bo off the stool and pulled his pants up. I quickly washed his hands, put his coat and hat on, and said, "We have to leave right now or he'll miss the bus." I picked him up and we ran out the door. Allen was storming back toward the house. "Here he is," I yelled to him, running with Bo in my arms.

"The bus driver is waiting. Come on, Bo." Allen grabbed him from me and ran him to the bus.

I went back in the house shivering. Khanh was standing by the front window with tears streaming down her face. "Oh, Khanh, Bo will be just fine," I said sympathetically putting my arm around her. "He is so excited to go to school." She walked away from the window and went back in her room.

Allen came back in the house huffing and puffing. "What in the hell took them so long?!"

"Sweetheart, calm down. They were trying to get stool samples."

"For an hour?"

"I don't know. They also had to take showers and get dressed."

"We'll have to get them up at five o'clock from now on if they're this slow."

"They'll get used to it. I think part of the problem was that Khanh didn't want Bo to go."

"Why?"

"I don't know but when I came back in, Khanh was standing by the window crying. I don't think she and Bo have ever been separated for long."

"Well, they'll have to get used to it."

"They will. It will just take some time. Remember they're in a foreign country and can't even speak the language. It must be terribly frightening to send your five-year-old son off on a bus."

We woke our own kids up and sent them off to school. Khanh still hadn't come out of her room, so I knocked lightly on her door. I didn't get any response, so I opened the door a crack and saw her asleep on the bed. She opened her eyes and smiled at me. I went in and sat down on the bed.

"How do you feel?" I whispered, patting her leg. She sat up and nodded. "I'm going to go to work," I said waving my hand as if saying goodbye. She nodded again. "Allen will be gone, too." She looked at me with uncertainty. I wrote my work number on a piece of paper. "My telephone number," I said pointing to the note paper. She still looked confused, so I got up, took her arm, and led her into the kitchen. I picked up the phone and said, "telephone" pointing to it. She nodded. "My number," I showed her the note pad and pushed the buttons that were on it. "You call me," I pointed to her and then to the telephone "and say, 'Sandy.'" She nodded. I walked back into her room and showed her the clock. "I will be home at eleven o'clock." She nodded her head in apparent understanding.

"Bo?" she asked.

"Bo is at school with Tong. They will not be home until about four o'clock." I showed her on the clock. She looked up at me alarmed. "It's all right. Tong is with him. Jack and Annie are at school too. Bo will have fun," I said slowly.

Tears filled her eyes again. "Khanh, I know this is hard," I said putting my arm around her. "We can go see him at eleven o'clock if you really want to, O.K.?" She pointed to the eleven on the clock and said weakly, "Bo?"

"Yes, we will go see Bo at eleven o'clock," I sighed.

Her face brightened and she nodded in appreciation. "For breakfast. To eat. There are apples, eggs, or cereal." She nodded her head in acknowledgment. "You have to eat something or the baby will not be healthy," I said sternly pointing to her stomach. She grinned and nodded her head once.

I got in the car and drove to work. As I was driving, a feeling of relief came over me. Maybe this was the start of settling back into our routine. I was worried about leaving Khanh alone. My mind started to imagine all the things that could go wrong: she forgets to turn the stove off, she gets sick, she goes outside and falls. How was I ever going to move them out on their own?

When I arrived at my office, there was a big flocked Christmas tree in the entryway and poinsettias sitting on all the desks. "Good morning!" Karen greeted me. "I'm glad you came in this morning. There's some cookies and cake in the conference room. Go get yourself some."

"Thanks, Karen. I think I will." As I walked down the hallway, several of the secretaries came and asked me how our refugees were doing. They wanted to know if there was anything they could do to help. It was the same group of people that had already done so much to help outfit and furnish Khanh, Tong, and Bo's new home. I thanked them for their concern. I wondered why it was that the people who had the least were usually the ones that helped the most.

I looked at the stacks of mail and messages on my

desk. "I can see it was really slow while I was gone," I told Karen with a cheerful sarcasm.

"Yeah. Real slow," she chuckled. "I did as much as I could myself." She handed me the pile of things that needed to be done first. "April called and said they were leaving tomorrow morning for Sun Valley and wouldn't be back until after Christmas."

"Oh great. I have to talk to Brent before he leaves. I almost forgot, I have to take him his Christmas present, too. When am I going to do it?"

"I don't know. I suppose you'd better do it today or you won't get a chance."

"You're right. Some of this other stuff will just have to wait. Can you call April and see if I can come over at ten o'clock?"

"Sure."

Brent and April Proctor were my biggest and certainly two of my favorite clients, so I looked forward to seeing them. I worked until nine fifty and then grabbed the present I had gotten for Brent and ran out the door. I stopped at the florist to get April a Christmas cactus. She loved flowers and plants of all kinds. When I got to their house, April opened the door and gave me a big hug. "We've missed you. Where have you been?"

"Oh, I've been in town. But I've been very busy. April, your house is so beautiful!" I exclaimed as I looked around. It was a large house that looked like it belonged in a magazine. There was a big Christmas tree in the living room decorated in pink and white with beautiful antique ornaments and small porcelain dolls. The tables and banister had holly around them, and there were pink, white, and red poinsettias everywhere. "I've never seen such a beautifully decorated house in my life."

"Oh, thank you. We're sure enjoying it. And thank you for the beautiful Christmas cactus. How did you know I liked plants?" she giggled.

We walked into the family room and there was another tree, decorated in traditional reds, greens, whites, yellows, and blues. Underneath the tree, there was a train going slowly around a track, tooting its horn every time it emerged from behind the tree. There must have been almost a hundred presents neatly wrapped under the tree and spilling halfway across the room. "Who in the world are all these presents for?" I asked in astonishment.

"Oh, they're for all our children and grandchildren. And some are for the people at work and the mailman and anyone else who wants one," April laughed.

"April, I'm going to call the paper and have them come and take pictures of your home. I've never seen anything like it. When did you ever have the time to do this?"

"At night. Until about two in the morning. I just love Christmas. The whole spirit of the season just fills me up and I can't sleep, so I decorate."

Just then Brent walked into the room. "Isn't this the most ridiculous thing you've ever seen?" he said gruffly.

"I think it's beautiful!"

"My wife. It's not enough for her to work all day, chase down seven children and grandchildren and take care of me in the fashion that I'm accustomed to. She also has to stay up the whole damn night decorating," he said harshly but with a grin on his face.

"Oh, Brent. Get in the spirit of things. You enjoy it as much as everyone else," April declared. Brent walked over and kissed her on the cheek. "You're right. I wouldn't have it any other way."

"Well, I brought you a present," I announced to Brent.

"Oh good. I'm glad you brought me one because as you can see, I won't get any others." We all laughed.

"You know, you're not the easiest person to buy for," I said.

"What do ya mean? I like everything."

"I know that's part of the problem. You already have everything. The only things you don't have, I can't afford. Take a guess at what's in this box."

He looked at the long narrow box and said, "That's easy. The only thing it could possibly be is a golf club."

"You old scrooge. How did you know?"

"What else could it be? It's certainly not a box of cookies or candy." He opened it and pulled out the putter. He looked it over carefully and said, "Thank you. Do you know, I lost my putter about two weeks ago and have been waiting for someone to turn it in but nobody has. I was going to go buy a new one tomorrow."

"You're joking. You probably have five putters. But even if you do, this one is unique because it has a bull engraved in the head. See?"

"How about a cup of coffee, Sandy?" April asked.

"Sure. I'll have a cup."

"Where have you been lately? Every time we've called your office the last few days, you've been gone. Takin' an early Christmas, huh?" Brent asked.

"No, I've been in town. I've just been really busy."

"Well, we're all busy this time of year."

"I know, but we're doing something a little unusual this year."

"Like what?"

"We're sponsoring a refugee family."

"You're what!"

"Sponsoring a refugee family. They're from Vietnam."

"What all does that encompass?" April asked seriously.

"A lot more than we thought," I laughed nervously.

"Is it your church that's the sponsor?"

"No. Just Allen and I."

"Wow! Do they live with you?" Brent asked in disbelief.

"Yes. They'll live with us until they're ready to move into their own apartment."

"How long does that take?"

"It just depends. With our family it will take a little longer than usual because the father stayed in Vietnam."

"He did? How many of 'em do you have?" Brent asked still in shock.

"A mother and her two sons ages nine and five."

"Do they speak English?"

"No. The older son speaks a little but not much."

"Why'd ya sponsor 'em?"

"Oh, for a lot of reasons."

"Wow, I think that's something. You'll go to heaven, that's for damn sure," Brent concluded with a serious expression on his face.

I didn't know whether to burst out laughing or not. As I studied his face, I could tell he didn't mean it as a joke. He was dead serious. Brent was seventy and had cancer. He had rarely been to church until he was diagnosed with cancer.

"Well, I don't think that alone will necessarily get me into heaven."

"Yes, it will. But I would never do anything like that."

"Why not?"

"You know. We can't just let anyone who wants to come into this country come in. The big cities are already overcome with dark-skinned people. And look at all the problems they've caused." Brent stood up and started pacing back and forth across the room talking to the floor with his hand on his chin. "I mean, a white person can't even walk down the streets of New York City anymore. And I know, because that's where I come from. It didn't used to be that way. When I grew up, almost everyone was American. Now they're lettin' anyone in. They're ruining the country. But I admire you. You'll go to heaven. That's for sure."

"Brent, I understand your frustration. I think we're all at the end of our rope with crime, drugs, and gangs in the cities. But the problems aren't all caused by foreigners entering the country."

"Oh, yes, they are. It wasn't that way when there were only white people here. I know 'cause I grew up in New York City."

"But many things have happened since then besides just dark-skinned people moving in. There are a lot of white people that commit crimes too. The problem is universal."

"Then why don't you ever see any white guys shooting people in the cities?"

"You do. It's just that there is probably a higher percentage of non-whites in the inner cities because they don't have the education or job skills necessary to get out."

"But that's what I mean. We should be teaching all of those people instead of letting new ones in. If we let everyone in, there won't be any room for us anymore."

"Brent, I know it's a big problem, and I don't know what the solution is. Most of the refugees that come to this country take jobs that most Americans don't want."

"That's because Americans earn more on welfare. If we'd cut 'em out of welfare, they'd have to work."

"I agree that the welfare system is out of control, but don't confuse problems with welfare with letting refugees in."

"I just think we have to start saying no. What about India and Africa and all the people starving in Bosnia? We don't have enough food and money to help the whole world. It's not fair to let your refugees in and not let some of those poor kids in Ethiopia or Somalia in. There's nothing we can do. It's just too big a problem."

My eyes began to fill with tears and I felt a big lump in my throat. It was difficult not to start crying. I felt like he was attacking Khanh, Tong, and Bo. How could anyone want to send them back where they might starve?

"Brent, I don't know what the answers are," I said in a shaky voice. "The only way I can explain it is to tell you a story that I once heard a preacher tell."

"Once there was an old man walking along the beach. Ahead of him was a little boy who was picking up sand crabs on the beach and throwing them back in the ocean. The man followed the boy for quite a while and watched the boy continue to pick them up and throw them back. When the man caught up to the boy he asked him, 'Son, why are you doing that? There are so many of them it doesn't make any difference whether you throw a few back in or not. You'll never be able to get all of them.' The little boy picked up a crab, looked at the man, and threw the crab back in the water. 'It made a difference to that one,'" he said.

"That's how I feel about my refugee family. They are so special and mean so much to me. If everyone in America would try to help just one person in need, we wouldn't have nearly the problems we have now."

"Well, I admire you."

"I need to get back to the office pretty soon. I spent a good part of yesterday calling dentists to try and find one that would see Khanh. She has thirty-odd cavities, infections throughout her mouth, and she has a hard time keeping food down. The nurse thought it might be her mouth that was making her sick. She also happens to be pregnant."

"Oh, that poor lady. Did you call Dr. Cook?" April asked.

"No, I don't know him. I called all the Fs through Ts."

"Brent, give me the phone. I'm going to call Dr. Cook."

She picked up the phone and dialed. "Is Dr. Cook in?" April asked. "No, I need to talk to him right away. This is April Proctor. I'll hold thank you."

"She's going to get him for me. When can you take her in?" she asked me.

"Any time. If you just get her an appointment, I'll make sure I get her there."

We waited for about ten minutes, and April finally said, "Hello Dr. Cook. This is April. Fine, how are you? Good. I have a big favor to ask of you. We have a refugee from Vietnam who is in desperate need of a dentist. Brent and I thought since you're such a caring person and it's the Christmas season, that you would see her right away."

Brent and I stared at April, watching her face for a clue as to whether he would see Khanh. "There's no way it can wait until after Christmas. This lady is pregnant and can't hold any food down. The nurse at Central District Health thought it was her teeth that were causing all the problems. She has to see a dentist immediately," April pleaded. "Oh, thank you very, very much, Dr. Cook. I knew you had a big heart." April held for about ten more minutes until the receptionist got on and asked if we could come Monday at ten o'clock. I told her to assure them that we would be there.

"Thank you so much, April. I didn't know what I was going to do next. I sure didn't want to spend all afternoon on the phone again calling dentists."

"I'm glad I could help. You'll really like Dr. Cook. He's taken care of Brent and me for years."

"I'd better run. Have a merry Christmas." I gave them a hug and left.

When I got in the car, it was eleven o'clock. I knew Khanh would be nervously watching the clock. As I drove in front of the house, I could see Khanh standing in the living room looking out the window. She had her coat on, ready to go.

We drove to Franklin School. When we got there, the boys were getting ready to go to lunch. Bo saw Khanh and ran up and hugged her. Tong smiled shyly at me. I asked him if he was having fun and he said yes. Mrs. Carhill greeted us warmly. "The boys are doing wonderfully. We're just on our way to eat," she said.

"Good. I'm glad they're doing well. We just came by to make sure everything was fine. Khanh was a little nervous sending Bo off on the school bus this morning."

"Oh, I can understand that. The only slight problem we've had is that Bo keeps getting up and walking out of the room whenever he wants to. He doesn't understand yet that he's supposed to stay in the classroom until recess. When he goes to recess, he holds Tong's hand the entire time."

"I'm sure he'll get more comfortable after he's been here a few days. Did they eat a good breakfast?"

"You know, I'm not sure. I didn't see them down in the lunchroom. I'll try to watch what they eat at lunch."

"Thank you."

"O.K., kids, it's time to go," said Mrs. Carhill.

"Come on, Khanh, it's time for us to go, too. Tell Bo goodbye."

Khanh was holding Bo as she started to leave with me. "You have to leave Bo here," I told her.

Khanh looked at me and shook her head. Tong started to take him from her, but Bo started to cry.

"Why don't you let him go home with her today?"

said Mrs. Carhill. "He's been here three hours, which is probably enough for the first day. He can come all day Monday."

"I think you're right. I don't want to go through a tearful afternoon again. We'll see you on Monday. Tong, you come home on the bus O.K.?"

"Yes. Goodbye," he bowed and smiled.

"Goodbye. Eat a good lunch." I gave him a big hug.

"Yes," he agreed as he left the room.

I took Khanh and Bo home for lunch. When we were done eating, Khanh and Bo went in their room and took a nap. I called some clients from the house until Allen got home at three o'clock and then I went back down to the office.

I was in charge of the annual Merrill Lynch Christmas Calls program the next morning, and I had to review our plans to make sure everything was ready.

On my way home from work, I stopped and picked up three plain red Christmas stockings and some colored felt. Everyone in my family had their own hand-decorated stocking that we hung on the fireplace. Khanh, Tong, and Bo had admired them many times, so I thought it was time that they made their own.

After dinner we got out the art supplies, and while I finished addressing Christmas cards, our refugees worked on their stockings. Bo was excited to help, but it only lasted about ten minutes until he got bored. Khanh chose the colors she wanted on her stocking and then proceeded to draw the design of a star and a Christmas tree on the felt. She cut the patterns out and glued them on carefully. Tong drew a Santa Claus first but decided he didn't like it, so he made a tree. He decorated the tree with colorful balls but decided he didn't like that either. Finally he settled on a big white tree without decorations on it. As he cut the tree out, his face was deep in concentration. He and Khanh were both perfectionists. Everything they did was done as if it was a statement of who they are. He glued the tree carefully to the stocking and then put little snowflakes around the tree.

While they worked on their stockings, we listened to Christmas carols. As the different carols came on ("Silent Night," "Away in a Manger," and "Joy to the World"), I looked at my refugees to see if any of the tunes seemed familiar to them. I couldn't imagine a Christmas without singing these beautiful carols. They had been sung by my ancestors for generations. I wondered if they had similar traditions in Vietnam. That night in bed, I thought about how fortunate we are to have such a rich history.

DAY 10: *Judge Not*

I always looked forward to Saturday because it was the only day of the week I got to sleep in. This morning, however, I had to be at the office by nine o'clock. I was the coordinator for our office's Christmas Calls program, which allowed low-income people to use our phone lines for free to call anywhere in the world. The mayor's office had asked us about four months ago if they could participate in the program. I had told my boss at the time that it was a political maneuver so the mayor, who was running for U.S. Congress, could get some good press. Since my boss was a big supporter of the mayor, he decided to let their office run the whole program. All we were supposed to do was provide phone lines and help the people dial the calls. The mayor's office wanted to invite the nursing homes, homeless shelters, churches, Salvation Army, etc., to participate in the program. They were in charge of arranging all the transportation, scheduling the phone times, handling the press releases, etc.

About a month before the program, I called the mayor's office several times to make sure they were doing their job, but nobody would return my phone calls. A couple of weeks later, my boss talked to the mayor's assistant and found out that they were having a hard time finding people interested in using the phones, but they assured us they would be ready in two weeks. Almost two weeks later, the mayor's assistant called to tell us our service wasn't needed in this community. We were stunned. Several people from our office spent the next few days calling the press and low-income agencies to make them aware of the program. We didn't have time to screen or schedule callers, so we just told them to come. We had no idea how many would show up.

Jack and Annie complained incessantly about my being gone all day Saturday, since it was only one of two days each week we had together. They wanted to go Christmas shopping, so I promised we would go the next day after church. I also agreed to let them help with the Christmas Calls program.

At ten o'clock the first callers started arriving. Many of them were from the homeless shelters and hadn't talked to relatives for at least a year. There were also refugees from all over the world. We placed calls to fourteen countries including Cuba, the Ukraine, Russia, and Azerbaijan. The fall of communism in the Soviet Union had recently taken place, and there weren't many phone lines into the Soviet countries or Cuba. It took several hours to get people through, but we managed to get at least one call placed for everyone that came.

Khanh, Tong, and Bo came down in the afternoon to use the phone lines. I was hoping they could call Saigon, but I found out there were no phone lines into Vietnam. Khanh brought her address book, however, and showed me the number of someone in France.

"You want to call France?"

She nodded. "That's right. You have a cousin who lives in France, right Tong?"

"Yes. Ummmmm. Khanh's brother," he replied.

"Khanh's brother?"

"Yes."

"All right. We'll try to reach him." I placed the call

and Khanh began talking furiously. Then she began crying. Tong got on one of the other lines and listened also. Soon he started crying, too. They talked for twenty minutes and then tearfully exchanged good-byes.

Next she showed me a number they wanted to call in Vermont. I remembered Tong telling me they also had cousins in Vermont. We dialed the number, and again Khanh and Tong sobbed. By the time they hung up, their faces were red and wet, and their eyes looked so sad. We tried to comfort them, but it didn't seem to help.

By the time the program ended at four o'clock, I was exhausted. Our office Christmas party started at six o'clock, and I didn't know how I would ever make it.

When I got home, I played with the kids for a while and then started getting ready for the party. Normally, I looked forward to the annual Christmas party. It was a festive time of year, and everyone was usually in the holiday spirit.

Annie came upstairs to watch me get ready. She picked out the jewelry she thought I should wear and gave me ideas on how I should fix my hair. For Annie, helping me prepare for the big party was the next best thing to being there.

I got ready rather quickly. I wore a plain red wool skirt and a cream blouse with lace around the neck and wrists. It was really rather boring compared to my usual attire. I hadn't had the time or desire to shop for a new Christmas outfit. Annie was quite disappointed that I didn't have something fancier.

Allen put on his suit and tie. We walked

downstairs and Khanh, Tong, and Bo stood up and stared at us with big smiles.

"Ooooh," Tong sighed. "Handsome," he said to Allen.

We all laughed. "Yes, handsome," Annie agreed.

Bo ran up and pulled Allen's tie and giggled. It was the first time they had seen us dressed up.

We had our nephew Stephen come to the house to stay with our kids. I was afraid to leave all of them with Khanh since she didn't speak English. We kissed all the kids goodbye and left. As we pulled out of the driveway, I stared at the skiff of snow that covered the ground. It was already dark, but the snow shone brightly in the headlights. It was a clear dark night with just a sliver of moon accompanying the infinite stars in the sky. It was a beautiful night. "I don't feel like going to the party," I said to Allen.

"Why not?" he asked surprised. "You always love the office Christmas party."

"I know. But this year I feel different. Watching our refugees go without so much, even without family, I just don't feel like celebrating. They sit home in bad health and homesick with nothing to give for Christmas, and we go out and eat, drink, and be merry."

"Sweetheart, I hope it hasn't ruined Christmas for you."

"It hasn't. It's just changed the way I want to celebrate. I would rather stay at home with our kids and refugees and make something or play games. I feel sad seeing everyone in expensive dresses, eating caviar and drinking champagne when our refugees have so little and their families back in Vietnam have almost nothing."

"But you've done a lot to make things better for
them. You've given them the opportunity for a good
education and good jobs, which will make their future
brighter. You should feel good about it. They're as well
off now as they ever have been."

"I do. But it's difficult to enjoy the luxuries of fine
food and drink like I could before. I think of how much
the money spent on it could buy for Tong's family in
Vietnam."

"Honey, you can sulk about all the starving people
in the world, but unfortunately there's not a whole lot
we can do about most of them. I don't want it to ruin
your Christmas. Let's just have a good time and forget
about the refugees for an evening. We haven't gone
out alone for a long time. Let's enjoy it."

"You're right. We will."

We pulled up to the Boise Art Museum and
parked. Merrill Lynch had rented the museum for
the evening and was having the food catered. We
went in and joined the line waiting to greet my boss
and his wife. Jim Steele was dressed in a tuxedo
and his wife, Jan, was in a long black chiffon dress.
We gradually worked our way through the line,
exchanging pleasantries, then went into the rooms
where the art work was displayed. As we walked
around and looked at the paintings, it struck me
that most of them portrayed sad or confused
people or scenes. Rarely was there one that
celebrated life.

We visited with our friends from the office and
their spouses. It was the only time of the year that we
saw most of the spouses. We listened to the gossip
concerning who was with whom and the revealing

dress that Sue was wearing. I kept glancing at my watch wondering if we could leave yet.

After wandering through most of the museum, I whispered to Allen, "Let's go."

"Why? I don't want to go yet. Besides we're having a sit-down dinner and they're expecting us."

"I know, but we could say I don't feel well and go somewhere by ourselves. We haven't been alone forever."

"But Sweetheart, we can't leave before dinner. Let's stay until after we eat."

"O.K.," I agreed reluctantly.

We ate hors d'oeuvres and drank cocktails for about an hour, until it was time to gather in the dining hall. Then we sat down at a round table with three other couples. They served our soup and salad rather quickly, but it took a long time to get our main course. I continued to glance at my watch periodically, hoping they would feed us early enough that Allen and I would have time to do something by ourselves. We hadn't had time to talk about anything except the refugees since they arrived, and I wanted a few minutes of peace and quiet to catch up on other things.

They didn't bring our dinner until nine o'clock. By then many of the people had been drinking liquor for three hours. The room was becoming loud and hot. I ate quickly and then whispered to Allen, "Let's go."

"I'm not done yet. Neither are you. You've hardly eaten anything."

"I'm not hungry. I just want to get out of here."

"Can you wait until I'm done?" he snapped back.

I went to the rest room and patted my face with a cold paper towel, then walked around the museum for five minutes. When I went back to the table, Allen said, "O.K. I'm done. Do you still want to leave?"

"Yes. Let me go tell Jim thank you."

I thanked my boss and his wife for the wonderful evening and claimed that we had to leave because one of the children was sick.

He insisted that we stay for a short play that the Shakespearean actors were going to put on, and we reluctantly agreed.

As I watched the play, my mind kept wandering to our children and refugees at home. I wished I could bring them to the party, but I would probably have ended up embarrassed as they observed all the excesses. I started feeling sad again thinking about their plight.

We didn't get away until ten thirty, which was late for us. We stopped for coffee, then drove to the top of one of the hills overlooking Boise. We found a secluded spot to park where we could see both the clear black night sky with all its glittering constellations and the vibrant sprawling city with its sparkling lights of white, red, and yellow.

"It's so beautiful," I said softly as we sat quietly engulfed in the whole scene. "We are so fortunate to be able to drive five minutes and enjoy such a spectacle. Think of all those people in New York City who can't even see beyond the high rise next door. No wonder they have so much crime. People can never get away from each other and observe nature. We have the best of both worlds. We can sit up here and enjoy nature and the bustling city all at once."

"Yeah. It's so quiet and peaceful up here. If it was

summer we could hear crickets, but in winter it's dead silence. This is good coffee, isn't it?"

"Yes. But it's starting to fog up the front window. We won't be able to see the stars and lights for long. I'm going to roll down my window."

"You'll freeze. It's too cold."

"I'll just do it for a minute to unfog the window."

"So what did you want to talk about?"

"Just coffee and windows and things."

"I thought you needed to talk to me about something more serious."

"No, I just wanted a few minutes without a hundred other people around. I better roll up the window. I'm shivering."

"Come sit by me and I'll warm you up."

I moved next to him and he put his arm around me. I looked up at him and our lips met spontaneously. My heart jumped. It felt like our first kiss eighteen years ago. It had only been ten days since we had been alone, but it suddenly felt like an eternity. Before I knew it, our passions had taken over and inhibitions melted away.

As we sat in the car afterward, Allen said, "Well, now the windows are really foggy. I'm plenty warm, how about you?"

"Me, too. Let's roll down the windows for a minute. We sat in a state of total relaxation until I broke the silence, saying, "That was really a stupid thing to do. What if a police car had pulled up and arrested us. Could you see us calling our refugees to bail us out of jail?" I laughed.

"We'll have to come up here to talk more often," Allen teased. "At least I can drink my coffee now. It's not so hot."

We sat in silence for a while watching the stars in the sky and the city lights. "You know, I was really hard on Khanh for getting married in the Philippines. Who knows why she did it? Maybe it was to feel the same way we just felt. Every human being wants that. Or maybe it was because she was by herself with two boys and she was afraid of getting raped. Maybe she thought she needed a husband to protect her and the boys, which would have been very practical. Or maybe it was because her emotions got away from her and she did something stupid."

"It's hard to say, but I don't think it's for us to judge. If she got married, I think we have to assume that she was in love. In any case what's done is done. We just have to make the best of it. It's midnight."

"It is? We better go home. Ben will get us up early and we'll probably have another long day, but I wish we could stay up here all night."

"We'd freeze. I'm already starting to get cold."

"I love you."

"I love you too, Sweetheart. Thanks for a wonderful night."

"Thank you." We embraced and kissed one more time.

DAY 11: *More Tears*

We got everyone up early and ready to go to church. Khanh felt sick again and was the only one who didn't go. During church Tong and Bo were both quiet, which I could not say for my three children. When we sang hymns, Tong joined along, singing loudly. He had a wonderful voice. I didn't know if he understood what he was singing, but he seemed to enjoy it. I whispered to Tong, asking him if he went to church in Vietnam. He said no but that his mother used to go to the temple. I asked if she was Catholic and he said no. I had read that most Vietnamese were either Buddhist or Catholic. Although Khanh had reported herself as Catholic in the refugee documents, I assumed Tong's mother must be Buddhist.

After church we stayed and had cookies and punch. My friends surrounded us, anxious to meet Tong and Bo. Many of them offered to help us with clothing, food, or furniture.

We went home and ate lunch, and afterwards I took Tong and Bo to get school supplies. Their lists included seven notebooks for Tong, pencils, pens, ruler, scissors, erasers, color crayons, paints, and markers, a school supplies box, tissue, PE shoes, stickers, etc. I'm sure kids from other countries learn just as much with a quarter of the supplies. Tong seemed bothered by something while we were shopping, but I couldn't tell what or why.

When we got all the new supplies home, Tong went to his room and shut the door. An hour later I asked him if anything was wrong, but he said no. I thought maybe he was tired from getting up early, so I encouraged him to go to sleep for a while.

I went downstairs and started looking through the ads in the newspaper for an apartment. I had no idea how much Khanh would have to spend each month. The cheapest apartments for low-income tenants ranged from $350-$450 per month. I called a few of them, but there was either no answer or there was a long waiting list. Most of the lower-priced apartments were one-bedroom, and they would not rent one-bedroom apartments to one adult and two children. I did find a few two-bedrooms for $375-$400, but none of them included utilities. By the time utilities were added in, the rent was closer to $500 without a phone.

It was two o'clock and I had promised Jack, Annie, and Ben that I would take them shopping. I didn't take Tong and Bo because I thought my kids needed some time alone with me. I told our refugees that they couldn't come because we were going to buy them a gift. They understood what gift meant and were very excited. We asked them what they wanted. Tong either couldn't think of anything or was too embarrassed to ask for something. Bo ran and got Ben's duplos and brought them to us. After Tong saw what Bo wanted, he became excited and ran and got Jack's Legos.

The mall was an absolute zoo. We didn't get Tong and Bo's presents because the toy store was too busy, but we bought several things, including a watch, a camera, and a new photo album. After shopping for two hours, we got ice cream cones and sat along a bench in the center of the mall watching some of the high school choirs sing carols. None of us said much—

we just enjoyed being together and basking in the holiday spirit.

When we got home, I found Tong lying on his bed, crying. I asked him what was the matter, but at first he wouldn't tell me. I offered to call Loc but he said no. After a while, he broke down and tried to tell me something about his cousin in Vermont, whom they had talked to yesterday. I couldn't understand what he was trying to tell me. He asked if he could call his cousin in Vermont again. I agreed and told him to get Khanh's address book to find the phone number. He jumped up and said, "No! Khanh no!"

"You don't want Khanh to know?"

"No," he said sharply.

"Tong, she's the only one that has the phone number," I gently reminded him.

"I get book," he said, and ran downstairs.

I followed him down, afraid that he was about to get himself in trouble. Khanh was in the family room watching TV with Bo and Ben. Tong disappeared into the bathroom and soon came out and walked nonchalantly back upstairs. I waited five minutes and then followed him.

"Look," he whispered as he pulled the address book out from under his shirt. He stuffed it back in, took my arm and led me into my bedroom and shut the door. He walked over to the telephone and dialed the number. Pretty soon I heard him talking furiously and subsequently he began to cry. He had a difficult time communicating because he was sobbing so hard. I sat on the bed and watched him, once again feeling helpless. He talked for about fifteen minutes, then went in my bathroom and blew his nose, splashed water on his face, and went back downstairs to put the address book away.

Returning to his bedroom, he laid back down on his bed and stared at the ceiling with that far-away look that I had seen so many times.

Concerned, I asked "What's the matter, Tong?"

He shook his head with tears in his eyes. "Please tell me," I encouraged him. "I can't help you if I don't know what's wrong," I continued softly as I rubbed his forehead. He stared at the ceiling as if he was in another world. I sighed, and left the room, closing the door behind me.

That night after dinner I insisted that everyone read. Allen listened to Tong read a book and tried to help him understand the meaning of the words he read. He could read well, but couldn't comprehend the words. I read to Bo and Ben, who had a longer-than-usual attention span. Jack and Annie read their books as they were required to every school night for a half an hour before bed. Since our refugees had arrived, we had gotten off our schedule, and the children were running us instead of the other way around.

I made the kids get in bed by eight o'clock since they had school the next day. Tong and Bo were excited to go back to school. Bo was particularly excited about riding the bus again.

I never did find out what was the matter with Tong.

DAY 12: *The Climax*

I woke Tong up at five thirty. He argued about having to get up, but I sternly told him to get out of bed and get ready for school. When he realized I was serious, he sat up, smiled at me and got out of bed. I sent him down to wake Khanh and Bo and told him that I did not want to rush for a waiting bus, as we had on Friday.

This morning went much better. Tong and Bo were dressed and ready to go at six fifty. Allen walked out the door with them, but suddenly Bo ran back in the kitchen and picked out two apples. He looked at me with an anxious face. "Yes, you can take those. Now hurry out to the bus." Khanh and I waved goodbye to them as they went out the door.

I got my children off to school and helped Khanh get ready to go to the dentist. About eight thirty, Dr. Cook's receptionist called and asked if we could change Khanh's appointment from ten to two o'clock. I reluctantly agreed.

Since I had the morning free, I decided to call about apartments again. I pulled out my list from the Sunday paper and started calling more numbers. All of the subsidized apartments were occupied and had long waiting lists. Looking through the ads again, I spotted a two-bedroom house near the university listed at $400 per month. I immediately called and learned that it was vacant. I arranged to go look at it at one o'clock.

I called the Refugee Center to find out whether our caseworker had calculated how much Khanh would have to spend on rent, but she hadn't reviewed her papers yet. I also called Crista at SOAR to see if she could help estimate Khanh's benefits, but she had no idea. I remembered that one of my friends from church owned a rental agency so I called him. He agreed to look through his listings to see if he could find something. He was sympathetic because he had sponsored a refugee family many years ago.

One of Khanh's obligations under the refugee program was to attend English classes. I called the Refugee Center and learned they were beginning a new class at eleven that morning. I would have to hurry to get Khanh there on time. I explained to her that she needed to get ready to go to the Refugee Center, but she shook her head no. I told her she had to go and went in her room to get her papers. For some reason she never wanted to leave the house. I wasn't sure if it was because she didn't feel well or because she was scared.

About a mile before we reached the Refugee Center, she started vomiting again. Fortunately, she had brought another airsick back with her. She must have taken almost every bag on the plane.

When we arrived, Khanh went in the bathroom and lay down for a few minutes while I put a wet paper towel on her forehead. A few minutes later, a receptionist retrieved us and led us to the classroom. The class had already begun, so when we walked in the room, everyone turned around and looked at us. There were about twenty-five students from different countries, ranging in age from eighteen to eighty. They were gathered around a long conference table. The teacher greeted us and then showed Khanh where to sit. I told Khanh I would be back at one o'clock to pick her up.

I decided to go to my office for a few minutes. As I drove to work, I marveled at the ability of one teacher to teach English to twenty-five students who spoke different languages. I had taken a year of French in high school and remembered how hard it was to learn a new language. How much more difficult it would be to be uprooted from your country, in addition to learning a new language and new customs. Western civilizations have a lot in common, but people from Eastern civilizations have an entirely different frame of reference. I likened it to situations where men and women have difficulty communicating because they are so different—their way of thinking, the way they were raised, and their motivations are often so different.

While I was at my office, I called one of my clients, Dr. Bell, who was disgusted because I had been out of the office so much. When I explained what we were doing, he felt guilty and wanted to help in some way. He offered to get them some clothes, so I told him Khanh needed maternity clothes and Tong and Bo needed jeans. He also inquired about what the boys wanted for Christmas, so I told him that Bo wanted Duplos and Tong wanted Legos.

I didn't get much work done before I had to leave to meet the landlord at the rental. When I got there, the landlord was waiting on the front porch. The house was a small green house with white trim around the window sills and a short white picket fence. It was old but fairly well maintained. The yard needed some work, but nothing that a little elbow grease wouldn't cure. The house was surrounded by duplexes and apartments primarily rented by college students.

"Hello, are you Sandy?" the man greeted me warmly.

"Hello, Mark. Have you had the house for rent very long?" I asked.

"Nope. Just about three days. Some college kids were renting it, but they finished at the end of the semester."

He unlocked the house and we went in. It was small, but clean. There was a living room, kitchen, one bedroom and a bathroom on the main floor. There was another small bedroom and a fruit cellar downstairs. It had been freshly painted and had new beige carpet throughout the main floor. The kitchen was old, but all the cupboards had been painted recently and the linoleum was new. It seemed perfect for our family. It was in a safe neighborhood, had two bedrooms, and a yard.

"The rent is $400?" I asked Mark.

"Yup, and it includes all utilities except water. The water should only run ya around $20 a month, though."

"Except for the summer."

"Yeah. Are you the one that'd be living here?"

"No, I'm looking for a mother and her two sons."

"Oh, well this'd be perfect. I'd need a cleaning deposit of $125, then they can move in."

"It sounds good. I'll call you back later this afternoon and let you know for sure. You don't have anyone else seriously looking at it, do you?"

"Nope, but ya never know when someone else will want it. But I'd rather rent it to a family than some more college kids. They kind of rip the place up, ya know."

"I might want to bring them down this afternoon, so I'll call you. Could you possibly meet us here around four o'clock?"

"Probably. Just call when ya know."

"All right. Thanks very much, Mark."

"And I thank you, Sandy. See you later."

Driving back to the Refugee Center, I mentally added the other expenses Khanh would have besides rent, water, and food. I figured that Allen and I could afford to pay $50 a month to help them with their rent and $25 for water if the Refugee Center gave them $350. But that would mean they couldn't have a telephone. Their medical expenses, bus tickets, and food were covered for the next few months. It became increasingly apparent that I should rent that house. The budget would be tight, but it would be possible for them to live by themselves. I was excited!

When I arrived at the Refugee Center, Khanh was still in class so I waited outside the room. Soon she came out with a new book and some papers. The teacher asked me to bring Khanh every day, so I agreed to do my best to get her there. Khanh said goodbye to a couple of other Vietnamese women she had met and we left for the dentist's. His office was only about two miles away, and since Khanh hadn't eaten lunch yet, I stopped at McDonalds and got her a fishburger, french fries and a Coke. She ate everything in the car on the way to the dentist's office. That was the most I had seen her eat since she had been with us.

Arriving at the office, Khanh sat down in the waiting room while I checked her in. As I was filling out the new-patient information, she came up to me and rubbed her stomach. "Don't you feel well?" I worriedly asked. She shook her head yes, so I asked the receptionist where the rest rooms were. I helped Khanh into their private bathroom, then went back to finish the papers. After I shut the door, I could hear her vomiting. Ten minutes later, she still hadn't returned to the waiting room, so I knocked on the door and asked her if she was all right. She opened the door and pointed to her mouth with a sour-looking face. "Do you want a toothbrush?" She nodded her head.

I asked the receptionist if they had a spare toothbrush that I could buy. She found me one with a small tube of toothpaste but wouldn't let me pay for it. I gave them to Khanh and went back in the waiting room. I sat down to read a magazine and had just opened it when Cindy from the SOAR office came in.

"Hello, how are you, Sandy?" she said catching me by surprise.

"Well, hi! What are you doing here?"

"Crista told me that you would be here with Khanh at two o'clock, so I thought I'd come by and see how you were doing. I also brought some things with me to help you find an apartment."

"Oh, thanks, Cindy. I feel like I'm going around in circles. I found a cute house by Boise State for $400 a month, but I don't know how much we can spend yet. Is there anyway we can speed the Refugee Center up a bit?"

"Not really. They're busy and it usually takes a couple of weeks. I'm sorry we haven't been much help finding an apartment. I think this list of low-income apartments with phone numbers will help you."

As I looked over the list, the receptionist walked

into the waiting room and said, "Sandy, would you like
to bring Khanh back now, please?"

"Sure. Do you want to come with us, Cindy?"

"I think I will. I have a couple of other things for
you."

I went up to the bathroom and knocked on the
door. "Khanh?"

She opened the door.

"It's time to see the dentist. Are you all right?"

She nodded her head and followed the
receptionist down a long hallway into a small room
with an old dental chair. The receptionist told Khanh
to sit in the chair and the dentist would be in shortly.
Khanh sat down nervously in the chair. She clenched
her hands tightly around the armrests. Her eyes were
opened wide in fear. She looked pale.

I lightly rubbed her head and tried to calm her.
"There's nothing to be afraid of, Khanh. The dentist is
just going to look in your mouth and check your teeth,"
I said trying to comfort her.

Tears began falling down her face. She quickly
wiped them away, embarrassed that I saw them.

"Oh, Khanh, don't worry. The dentist isn't going to
hurt you." I stood next to her chair with my arm
around her as the dentist's assistant came in.

"Hello, are you Khanh?" she said without emotion.

Khanh nodded suspiciously.

"What are we going to do today?"

"Dr. Cook has agreed to see Khanh because she
has a lot of cavities and has been sick. The nurse at
Central District Health said her mouth was badly
infected and was causing her to vomit."

"When was her last check-up?"

I stared at the assistant in disbelief. "I have no idea. Maybe never. She's only been in this country a week."

"Are you sure Dr. Cook knows that?"

"Absolutely."

The assistant put a blue paper cover-up around Khanh's upper body and pumped the chair up. Khanh jumped and flung her arms spontaneously, grabbing the chair tightly. "It's O.K.," I assured her putting my arm around her again. The assistant turned a bright light on over the chair and laid it back a little. Khanh started crying silently again, quickly wiping away her tears.

"How did the nurse know she had so many cavities? Did you bring her x-rays?"

"I don't even know if she took x-rays. If she did, I've never seen them."

"She had to take them to know there were that many cavities."

"She said you could see them just by looking in her mouth."

The nurse asked Khanh to open her mouth wide and tilt her neck back. "She doesn't understand English," I said, as I helped her lay her head back. I opened my mouth and pointed to her. Khanh opened her mouth reluctantly. The assistant grabbed a long metal stick with a sharp pick at the end and looked in Khanh's mouth. She used the pick a couple of times to prick her teeth and then let out a big sigh. She left the room and told us that the dentist would be in soon.

Khanh started to get out of the chair, but I said, "No, we're not done yet. The dentist still has to see you." She looked at me perplexed and sat back down.

A couple of minutes later, the assistant came back in and said Dr. Cook wanted to see the x-rays. I told her I would call Central District Health and ask if they took any.

I called CDH, but the receptionist said they didn't even have an x-ray machine. I went back and told the dentist's assistant that Khanh had not had x-rays taken. She let out a big sigh and said disparagingly, "I don't think there's anything Dr. Cook can do for you, especially since the patient can't even understand anything he says."

"That shouldn't be a problem, because I can interpret for her," I replied somewhat sarcastically.

I went back in the room with Khanh, and shortly after the dentist joined us. "Hello, I'm Dr. Cook," he said politely.

"Hi, Dr. Cook. I'm Sandy Dalton and this is Cindy Tyler from SOAR and Khanh Trinh, our refugee. I want you to know how grateful we are that you agreed to see her. I called at least forty dentists and couldn't get one to help her. She's been sick ever since she arrived over a week ago, and the nurse at Central District Health thought it might be because of her teeth. She said there were infections throughout Khanh's mouth. To further complicate things, she is pregnant and hasn't been able to hold much food down."

"Oh boy, I don't know what I'll be able to do. Why didn't you fill out the patient chart? Do you know anything about her health history?"

"The nurse at CDH said that she is malnutritioned, and somewhat dehydrated, but doesn't seem to have any serious diseases."

"Well, let me take a look and see what we can do,"

he said reluctantly. He gently tilted Khanh's head back and opened her mouth. He picked up his small mirror and the same pick the assistant had used. He looked around her mouth, occasionally pricking a tooth. He had gray hair with a small bald spot on his head and old-fashioned, gray, wire-rimmed glasses. He had a reserved, almost arrogant air about him which is typical of so many doctors and dentists.

After he examined Khanh's mouth for a few minutes, he set his instruments down and told her she could close her mouth. He sat on his round swivel chair and stared at the table covered with a white cloth and filled with shining silver picks, mirrors, and needles for several minutes. Finally he wearily said, "I don't know what I can do. She's going to have to see an oral surgeon. This is way beyond my level of practice. I think all of her teeth are so badly decayed that it's too late to save any of them. Her mouth is so infected that she must be in terrible pain. Does she complain about her mouth hurting?"

"No, she never complains. She just indicates that her head or stomach hurts," I answered weakly. I was horrified. What did he mean it's too late to save them? She was only twenty-six.

"She probably just doesn't want to complain. I can't imagine that her mouth doesn't hurt. I mean, look at it," he said sympathetically. He turned his big overhead light on again, tilted Khanh's head back and opened her mouth. I stared into her mouth in disbelief. I had never seen or even imagined a human mouth could look so awful. All of her teeth were so rotten they were just little black stubs. There were wide spaces between some of them where teeth had been pulled or had chipped away. All of her gums were swollen and red, probably from the infection. I felt light-headed and sick to my stomach. I stepped back, afraid that I was going to pass out. "I'll be right back," I said softly, patting Khanh's leg. She was crying again. I stumbled out of the room and walked blindly down the hallway. "Are you O.K.?" Cindy asked, grabbing my arm. I opened the bathroom door and went in. Cindy followed me. As the door shut automatically, my back slid down the wall and I collapsed to the floor. "Oh my God, I can't stand it anymore," I sobbed. "I just can't take anymore. I can't stand any of it anymore. It's all too awful. I just can't take it. God, why does it have to be this way?" I yelled. "Why? Why? Why?"

"Sandy, it's O.K.," Cindy said with a petrified look. "It'll be all right."

"No, it won't. Don't you see? It won't. There's nothing I can do to make it all right. She's only twenty-six. I can't give her new teeth. I can't make it so that Tong can grow up with his family. I can't bring Khanh's husband and baby's father here. I don't have any power. I just sit and watch it all. I can't stand it anymore. Oh my God, I love them too much. I just can't stand it anymore," I sobbed and pulled at my hair. "It's all so unfair. It's just not right. Why does it have to be this way?" I moaned and buried my face between my knees.

Cindy patted my back and said, "Sandy, it's all going to turn out O.K. They'll be happy here. I promise they will. You should see other families from Vietnam that have settled here. They've lost children and parents and have terrible health, but they're happy. It will work out just fine, you'll see. You'll get used to it in a little while and these things won't bother you so much."

"That's the worst part of it, though. Don't you see?" I said like a robot staring at the floor. "You get used to it. We all get used to it. The more terrible things we see, the more we accept them. That's the problem. We get used to it. Before long, living half a world away from his family seems like nothing because there are some kids who don't have a family at all. We all desensitize ourselves. Well I'm not going to. It's too awful. I'm not going to pretend that what my refugee family has been through is nothing because there are worse cases. I know there are worse cases, but not among people that I love."

I sat in a state of semi-consciousness, trying to clear my mind of the echoes bouncing from one side of my head to the other repeating, "Why? why? why?" A few minutes later, I broke the silence and weakly said, "I'm scared of myself. I'm going to do the same thing—I know I am. I'm going to get used to it. I'm not any different than anyone else. I can't stand it. I can't live any other way. We numb ourselves because our hearts can't deal with it any other way. It just hurts too much when it's someone you care about."

I stood up and splashed my face with cold water. I patted it dry and got my red lipstick out. I rubbed a tiny bit on my finger and smoothed it on my cheeks. Then I put some on my lips. "There, I don't look so much like a mummy," I said.

Cindy laughed. "You didn't look like a mummy. You just looked like someone who has been through a lot lately. I'm going to start helping you more. Crista should have offered to help you find an apartment."

"That's O.K., Cindy, really. You and Crista have lots of other refugees to help. Allen and I will do just fine. You've done so much more than we have. You devote your whole life to helping them. Please don't feel like you haven't done enough."

We walked back to the room Khanh was in. She was there by herself. She sat up and started to get out of the chair. I let her. "Here, sit here, Khanh," I said, pointing to the only other chair in the room. She looked at me suspiciously, with my red eyes and tear stained face. Dr. Cook came back in and also gave me a strange look. These people probably think I'm some flighty blonde, I thought.

"I don't know what to do," Dr. Cook announced. "She has to have some antibiotics immediately to clear up the infection, but I don't have any health history on her. Is there an interpreter somewhere that can ask her a few questions for me?"

"I'll call around and see if I can find one," Cindy offered.

"When you get home, I want you to either call Dr. Richard West or Dr. Wayne Benes, who are both oral surgeons and try to get her in right away. Tell them I referred her. Let me know if you can't get her in soon."

"All right. Thank you very much, Dr. Cook."

He left the room, and we waited for about a half an hour for Cindy to come back. She was unable to find any Vietnamese interpreters. Dr. Cook came back in and scratched his head when he heard the news. "I don't know what to do. I doubt she has ever taken any antibiotics. About the only thing I'd want to prescribe in her condition is penicillin. It'll clear the infection right up, since her body has never had it before."

"Dr. Cook, I can get an interpreter tonight either on the phone or at my house and make sure she's not allergic to anything."

"Well, O.K. I'm going to go ahead and prescribe her some penicillin, but don't give any of it to her until you've had an interpreter ask her if she's allergic to any medications. Then please call me tomorrow morning and I'll check off her chart. I'll give you a photocopy of her chart and you can have the interpreter ask all of these questions, O.K.?"

"I promise I will."

"You realize that I could lose my license for this."

"I understand. I promise I won't give her any until I've completed this questionnaire."

"Now, may I please have her medical card?"

"Oh, I forgot to tell you. It's in the mail. It's supposed to be in my mailbox today. I promise I'll call you within the next day or so with the number."

He stared at me in surprise and disgust, but then he looked at Khanh. He looked back at me and said, "Take good care of her and see to it that she eats. Once she starts taking this penicillin, she should start holding food down within a day or two. If she doesn't, be sure and take her back to CDH right away."

"I will. Thank you so much, Dr. Cook. I don't know what we would have done without your help. Have a merry Christmas."

"You too. Goodbye, Khanh," he bowed in respect.

As we walked out Cindy said, "There's only one problem."

"What's that?"

"You're not going to be able to find a pharmacy to

fill that prescription without a medical card. It could be a week or so before you get it."

"Oh, I'm not worried about that. I'll just pay for it. I'm not about to wait a week to get Khanh started on the penicillin. I don't think it's that expensive anyway."

"But you shouldn't have to pay for it."

"Why not? We're the ones that sponsored them. Better us than the taxpayers. We can afford $10 or $15 for medicine. Thanks so much for getting me a list of apartments. We're going to look at the house by the university this afternoon, and if that doesn't work, I'll start calling your list tomorrow."

"Be sure and let me know if you need anything. I'm going to start helping you more from now on. You got the most unusual case I've ever seen."

"Thanks, Cindy, but you really have done a lot already. Have a good day, and I'll talk to you soon."

I stopped to fill the prescription and bought a few groceries on our way home. As soon as we got home, Khanh went in her room to lie down. I tried to call Loc but couldn't reach him. I felt so drained that rather than go to work as I should have, I went upstairs to rest and fell sound asleep.

The next thing I knew, Annie was in my room laughing, "Mom, what are you doing sleeping?"

"Oh, Honey, are you home from school already?"

"Yeah, Mom, don't you feel good?"

"I feel fine. I was just so tired I had to lie down."

"Mom, I really had fun at school today."

"You did, Sweetheart? What did you do?"

"Well, first we didn't have to have our spelling test because our teacher got sick and we had a substitute. And she was really nice. She let us watch a movie."

"Really! What movie?"

"*Prancer.* And it was so good, Mommy. Can we rent it sometime?"

"We'll see if we can find it."

I glanced at the clock and it was three thirty. I jumped out of bed and asked Annie, "Is Khanh up?"

"I don't know, Mom. I just got home. I haven't seen her."

"I'm supposed to take our refugees down to look at a little house for rent at four o'clock. I better get going or we'll be late."

I went downstairs to look for Khanh. When she opened her bedroom door, her eyes were red and face wet. "Bo?" she asked me anxiously.

"Oh," I sighed in relief. "Bo will be home in about fifteen minutes. When he gets here, we need to go in the car," I said as I waved my hand goodbye. She just stared at me, then sat back down at the desk and continued writing a letter. I sat on the bed for a minute and watched her. Every minute or so, she would interrupt her writing to sniffle and wipe her nose. I supposed she was writing to her husband. I got up and left, closing the door quietly.

Tong and Bo didn't get home until about four o'clock. As soon as they walked in, I set their backpacks down and led them to the car. Khanh resisted going and didn't want Bo to go, but I told her we all had to go. I got her coat out, handed it to her, and escorted her to the car. The house was only about two miles away, which was one of the things I liked. Not only was it close to our house, it was also close to my and Allen's offices. Before we left, I had called the landlord to remind him that we were coming. He said he would be sure to be there because he wanted to rent it to us today.

When we pulled up in front of the house, the landlord was sitting on the front porch again. We got out of the car and went up to the front door.

"Hello, Mark," I cheerfully said. "This is Khanh, this is Tong, and this is Bo." They all three bowed their heads and smiled. "They don't speak English yet. They've only been here a little over a week."

"They're not going to stay here, are they?" he asked, concerned.

"Well, yes. That's who I'm looking to rent a house for."

" I'm sorry, Ma'am," he stuttered, "but I've already rented it."

"What do you mean? I just talked to you five minutes ago and you told me you wanted to rent it to me today."

"But right before you came, another person that came earlier decided to rent it. They just called me and I promised it to them. I'm sorry, Ma'am."

I didn't know what to say. I knew he was lying, but I didn't want my refugees to know what he was doing. They had been discriminated against all their lives because they were part American, and I didn't want them to know that some Americans would discriminate against them because they were part Vietnamese.

"Can we look at it anyway, in case the other person changes his mind?"

"Nope. I didn't even bring the key with me."

I stared him straight in the eyes and told him, "If that's the way you want it, have it your way. You'll regret it someday."

"Now, what's that supposed to mean? I can't help it if someone come to rent it before you."

"We'll see. I'll check back within a couple of days just in case nobody's moved in yet. We're second in line, right?"

"Well, yeah, I think that's right. But my new renters won't be movin' in for a bit, so there's no reason to check within a couple of days."

"Goodbye, Mark."

I headed back to the car with Khanh, Tong, and Bo following me. When we got in the car, I told Tong the landlord had lost the key. I tried to maintain my composure.

When we got home, I tried to call Loc, but his wife said he wouldn't be home until six o'clock. She said he would call me then. We ate dinner, and sure enough, at six o'clock Loc called. I explained the problem with Khanh's mouth, and he agreed to ask her the questions that were on the dentist's form. It was cumbersome because I had to read Loc each sentence first then hand the phone to Khanh while he translated it. Next she would hand it back to me, and he would tell me what she said. It took a long time to finish the twenty questions. As I expected, she wasn't aware of any allergies and hadn't had any of the diseases listed. I thanked Loc and as soon as we hung up gave Khanh her first penicillin.

That night while lying in bed, I told Allen what had happened at the rental house. I was still fuming. "I think I'll file a complaint with the Human Rights Commission tomorrow," I said in disgust.

"Sweetheart, it won't do any good. If he's that big of a jerk, it's better not to have our refugees rent from him anyway. He would just make it miserable for them."

"I know, but you should have seen the way he looked at them, like they were some kind of animals or Martians from space. Why would he care if they're Vietnamese?"

"Some people are just jerks. No matter how much you try to reason with them, they're just jerks. Don't worry about it. We'll find them a place. I'll help you call around tomorrow."

"It would be so much easier if we knew how much we had to spend."

"I know. But don't worry. We should find out any day now."

"Don't you ever worry about anything?"

Allen looked at me and grinned. "Remember what you always tell me, 'Do not be anxious about tomorrow, for tomorrow will be anxious for itself. Let the day's own trouble be sufficient for the day.'"

I laughed. "Good advice. I'm going to bed. I hope tomorrow goes better. Today was a rough day."

"Tomorrow will be better. I promise. Goodnight, Sweetheart. I love you."

"I love you, too," I said, as I kissed him goodnight.

DAY 13: Why?

When the alarm went off, I hit the snooze button a couple of times. I had tossed and turned all night and lain awake staring at the ceiling for a couple of hours. I just couldn't get the events of the day out of my mind. I finally fell back to sleep at five o'clock.

I knew it would be a long day. The kids had their school Christmas program at seven that evening which wouldn't get over until nine o'clock, so everyone would get to bed late.

The morning ended up going pretty smoothly. Since I got up late, I told everyone they needed to hurry and they thankfully cooperated. We got Tong and Bo on the bus without making the bus driver wait. Then we got our kids off to school and Ben to his grandma's. Allen decided to stay home with Khanh until eleven o'clock and then take her to English class. That gave me most of the day to spend at my office.

It felt good to be back at work, although I found it difficult to concentrate—worrying about Khanh, Tong, and Bo.

I got home about four thirty and hurried to make dinner. After we ate, I helped Jack and Annie get dressed for their Christmas program and asked Khanh, Tong, and Bo to go with us. I tried to explain to Tong that it was Jack and Annie's program, but all he really understood was that we were going to church. He and Bo wanted to go, but Khanh insisted on staying home. I didn't understand why Khanh never wanted to go to church with us. Her immigration papers had clearly stated that she was Catholic. She also wouldn't let Bo go, which caused lots of tears, especially since Tong got to go.

We arrived at St. John's Cathedral early so we could find seats near the front. It was a beautiful old church, with a large rose-shaped stained glass window in the front and stained-glass windows all along the outside walls of the church. It wasn't overly ornate, like many Catholic churches. It had the grandeur of the greatest cathedrals with the simplicity of the most humble churches. One of the pleasures we received from sending our children to Catholic school was that the annual Christmas program centered on what Christ's Mass was all about.

While we were waiting for the program to start, Tong kept taking his shoes off. I had to remind him several times to put them back on and leave them on. He asked why and I told him it was because he was in church. He explained that in Vietnam, people don't wear shoes inside the temples, but I responded that this wasn't a temple, it was a church. He was getting bored, so he picked up one of the hymnals and started looking through it. He was reading quietly to himself when he gently nudged me and pointed to the word "grace." He shook his head and said, "No understand."

"Um. Forgive? No. God?" I pointed up.

Tong said, "Yes, God."

"Um. God's favor, God's love. Love?"

"Love. Love," Tong shook his head and wrinkled his nose.

"Um, love," I crossed my arms over my heart. "I love Allen," I said putting my arm around him. "I love Jack, Annie, and Ben. Tong loves his mother, father, and brothers."

"Oh, yes. Love," he crossed his hands over his heart. "Yes, love," he repeated with a smile.

"I love Tong," I smiled as I crossed my hands over my heart.

"Yes," Tong smiled back.

He resumed reading the hymnal, but soon pointed at another word, "soul." "No understand."

"Soul. Ummm. Heart," I pointed to my heart. "Thump, thump, thump," I patted my hand against my heart in a rhythm. Heart?" Tong looked at me puzzled, so I took his hand and put it over his heart. "Thump, thump, thump, Tong's heart."

"Oh, yes, heart."

"Soul is kind of like heart. Umm. Mind?" I pointed to my head. "Mind." I pointed to Tong's head. "School. Learn. Think."

"Oh, yes," he smiled.

"Soul, like heart and mind together." He looked confused again, but I couldn't think of how else to explain what soul meant. I had no idea if he had a Vietnamese reference that he could associate with soul.

Tong started reading the hymnal again. I was hoping he wasn't going to ask me any more difficult questions. Soon however, Tong pointed to the word, "faith." "No understand."

Oh boy, I thought. "Allen, explain faith to him," I said exasperated. Allen attempted to explain it to him, but unfortunately not to Tong's satisfaction. "Sandy, faith?"

"O.K. Ummm. Believe? Do you understand believe?"

"No," Tong shook his head.

"All right. God, yes?"

"Yes."

"O.K. God, yes?" I smiled and pointed up. "God, no," I said with a frown and pointed to the ground.

"God, no," Tong pointed to the ground.

"Ummm. I don't think you understand. I," I pointed to myself, "I believe in God." I pointed up. "Allen believe in God." I pointed to Allen and then up. "Tong believe in God?" I looked at him with a questioning face.

"Yes," he smiled.

"Good. Tong believe in God," I smiled and he nodded in agreement. "Tong have faith in God," I nodded back. "Tong believe and have faith in God."

"Yes," Tong smiled and started reading the hymnal again. Fortunately for my weary mind, the principal entered the stage and started the program. Each of the classes either sang songs or put on a play. During the songs Tong tapped his foot along to the music, seeming engulfed in it.

By the time we got home, it was nine thirty, and Khanh and Bo were asleep. Jack and Annie were so wound up that it was hard to get them to bed. Tong wasn't ready for bed either. He wanted to go in Allen's den and write a letter to his brothers, so I let him. "You have school very early though, Tong," I reminded him. He nodded in acknowledgment.

As I climbed in bed, my mind kept drifting back to the why? question. Why do some people have things so rough and others like me have it so easy? Why were Khanh, Tong, and Bo born in Vietnam and my family and I born in America? It's nothing that either Khanh or I did. It just happened. Why are some babies born brain-damaged and others like mine born healthy? Why is the world so unfair? Why? why? why?

It had been a long time since I had gotten hung up on the why? question. I remembered the last time I tried to solve the big question, the only thing I found that helped was reading the Book of Job. Now, I didn't have time to re-read the whole thing, but I did read the ending where God gives Job the best answer there is to the why? question. As I read the beautiful flowing prose, I didn't necessarily have the answer, but I felt a lot better. I kissed Allen goodnight and fell asleep in peace.

DAYS 14 & 15: *The Decision*

I had a hard time getting the kids up, since they stayed awake too late the night before. This was also their last week of school before Christmas break, and somehow it seemed like their longest week. I was glad I wasn't a teacher.

We managed to get the kids off to school, although Tong and Bo almost missed the bus again. Allen had made Khanh an appointment at the oral surgeon's for nine that morning. I gave Khanh her second dose of penicillin and had her drink a cup of tea and eat some saltine crackers. Then I put together a few homemade airsick bags by stuffing baggies inside of small paper sacks. When I handed them to her, she looked them over and laughed. She went in the pantry and got a package of potato chips, handing it to me.

"Do you want to take this?" I asked.

She nodded, so we put them in my purse and left for the oral surgeon's office, which was on the other side of town.

It was a beautiful, clear, warm morning. There was still a bite in the air, but the heat from the sun, which was coming over the horizon, had already melted the frost. I stopped and got my cup of coffee. When we started driving again, I rolled Khanh's window down just an inch. I thought a little fresh air might help prevent her from getting sick.

At the oral surgeon's I filled out the same medical form I had filled out twice before, only this time I actually knew most of the answers. We waited almost an hour before we saw the doctor. I had taken some work with me, and Khanh looked at magazines, which she seemed to enjoy. When the nurse finally called us, we went back to one of the examination rooms, and Khanh sat down in a much more modern dentist's chair than the one before. The room was decorated in mauve and light blue with plush carpet and wall paper. As we waited for the oral surgeon, Khanh seemed much more at ease.

The doctor came in about ten minutes later and introduced himself with a warm smile. I explained her medical situation, including the fact that she was pregnant. He said he had treated many refugees and was quite familiar with most of their problems. He laid Khanh's chair back, turned on the bright overhead light and gently opened her mouth. He studied it for a few minutes, then turned the light off and said, "Dr. Cook was right. Almost all of her teeth are so far decayed that I don't know if I can save any of them. However, I won't do anything while she's pregnant. We'll see how she feels after she finishes the penicillin, and if we need to, we'll treat the pain. But I won't pull any teeth until after the baby is born."

"How will she eat without any teeth?"

"We can fit her with dentures. They won't be perfect, but they'll be better than what she has now. Has she been complaining about the pain?"

"No, she acts like her head and stomach hurt sometimes, but not her mouth."

"As bad as it looks, I'm sure it hurts. She probably just doesn't want to complain."

"That's what Dr. Cook said. Well, we appreciate you seeing her on such short notice."

"I'm glad I could help. I wish there was more I could do now. You be sure and bring her in after she delivers. We might even have to admit her to the hospital if we pull all her teeth at once. In the meantime, call me if she starts complaining about the pain."

"O.K. Thanks again."

"Goodbye, Khanh," the doctor waved.

I decided to take Khanh over to the Refugee Center for English class. I waited with her until class started and then I went to my office. Allen agreed to pick her up at one o'clock so I could work the rest of the day.

I called Lyle to see if he had found a rental for our refugee family. He said there was a one-bedroom apartment about a mile from our house that rented for $375 without utilities. I told him I would go by and look at it. Allen had already called some of the apartments from the list Cindy had given me, but to no avail. If this apartment of Lyle's didn't work, I had no idea what we were going to do.

On my way home from work, I stopped by the apartment. It was near the end of a cul de sac, only a block from a little mall that had a grocery store and laundromat, and only a block from our church. There was a big city park a few houses away. Although the location was good, the building, which was a converted old house, was quite run down. There were weeds growing in the yard and litter dotting the grounds. I opened the door and saw a couple of small bikes and some other toys in the long, dark hallway. I didn't have a key to the apartment, so I turned around and left.

When I got home, we decided to order a pizza for dinner. While we were waiting for it to be delivered, I went outside and checked the mail. There was a letter from the State of Idaho, Department of Health and Welfare. I quickly opened it and read it. There was a lot of information concerning particular programs which Khanh qualified for. After sifting through all the papers, I determined that she would get $325 for rent, $200 in food stamps, and medical cards for all three of them. That was it. Khanh would simply have to get a job.

I called Lyle back and told him we would probably take the apartment. He explained that though the landlord would normally only allow an adult and one child in the apartment, he would let us rent it, since we couldn't find anything else. There was a $200 security deposit plus the first month's rent that was due in advance. We had been given $150 per refugee as a one-time payment to help with expenses, so we figured we would use that and pay the balance ourselves. He said we could move in right away, so I told him we would move them in the next weekend.

Allen and I sat down to prepare a budget for Khanh. When we added all the expenses up, they were $150 a month short. We committed to help them until Khanh got a job, and then again for a while after the baby was born. We were prepared to do it because we were fortunate to have good jobs. We also knew when we signed up for a single mother with two sons that they would require more help than most.

The next day after school I took Tong and Bo to see the apartment. Khanh was sleeping. Since I hated to wake her up, I left her home. I got the key from Lyle, and we went in and looked around. It was very small and old. There was one small bedroom, a kitchen, a room that served as both living room and eating area, and a small bathroom. I tried to explain to Tong that this would be their home, but I wasn't sure if he understood. "Is it O.K.?" I asked him.

"Ummmm, no," he shook his head.

"Is it too small?"

He looked at me perplexed.

"Too little?" I asked.

"No understand," he answered in frustration.

I made a small room with my hands and said, "little," then made a big room with my arms and said, "big."

"Oh, no," he laughed. "Ummm, in Vietnam, ummmm, very small. Ummm, many people."

"You have many people in your house in Vietnam?" I asked slowly.

"Yes. Very small."

"How many bedrooms does your house have?" I asked pointing to the bedroom.

"Ummm, no bedrooms. Ummm, one room, and ummm, one cook room."

"Oh, only one room and a kitchen?"

"Yes. Cook room, ummm, no house."

"The cook room is not in the house?"

"Ummm, no, ummm, very hot," he said blowing his fingers.

"Oh, it is a separate building? Not in same house as other room?"

"Yes, ummm. Very small."

"How many people live in your house?"

"Ummm mother, father, three brothers, ummm many cousins."

"Where did you all sleep?"

"Ummm." Then he laid out the sleeping pattern of the whole family. I counted eighteen people that lived in his small, one-room house.

"Did you sleep on a bed?"

"Ummm, no bed. Two small boys on, ummmm, no bed," he shook his head and wrinkled his face. "Ummm, bed. No bed," he shook his head again.

"You mean a mattress?"

"Yes! Yes! Two cousins on mattress. One mattress in house."

"Oh, there was only one mattress? Did you sleep on the floor?"

"Yes," he nodded.

"Oh, Tong," I said as tears filled my eyes. "Did you have enough food to eat for all eighteen people?"

"Ummm, no," he said sadly, dropping his head.

"Let's change the subject. Is this O.K. for Khanh, Tong, and Bo?"

"No. Sandy and Allen house."

"You want to stay at my house?"

"Yes," he smiled.

"But Tong, you have to have a house of your own. One for you, and Bo, and the new baby. Like in Vietnam, Tong's family all in one house. It is better that way."

"No," he shook his head firmly. His eyes started to fill with tears, and he walked out of the apartment.

"Come on Bo, let's go," I said exasperated. As we drove home, Tong looked out the window and ignored me.

When we got home, Tong went up to his room. I looked through the things he had brought home from school. He had made three beautiful paper Christmas ornaments. One was a rectangular building with a window, door, and a Cross trimmed in gold glitter. It didn't look like most typical American churches with tall pointed roofs or steeples, but it was a church that Tong identified with. He had also made a Christmas tree and a small, white snowflake. Annie saw them and exclaimed, "Oh, Mommy, look at these beautiful ornaments. Can I put them on the tree?"

"Yes, but be careful so they don't tear."

She laid one on the children's tree and the other two on the family tree. I went upstairs to tell Tong how pretty his ornaments were, but he was lying on his bed crying. "What's the matter, Tong?"

He looked at me with a drawn face, and asked humbly, "Telephone cousin?"

"You want to call your cousin?"

"Yes."

"The one in Vermont?"

"Yes."

"Did you keep her number?"

"I remember."

"All right, let's go call her." We went in my bedroom and closed the door. He shut his eyes tightly and slowly repeated the telephone number as I dialed. I couldn't believe he remembered the number, but we managed to dial the right one. When his cousin answered, I gave the phone to Tong. He talked furiously, at times crying, and at times almost yelling in desperation. I sat patiently and waited while he talked for fifteen minutes. When he hung up, he told me, "Tong, cousin house, Vermont."

"What?"

"Ummm, cousin in Vermont. Tong, Khanh, and Bo Vermont."

"You want to go to Vermont to see your cousin?"

"Yes. Tong house in Vermont."

"You want to move to Vermont?"

"Yes."

"Tong, I don't know if you can. We're your sponsors. You don't want to stay in Boise with Allen and me?"

"Sandy," he pleaded. "Family in Vietnam want Tong in Vermont."

"Your family wants you to move to Vermont?"

"Yes."

"How do you know? You haven't talked to your family."

"Mother say, ummmm, in Vietnam, Tong in Vermont."

"Your mother told you to move to Vermont with your cousin when you arrived in America?"

"Yes," he nodded firmly.

"Oh boy, Tong. I don't know what to do. It costs lots of money to move to Vermont."

"Yes."

"I'll call Loc and see if he can come over tomorrow night, so we can talk about this."

"No Khanh."

"You don't want me to tell Khanh?"

"No."

"Well, we're going to have to tell her if you move to Vermont."

"Loc tell Khanh."

"All right, I'll call Loc," I said shaking my head in frustration.

I called Loc. He reminded me that there was a Christmas party for Vietnamese refugees at the Refugee Center tomorrow. He wanted us to take Khanh, Tong, and Bo, so I told him we would. He agreed to come over after the party.

That night when we got in bed, I explained to Allen that Tong apparently wanted to move to Vermont. Allen was just as surprised as I was. "Sweetheart, what am I supposed to do? I told Lyle we would rent the apartment and move them in on Saturday. I was going to take Khanh to the apartment and teach her how to go to the bus stop and ride the bus tomorrow. Once again all of my plans are totally up in the air. I don't know if they can leave Boise, since we're their sponsors. How can we be responsible for them in Vermont?"

"Sweetheart, calm down. We'll call Cindy tomorrow and see what she says. If she says they can move, I think we should try to accommodate their wishes."

"But, Allen, Khanh doesn't even know about this. I wonder why Tong waited so long to tell us? We don't know these people in Vermont. We can't move all the furniture and stuff we got for them three thousand miles. How are they supposed to get back there?"

"I don't know. Let's not worry about it until we know what's going on."

"But what am I supposed to do in the meantime? Move them into their apartment, and then move them out a week later?"

"No, we'll call Lyle tomorrow morning and tell him we're not sure if we want the apartment. If you explain the circumstances to him, I'm sure he'll understand."

"But Allen, he's already gone out of his way to accommodate us, and now I'm going to tell him to hold the apartment for a few more days in case we need it?"

"Yes. If he can't, we'll find another one."

"That's easy for you to say. Do you know how hard it was for me to find this place?"

"I know, but we'll find another one."

"Sure, we'll find another one," I sarcastically said, storming into the bathroom and slamming the door.

"Sandy, what's the matter with you?" Allen asked, trying to unlock the door.

"Nothing, just go away," I cried. I sat on the bathroom floor and sobbed.

"Sweetheart, please unlock the door. What's the matter?"

"Nothing, just leave me alone."

"Look, I'm sorry if I said something wrong. Please come out."

"I will in a minute. Just go back to bed."

I sat on the floor for a few minutes and wondered why I ever got into this mess. It wasn't like the literature said it would be. Every time things started to settle down, some major new event took place. I was getting sick and tired of it. I sat in the bathroom and felt sorry for myself for a few more minutes, then went back to bed.

"Sweetheart, why did you get so upset?"

"I don't know. Part of it is that it hurts my feelings that Tong wants to move away. I thought he would want to stay by us."

"Sandy, I'm sure he would like to stay by us, but if his family in Vietnam told him to move to Vermont, he's obligated to fulfill their wishes. And remember they're half a world away."

"I know, but I've gotten so close to them, especially Tong, that I don't want them to move away. If Tong moves, maybe Khanh and Bo could stay."

"I understand how you feel, Sweetheart, but it's also important for them to be near their family. We don't even speak their language, let alone understand their customs. Think how you would feel if you were in their situation. I don't think it would work to have Khanh stay and Tong move. Think of all the legal ramifications."

"I know. I just feel bad. And from a practical view, I don't know how it's going to work. I guess we'll see what Cindy and Loc say tomorrow."

"That's right. We have to do what's best for Khanh, Tong, and Bo."

"I know. I'm so tired. I just want to go to sleep. Goodnight, Allen. I love you."

"Goodnight, Sweetheart, I love you, too," he said as he leaned over and kissed my cheek.

That night, like so many nights in the previous two weeks, I tossed and turned. I had only known this family fifteen days, yet I felt they were a part of me. How could I feel so bad about them leaving when they had only been here such a few days? It reconfirmed my conviction that the human heart can love an infinite number of people an unlimited amount and still have room to love one more. Why then can't human beings live together in peace?

DAY 16: *A Time to Seek and a Time to Lose*

I woke Friday morning to find Jack and Annie already awake and dressed. "Why did you get up so early?" I asked.

"Because, Mom, today is the last day of school and we have a Christmas party, and only a half day!" Jack gleamed.

"I hope you don't get tired later on today. Jack, will you go wake Tong, please? Tell him to go get Khanh and Bo up."

"O.K., Mom," Jack readily agreed, which was highly unusual.

Before long, the whole household was bustling. Nobody complained about waking up or going to school. Even Tong said that he and Bo had parties. "I guess we're the only ones that don't get to have a party, Allen."

"You're wrong, Mom. Remember, we have a party late this afternoon at the Refugee Center."

"Oh, that's right. Tong, this afternoon, party at Refugee Center. Loc wants you to go."

"Yes," Tong nodded with a smile.

After we got all the kids off to school and Allen left for work, I sat down and made a Christmas shopping list. It was already Friday, and Christmas was next Wednesday. I didn't have many presents bought—if I waited any longer, the crowds would be unbearable. I also made a list of what I needed to do to get my refugees moved into their apartment.

While I was waiting for the stores to open, I made a salad for the party at the Refugee Center and read the paper. At nine o'clock, I called Lyle and told him that I still wasn't sure if we were going to rent the apartment. He said that he understood and would try to keep it open a couple more days.

At ten o'clock I headed for the mall. I tried to convince Khanh to come but she wouldn't. I explained that I would be away for two hours and gave her Allen's phone number if she needed anything. Since I knew I didn't have much time, I tried to buy everything at a few stores.

I returned home in under two hours. Khanh helped me get all the presents wrapped before the kids arrived home. She wrapped only three presents while I wrapped twelve, because she was so deliberate in every thing she did. She measured the paper to within a quarter inch of what she needed, and cut it in a perfect line. When she put tape on, she measured it carefully. She took great pride in each gift she wrapped. While Khanh carefully wrapped her presents, I sloppily cut crooked lines, slapped tape anywhere it seemed most convenient and finished each present off with a store-bought bow. She put several different colors of ribbon on and made her own bows. She was definitely cut out to be an artist, I concluded—it's just that she never got the chance.

When the kids arrived home, they were full of energy and excitement from their last day of school. Jack and Annie brought cupcakes and balloons home. Tong and Bo had candy canes.

I asked Jack and Annie if they wanted to help wrap our refugees' presents. They yelled jointly, "Yeah!"

"Tong and Bo, you have to go in the other room. We're going to wrap your presents," Annie teased.

They looked at me mystified. "Presents, gifts? For Tong and Bo," I repeated.

"Oh!" Tong exclaimed and smiled. He repeated this important information to Bo, who giggled and jumped up and down.

"Come on, Bo, you go in my room and don't peek," Jack said kindly, leading him up the stairs. Tong followed him with a big grin on his face.

After we wrapped their presents, we hid them under the tree, then called Tong and Bo. They came running eagerly down the stairs and started hunting for their presents. When they found one, Tong would exclaim, "Ohhh, Bo gift!" Then Bo would quickly grab it and shake it, trying to guess what it was. Bo started to open a couple of them, but we stopped him before he got far. He didn't understand why he had to wait.

Later in the afternoon, I told everyone to get ready to go to the Christmas party at the Refugee Center. I had Tong tell Khanh, but she wrinkled her face and shook her head no.

"Yes, Khanh. It will be fun. There will be lots of other Vietnamese refugees there." She shook her head no again, then took Bo in her room and changed his clothes. Before we left I encouraged Khanh one more time to come, but she still refused, so we left her home.

When we arrived at the party, there were already about fifty people there, few of whom spoke English. They were from all over the world. There were several Vietnamese, so I took Tong and Bo up to introduce them. They talked back and forth, occasionally looking at Allen and me and smiling. We smiled back but had no idea what they were saying. We went through the buffet line to get our dinner. There was a tremendous variety of dishes from many countries. Most of them I had never seen before. They seemed to have two things in common: no meat or chicken and lots of rice or noodles. While we ate, Tong kept his eye on several teenage girls who were listening to loud music on the boombox and dancing.

"Tong, quit watching the girls," Allen kidded.

He laughed and said, "Chinese. Handsome."

"Pretty," I corrected him. "Where is the music from? Vietnam?"

"No, China."

"Do you speak Chinese?" I asked.

"Yes, not good. Father, ummm . . . in Vietnam, ummm . . . Chinese."

"What?"

"Father in Vietnam Chinese," he said slowly.

"Your father in Vietnam is Chinese?"

"Yes."

"Why don't you ask one of the girls to dance?" Annie teased. "Come on, Tong, go dance," she pushed him.

"No," he shyly answered.

By the time we finished eating, there were hundreds of people there. We didn't see Loc and his family, so I was afraid they wouldn't come to our house.

Shortly after we returned home, however, the doorbell rang. It was Loc and his family. I hadn't talked to them for several days. So much had transpired that I felt I had a lifetime of catching up to do.

After we exchanged greetings, I explained the

difficulty we were having finding an apartment. I recounted the problems with Khanh's teeth, including possibly having to hospitalize her after the baby was born in order to pull all her teeth at once. Then I told them about Tong calling his cousins in Vermont on two different nights and crying, and that Tong had announced that he wanted to move there.

"Loc, can you talk to Tong and see what he wants to do? He said his mother wanted him to move to Vermont when he arrived in America," I said.

"O.K., I'll talk to him," Loc agreed. I brought everyone drinks and we sat down in the living room. Then Loc began a long conversation with Tong. Khanh and Bo didn't say anything; they just listened. A few minutes into the conversation, Tong started to cry again. His face was serious and the tone of his voice harsh.

Finally, Loc turned to Allen and me and said, "Before Tong left Vietnam, his mother told him that she wanted him to move where his cousin lives, which is in Vermont. His cousin has only been in America for one year, but has a job and an apartment. She has two grown sons and a ten-year old daughter who live with her. Both her sons have good jobs. In Vietnam, family is extremely important. You see, the Vietnamese consider their extended family, including cousins, to be as important as Americans consider their immediate family. Tong feels sad because he doesn't want to leave you, but he wants to honor his mother's wishes. He wants Khanh to move so his cousins can help her while the baby is small."

"I wonder why they didn't find a sponsor in Vermont, since that's where they wanted to go?" I asked.

"Tong said it took them a long time to get a sponsor, and they didn't want to risk not getting another one."

"I called Cindy today, and she said they can move anywhere in the United States they want once they're here. There are several big problems though: how are we supposed to get them clear back to Vermont, and how much is it going to cost?"

"The only way we could send them is by plane," Allen commented. "There's no way we could send a pregnant mother and two children that don't speak English by bus or train."

"But, Sweetheart, if we send them by airplane, what are we going to do with all the stuff for their house?"

"That won't be a problem, I guarantee it," Loc answered quickly. "There are lots of refugee families that need furniture, clothes, and kitchen items. There's a family that arrived two days ago that doesn't have any furniture in their apartment. They have a baby who is only three months old, and they're all sleeping on the floor."

"I'm sure that's true, and I would love to help them," I said with a lump in my throat. "But this stuff was collected especially for our refugee family. We've been gathering it since we committed to sponsoring Khanh, Tong, and Bo months ago. It's not only stuff from our own house, but from our familys' and friends' houses, too. We want them to have it in their home. Otherwise, they'll end up with a bunch of things from people they don't even know," I rambled on, primarily talking to myself.

"Sweetheart, it's not that big a deal. They'll still get

nice things. And remember, what we're giving them certainly isn't new," Allen chuckled.

"Yeah, but it's special stuff we spent a lot of time picking out," I said with tears in my eyes. "If they get all new things in Vermont, I won't have any input in their home," I added almost incoherently.

"Sandy, we have to do what is best for them. Tong has made it clear he wants to be with his cousins," Allen said.

"I know. And I don't blame him. They have nothing else except their family. Especially with Tong's father, mother, and brothers so far away, it's important for him to be near his cousins. It will also be good for Khanh to have someone in her family to help with the baby. But I wish they could take the things we got for them. Oh well, it's just stuff. They'll have the most important thing, which is each other."

"Loc, please ask Tong if he's discussed moving to Vermont with his cousin. You also better ask Khanh if that's what she wants," Allen said.

Loc talked to Khanh and Tong for a few minutes, then reported, "Tong said his cousins want them to move to Vermont. Khanh is not so enthusiastic about moving. She would rather wait until after the baby is born. She didn't know that Tong's mother wanted him to be with their cousins. Tong said he wants to go even if Khanh stays here."

"Should I call the airlines to see how much three tickets would cost?" I reluctantly asked.

"I think so," Allen replied.

I called United Airlines. They had a special through Christmas Day of $350 with no advance purchase requirements. If we waited until after

Christmas, the tickets would be over $800 each. There was a flight from Boise to Chicago with an hour layover in Chicago and then direct to Burlington, Vermont. The operator checked seat availability and the only day she could book all of them was Christmas Eve at six twenty a.m.

"Can I give you a call back in a few minutes?" I asked her.

"Ma'am, there are only four seats left and I can't guarantee they'll be available when you call back," she replied.

"Can I have you hold the seats and I'll go pick up the tickets tomorrow?"

"I'm sorry, I can't do that, ma'am. This is a special fare and you need to pay for them before we issue them."

"Then can you hold on for a minute while I talk to my husband?" I graciously asked.

"All right," she agreed.

I explained the situation to everyone.

"I wonder if Khanh's cousin can help pay for the tickets," Loc commented.

"Allen, we could use the $450 we received for resettlement expenses instead of using it for the apartment, but that would still leave us $600 short."

"Yeah, but we also have to consider if they stay here, we're going to give them $125 or so a month to live. It won't take many months to reach $600. And I think the important consideration is that Tong wants to move and Khanh needs the support of her family in her condition."

"Loc, why don't you tell Khanh that we can get

them plane tickets to leave in four days and see if she wants to go?"

While Loc talked to Khanh, I told the ticket agent I was almost ready, and thanked her for being patient. During Loc's conversation with Khanh, Tong suddenly interrupted and pleaded with Khanh in a passionate tone. Khanh began crying and responded with an equally emotional defense. Tong and Khanh were both crying now.

Loc explained, "Khanh wants to go if Tong is going, but she is sad to leave you. She said you have done so much for her."

"What do you think Loc? Should we send them?" I asked in desperation, hoping he would make the decision for us.

"I think it is too much money for you to spend. We should call her cousins and see if they can help pay at least half of it. If you can afford to pay the rest, I think it would be best for Khanh, Tong, Bo and the new baby to be near their family."

"Do you agree, Allen?" I asked.

"Yes. I think you should go ahead and get the tickets."

I looked at Khanh, who still had tears running down her face, and at Tong, who had a sad but courageous expression. You are truly the man of this family, I thought as I stared at him, feeling the overwhelming pride a mother feels when her son has done something extraordinary. Tears filled my eyes and I wanted to hug them and beg them to stay. But I knew if I really loved them, I had to let them go. I returned to the phone, and taking a deep breath slowly said, "We'll take the tickets."

After I hung up the phone, I sat down in a chair, my legs weak. I went back in the living room. "Loc, tell them I bought the plane tickets. They're leaving Tuesday morning at six twenty a.m."

Loc relayed the information, and Khanh and Tong started crying again. Khanh talked to Loc for a while, who then repeated what she said. "Khanh thanks you from the bottom of her heart for all you have done. She remembers arriving at the airport so afraid and being comforted by you. She thanks you for taking care of her while she was sick and for starting the boys in school. She will miss you very much."

"Tell her we will miss her, Tong, and Bo, also, but that we will call them often, and they can come back and visit."

Loc repeated what I said and then added, "I think I should call their cousins."

"Good idea," Allen responded.

Tong dialed the number and handed the phone to Loc. He talked for quite a while. After he hung up he said, "Their cousins are very excited that they are coming. They will live in the cousins' apartment for a while until they're ready to move out on their own. I asked if they could afford to pay half of the plane fare and she said they could, but they could only send a few dollars a week."

"Did you tell them when Khanh, Tong, and Bo will arrive?"

"Yes, they will pick them up at the airport."

"All right. Well, I guess we're done."

"Yes, and my family and I must now leave. We were supposed to be somewhere fifteen minutes ago," Loc said as he stood.

"Oh, I'm sorry, Loc. Thank you so much for coming."

"We're glad we came. I will call you in a couple of days to see if you need anymore help."

"Thank you, Loc and Mai. I don't know what we would have done without you." They left, and our refugees went to their rooms. I left them alone for several hours.

Before Tong got in bed that night, he came to me, bowed, and said, "Sandy, thank you."

"Oh, you're welcome, Tong," I said, embracing him. "I love you." As I stared at him, it seemed that I had raised him since birth. That beautiful glowing face and sparkling eyes were so full of life and hope. "You will be a great man someday," I softly said. "Your family would be proud of you," I added, hugging him again.

I got the kids in bed, then put on my pajamas and heavy bathrobe and went out on the deck off our bedroom and sat down. It was bitterly cold and my body shivered in rebellion. At times, when life seems too complicated, I have to get outside in the fresh air amongst the stars so I can think clearly. I reflected on the day's events and how rapidly everything had changed. Yesterday, I had the weight of three, almost four, people's lives on my shoulders. I also experienced the joy of helping them and watching them develop. Tonight the overwhelming responsibility for their immediate welfare and their future failures and successes was mostly lifted. Their family would assume that position, which was right. But I had also lost the ability to shape three very special people's lives. It was like watching your children go off to college and knowing that their future was now in their hands, that you had done everything you could and your primary contribution to their lives was over. Oh Lord, I cried, thank you for bringing these people into my life, even though for only twenty days. I was reminded of one of my favorite passages from Ecclesiastes which seemed appropriate not only for my refugees, but also for our countries:

> For everything there is a season, and a time for every matter under heaven:
> a time to be born, and a time to die;
> a time to plant, and a time to pluck up what is planted;
> a time to kill, and a time to heal;
> a time to break down, and a time to build up;
> a time to weep, and a time to laugh;
> a time to mourn, and a time to dance;
> a time to cast away stones, and a time to gather stones together;
> a time to embrace, and a time to refrain from embracing;
> a time to seek, and a time to lose;
> a time to keep, and a time to cast away;
> a time to rend, and a time to sew;
> a time to keep silence, and a time to speak;
> a time to love, and a time to hate;
> a time for war, and a time for peace.

My time was up in three short days. I had to make the most of it.

DAY 17: *Full of Life*

I woke up Saturday morning with lightness of heart and renewed vigor. I knew I only had three days left with my refugee family. I wanted to make the most of them. I hadn't realized until now just how much the tremendous responsibility of helping my family adapt to America and dealing with all their emotional problems had weighed on me.

Ben woke me at seven o'clock and Jack and Annie came downstairs shortly after. When Tong came downstairs at eight thirty, he had a big smile on his face and looked more relaxed than I had seen him. He helped me cook breakfast, commenting several times about his father's cooking in Vietnam.

Bo got up shortly after and was hungry. Rather than eat the breakfast we had made, Bo wanted a piece of bread with peanut butter on it, so that's what I made him, giving him an apple, too. Khanh saw what Bo was eating and wanted the same. She ate all her bread, an apple, and drank a glass of milk. I figured the penicillin must be working.

After breakfast, I called Lyle and told him we wouldn't need the apartment. He was understanding and was sure he would be able to rent it without any problem. When I hung up, I asked the kids if they wanted to go with me to run errands. Everyone wanted to go so we all piled in the van. I tried to get Khanh to go, but as usual she didn't want to. First we went to Tong and Bo's school to get their school supplies. As expected, the school was locked up and nobody was around. Tong was upset, so I told him: "Tong, I will come back after Christmas break and get your pencils, notebooks, crayons, etc. and mail them to you in a box. Do you understand?"

"You mail?"

"Yes, I'll mail all of your and Bo's things that are in the school, but not for two weeks," I pointed to the school and put up two fingers. "Do you understand?"

"Yes," he said, smiling.

Next we went to the airport to pick up the plane tickets. Tong and Bo loved the airport as much as any kids. They watched the airplanes, helicopters, and Air Guard jets take off and land while I got the tickets. I explained to the lady issuing the tickets that my refugees did not speak English and I was concerned about them getting on the right plane in Chicago. She made a note of it in her computer and assured me that they would have a representative waiting for them at the gate at O'Hare. As we left the airport, Ben cried and Bo tugged at my arm, begging to stay. Next we stopped at the grocery store, where I bought some stamps and envelopes for Khanh and Tong. Our last stop was at the photography shop, where I dropped off the film I had taken of Khanh, Tong, and Bo in front of their Christmas stockings.

When we got home and started making lunch, Tong and Bo couldn't believe we were actually going to eat again. Neither of them ate anything, but Khanh had a bowl of Japanese noodles and another apple. "Khanh, you're eating so much better," I smiled. I put my hand on her forehead and asked, "Are you feeling better?"

She smiled at me and nodded her head. "Good, it must be the medicine," I commented. I showed her the bottle of penicillin. She nodded her head again. Soon after we finished eating, the telephone rang. When I answered it, I heard a bunch of people speaking what I assumed was Vietnamese in the background. "Hello," I said. I couldn't understand anything, so I put Khanh on the phone. She talked for ten minutes, and all I could think about was that her cousin had changed her mind and didn't want them to move to Vermont. Khanh finished talking and handed me the phone. "Hello," I cautiously said.

"Hello," came an American voice on the other end.

"Oh, you speak English," I said, pleasantly surprised.

"Are you Sandy?"

"Yes."

"I'm Mark, a missionary with the L.D.S. Church. I'm trying to help Tong's cousins get ready for Tong and his family."

"Oh, good. I'm relieved that they still want them to come."

"Yes, they're very excited. They'll be arriving on Tuesday, December twenty-fourth around three o'clock. Is that right?"

"Yes." I gave him the flight number and airline. "They're going to live in the same apartment as their cousins for now, right?"

"Yes. It will be crowded, but they're used to it. They were so excited they couldn't sleep last night."

"Do they know that Khanh is pregnant?"

"Yes."

"Oh good," I answered, once again relieved. " I'll probably send two or three big boxes filled with clothes and Christmas presents with them. Is that a problem?"

He asked Khanh's cousin, and she said it was all right.

"I want to thank you for helping them," I said.

"I'm glad to do it. We'll see Khanh and the boys on Christmas Eve."

"All right. Thanks again and have a merry Christmas."

"You, too," he answered, before hanging up.

"Is everything O.K.?" Allen asked.

"I think so," I answered.

"Oh, I forgot to tell you that while you were gone this morning, Dr. Bell and Shirley dropped by some presents for Khanh, Tong, and Bo."

"Oh good," I answered.

Jack overheard me in the kitchen and immediately yelled, "Did you hear that Tong and Bo? More presents for you!" All of them ran to the Christmas tree and went through the ritual of shaking, feeling, and trying to guess what was in each package.

That afternoon Khanh and I went through all the clothes I had collected for her and Bo. We ended up discarding half of them because there wasn't enough room to send them. Khanh kept taking all the shorts and summer tops out, but I tried to explain to her that it would get hot in the summer and they would need them. She also didn't want to take the snow boots I had gotten for her and Bo. I tried to explain that it was colder in Vermont than in Boise, but I didn't convince her. She took them out of the box when I left the room.

I showed the photographs I had gotten developed to Khanh, Tong, and Bo. I cut out one of the pictures of the three of them and put it in a picture-frame ornament I had bought. Then I put a photo of Bo in an ornament for Khanh, and one of Tong in an ornament which I gave to Tong to give to his mother. I gave a copy of all the photos to Khanh and Tong. She kept giving them back to me, not understanding they were hers. I showed her that I had the same photos and told her to send some of hers to her husband in the Philippines and Tong's family in Vietnam. Tong picked out a photo of him, Bo, Jack, Annie, and Ben eating candy canes next to the kid's Christmas tree to send back to Vietnam.

That night, we took them to the Vietnamese restaurant for dinner. They seemed to be tired of the worldwide cuisine we had been feeding them. In the sixteen days they had been with us we had fed them Italian several times (usually pizza, which they liked), Mexican (tacos which they weren't fond of), German (sausages and sauerkraut, which they hated), Chinese (really American stir-fry), and American (hamburgers, fish and chips, and roast).

We explained to the waitresses that our family was moving to Vermont. They were sad to see them go but happy that they would be with their family. After we finished eating and said good-byes to our Vietnamese friends at the restaurant, we drove to the Grove in downtown Boise to see the Christmas lights one more time. It was a clear crisp night, so we walked around for a few minutes, enjoying the huge lighted tree and brightly lit buildings.

Tong shivered and said, "Cold."

"Yes, cold, but invigorating," I answered.

"What?"

"Invigorating," I laughed. "Ummm, energy?"

"No," he shook his head indicating his lack of understanding.

"Ummm, vigor. No, ummm, full of life," I threw my hands up and yelled.

"What?" He asked, looking alarmed, probably wondering if I had lost my mind.

"Tong, don't be so serious," I laughed with my teeth chattering. "Full of life!" I picked up his arms and threw them high in the air.

"Yeah, Tong. Full of life!" Annie yelled and jumped up and down.

"Yeah, Tong," Ben carried on. "Life," he jumped up and down and twirled around. Then Bo started to giggle and throw his arms up and twirl around.

"Yeah, Tong, come on. Invigorating!" I yelled twirling around and laughing. We all started turning circles and yelling, "Invigorating!" Jack and Bo got carried away and twirled so fast they fell down. Allen stood by the tree, halfway hiding out of embarrassment. "Come on, Daddy!" Annie yelled. "Aren't you full of life?"

"You guys are embarrassing," he sighed. "These people must think you're escapees from the nut house. It's freezing cold out here. Let's get back in the car."

"But if you'd jump up and down and turn circles, you would warm up," I teased him.

"Come on. Let's go."

"We're having fun," I laughed, "and the kids are so wound up they need to get rid of some energy."

"O.K., but I'm going back to the van with Khanh," Allen answered.

The kids danced around the big tree yelling

"invigorating" and "full of life" a few more minutes. Tong eventually joined in.

When my legs started turning numb, I announced it was time to leave. All five of the kids argued, but when I agreed to go home and play Legos, they reluctantly piled in the van.

We played Legos for several hours, building a little city with houses, roads, a firehouse, and a police station. At ten o'clock, I made everyone get ready for bed.

"But, Mom, we can't put the city away. It took us a long time to build," Jack whined.

"All right, we'll leave the city up for a few days."

"Can we read for a few minutes?" Annie asked.

"O.K., but only for a few minutes. Everybody has to be in bed within five minutes or there's no reading."

They quickly got their pajamas on and climbed in bed. I read to Bo and Ben, and Allen listened to Tong read. Tong could read aloud quite well. He pronounced the words distinctly and understood the punctuation, but after reading several pages he laid the book down in frustration and said, "No understand."

"You don't understand?" Allen asked.

"No," he shook his head and wrinkled his face.

"Show me which words you don't understand and I'll help you with them," Allen encouraged him. He skimmed his fingers over the whole page and said, "No understand. Read, but no understand." He got up and went to his bed.

"I'm sorry, Tong. It will take time. The more you read, the better you will understand," Allen said patting him on the back.

"Let's all go to bed now. It's getting late," I said.

Allen and I gave all the kids a kiss goodnight and tucked them in. Before I went to bed, I watched my video of Pavarotti. As I listened to him sing the Christmas carols that I had heard so many times, I realized that the Christmas season was almost over and I had missed many of my favorite holiday activities. I loved to take the kids to the holiday parade, go to Handel's *Messiah* at the cathedral, and *The Nutcracker* ballet. I had missed many things this year that I hadn't even realized I had missed until now. But I quickly shrugged it off because I knew all those things would be back next year and all the years following. I was just thankful that my refugee family had been with us this Christmas season. I would probably never have all of them during the holidays again, and I wanted to enjoy them and help them as much as I could.

DAY 18: *Freedom and Neglect*

The alarm went off early because I wanted to take my refugees to the Catholic church service. A Vietnamese priest visiting from Canada was performing a service in Vietnamese at ten o'clock. I lay in bed wondering if my refugee family would know how to follow the service—when to kneel and how to take communion. Since the service would be in Vietnamese, I knew I wouldn't be any help. I decided to take them to see the priest before the service.

I called the church and asked for Father Knee. The secretary said he wouldn't be available until after the service, but suggested I call Father Knee's cousin. I called his cousin, who invited us over to her house at noon when Father Knee would be there. She said there would be another Vietnamese service in the evening.

Allen was going to take Jack, Annie, and Ben Christmas shopping at noon, so it worked out well for me to take Khanh, Tong, and Bo to meet Father Knee. When we were ready to go, Khanh shook her head, indicating she was not going. I firmly told her that she had to go. We got their papers together, made another airsick bag and headed for the home of Father Knee's cousin. We drove by a McDonalds and Bo yelled, "Coke." Khanh tapped my arm and pointed to McDonalds.

"You want to stop?" I asked her.

She nodded in agreement. It was Sunday morning with little traffic and plenty of time, so I stopped and let them eat. I explained that McDonald's had chicken or fish sandwiches, but they wanted hamburgers. We ate in the restaurant, and Bo played outside on the playground for a few minutes before we got back in the car and drove to see Father Knee.

Father Knee's cousin greeted us cheerfully and led us to the kitchen where four young girls and an older lady were making egg rolls. They had a huge pan of rice mixture in the center of the table, which they were wrapping in egg roll skins. It was obvious they had done it many times because they were quite skilled at making them.

They talked to Khanh, Tong, and Bo for over a half an hour until Father Knee walked through the front door. He was a small man, about forty, with black-rimmed glasses and a pleasant smile. He apologized for being late and thanked us for coming. While he went and changed into jeans and tennis shoes, his cousin took us into the family room at the back of the house, where it was private. Khanh sat in one chair with Bo on her lap and Tong sat next to me on the couch.

When the Father came in, he sat in a chair opposite us and asked what he could do for us. I answered, "Khanh, Tong, and Bo just arrived in America eighteen days ago. Their immigration papers indicated that they were Catholic. I've tried to take Khanh to church several times but she never wants to go, so I'm not sure if they're really Catholic. I would like to take them to your Mass, but I don't know if they've ever been to church before. I was hoping you could talk to them about church and other things."

"What kind of other things?"

"I'm not sure. They're moving to Vermont Tuesday morning to live with their cousins, and I may not see them for a long time. I'm worried about them going, although I'm not sure why. I guess I feel responsible for them and I care a lot about them. I just want them to realize that America is a wonderful place, but there are things they have to watch out for," I rambled on. "Why don't you explain that you're a Catholic priest and I asked you to talk to them for a while."

He conversed with my refugees for several minutes then said, "I asked them if they have been baptized and they said no. I asked them if church was an important part of their life and they also said no. They have never been to a Catholic church."

"Well, I'm glad I didn't take them to Mass," I disappointedly replied. "Tell them when they move to Vermont they will meet many good Americans and some not-so-good Americans. Tell them that they cannot trust everyone."

Father Knee talked to them again for a while and reported back. "Khanh says to thank you very much for all you and your family have done for them. They are very sad to leave you and hope that you and your family remain healthy."

"Tell them that we are so glad we sponsored them—that we have enjoyed having them stay with us. Tell Tong and Bo that it is important to study hard at school so they can go to college and get a good job someday. Also tell them that in America they are free to go to any church they want to, but I want them to go to some church because many people at church will help them."

Father Knee talked to them again and then said, "I explained that they will have many freedoms in America that they have never had before and that it's important to exercise those freedoms. I also reminded them that a good education is critical and that it's one of the reasons they came to America. Is there anything else you would like me to tell them?"

"Oh, I don't know," I sadly said. "How can I teach them all about life in America and warn them about all of life's pitfalls in fifteen minutes? There are many things I want to tell them, but they'll just have to learn by experience. Tell them that I love them and if they ever need anything they should call me and we will help them." My voice cracked and I could feel a lump in my throat.

Father Knee talked to my refugees for a long time and then blessed them and prayed for them to have a safe trip. "Thank you so much for bringing them to see me. I think it's important for them to realize that there are Vietnamese Christians. When the Communists took over, they forbade worship of any type. Khanh likely grew up without any religious experience unless her family secretly worshipped, which it doesn't sound like they did. I would encourage you to contact the Catholic church in the town they're going to and have them visit. Are you Catholic?"

"No, I'm Lutheran, but I'm sure they think I'm a Catholic, which is fine. There's not that much difference anymore and it's too confusing trying to explain it to them."

"Thank you for sponsoring them and for taking such good care of them."

"Thank you for seeing them today. Have a merry Christmas."

"You too." As we left he told Khanh, Tong, and Bo to have a merry Christmas in Vietnamese.

That night for dinner I fixed beef stew. It was one of the few meals I had made with beef in it. I had tried to mainly serve fish and chicken because that's what Khanh, Bo, and Tong ate in Vietnam. However, when I looked through the kids' and Khanh's school papers, I noticed that one of Khanh's papers asked what her favorite food was. She answered beef. I laughed to myself because I had assumed just the opposite. In Vietnam, beef was probably like lobster in Boise—a delicacy because it was not raised locally.

I looked through Tong's school work and could tell that he was an intelligent boy. He got 100s on all of his math papers. He was also doing well in English and spelling. The only subject he seemed to be struggling with was history.

As I looked through Annie and Jack's work, I pulled out a story which Jack had written. The title of it was "The Forgotten Child." The teacher had given him an A on it and commented that it was an excellent paper. As I read it, my stomach started to burn. The story was about a boy named Daniel whose family adopted two more boys. Once the new boys were in the house, Daniel's parents quit paying attention to him and spent all their time with the new boys. Daniel had to give up his bedroom so the new boys could sleep in it, and he didn't get any toys for Christmas. The story ended with Daniel running away from home and going to a new family that didn't have any other boys. Tears fell down my face as I realized how much I had neglected my own children. I knew it wouldn't be for long, but they had probably felt like it was forever.

That night after dinner, we watched *Santa Claus, the Movie.* Jack sat on my lap and watched it with me.

He stayed there the entire movie, which was unusual for him. I whispered to him that I missed being with him and it would only be two days until he and Annie and Ben would have me to themselves again. He nodded his head.

DAY 19: *The Joy of Christmas and the Gift of Life*

I woke up Monday morning and realized how much I had to do to get my family ready to move. The kids were out of school, so Allen agreed to stay home with them for the day. After breakfast I took Khanh, Tong, and Bo to the SOAR office to tell Cindy and Crista they were moving and to photocopy all of their documents so I could send the originals with them and keep a copy for me. There were so many papers, it took me an hour to copy them all.

Our next stop was Central District Health for copies of the records they had from Khanh's examination. We waited for an hour, but they never found any record of her ever being there.

We returned home and ate lunch. Then I called Allen's mother and father, and my parents and sister, to invite them over for a Christmas party tonight for our refugees. The rest of the day we spent packing as many of their new belongings as we could. Loc came by to tell Khanh, Tong, and Bo goodbye and to see if they needed him to interpret anything. I asked him to review their schedule with them and make sure they understood how to call me collect if they needed to. He left us some candy and sparkling grape juice for Christmas.

The day flew by. I had to rush to get dinner before our guests arrived. We ate quickly and had just gotten cleaned up when the doorbell rang. It was Allen's mom and dad, whom our refugees already had met several times. They brought some presents for Khanh, Bo, and Tong and put them under the tree. Soon after, my mom and sister, Debbie, arrived. They also brought several presents for each of the refugees.

I sat down under the tree and separated all the presents which belonged to Khanh, Tong, and Bo. They took up half the living room. We had our refugees sit in front of the presents so we could take their picture, but Khanh motioned for Allen's parents and my mom and sister to sit next to them, so we took a photo of everyone. Allen also took movie pictures throughout the festivities.

Annie and Jack handed one present to each of them to open. Khanh seemed embarrassed by all the presents and kept shaking her head in disbelief. The first presents they opened were sweatshirts. Khanh, Bo, and Tong thanked Allen's parents profusely, then tried the sweatshirts on. The next present Khanh opened was some turtlenecks, which she didn't seem to want. We explained that it was very cold in Vermont and she would understand why we bought them for her when she got there. Tong opened his next present, a big tub of Legos. "Ohhh, Legos!" he exclaimed jumping up in excitement.

"Yes, Tong, Legos for you," Allen's mother smiled.

"Just think, Tong. Now you can build your own cities anytime you want," Annie cried.

"Yes, thank you very much!" he said graciously to Allen's parents.

Bo fidgeted with anticipation as he watched his mother and Tong open presents. When his mother finally told him it was his turn, he jumped up and down in glee. Khanh and Tong had carefully unwrapped their packages, cautiously removing bows and tags and careful not to rip any of the paper; however, Bo grabbed his present and ripped the paper off as fast as he could. When he saw it was a soccer ball, he tossed the paper aside and jumped up and down expressing his joy in Vietnamese over and over again. He tried to extricate his ball from the box but quickly turned the task over to Allen's dad. While he was waiting for the ball, he and Ben ran down the hall and through the kitchen giggling.

Khanh opened the rest of her presents, which included some more sweatsuits and a couple of maternity dresses, an instamatic camera, a watch, the photo album I had gotten her, and the Christmas tree ornament with Bo's picture in it. After she opened the ornament, she put her head in her hands and cried, overcome with emotion from all the presents. She graciously thanked each person who had given her a gift and insisted on more photos taken with everyone.

Tong's presents included pants and shirts, an AM/FM radio and cassette, a couple of tapes, a watch, a globe, a game, a small electronic keyboard which he had asked for, and the Christmas tree ornament with his picture in it. "Tong, this is for your family in Vietnam. For their Christmas tree. Understand?"

He nodded his head and smiled, carefully clasping the ornament in his hands. "Thank you very much."

Bo was so wound up, Khanh kept yelling at him to slow down, but to no avail. His gifts included pants and shirts, a big tub of Duplos, several color books and crayons, some puzzles, including a map of the U.S., and some games. Each time he opened a present, his eyes grew bigger and he giggled and started jumping up and down. This caused tremendous anguish for Benjamin, who didn't understand why Bo was unwrapping all these wonderful presents and Ben couldn't unwrap anything. We finally had to let Ben open one, which generated complaints from Jack and Annie. I explained this was Tong and Bo's only Christmas and reminded them that they would have three Christmases as usual: one on Christmas Eve at my parents' house; one at our house on Christmas morning; and one at Allen's parents at noon on Christmas.

We had some cookies, and then our families said goodbye to Khanh, Tong, and Bo. In every letter Khanh has written me from Vermont, she has always asked if our parents and my sister were well.

The kids were so wound up, it was hard to get them settled down and ready for bed. Tong and Bo wanted to play with their new toys, but we insisted they read for twenty minutes before bed instead. We had tried to get them in the habit of reading before bed every night.

While the children were reading, I put on my pajamas and bathrobe. I looked out the window in awe as stars twinkled all over the sky like glitter. I couldn't resist stepping outside, so I went out on the deck and inhaled a deep breath of cold, fresh air. There wasn't a cloud in the sky. It was such a glorious night that I was torn between my body begging me to go back into the warmth and my heart pulling like a magnet to keep me outside in the beauty of the night sky. As my body started to win out, I heard a quiet knock on the glass door. Startled, I jumped and turned around to see Tong with his huge smile waving at me through the glass. I opened the door and greeted him warmly. "Hi, Tong, do you want me to help you read?"

"No, Sandy. No read," he shook his head. He walked outside and looked out at the sky. "Ohhhh," he said, as he slowly moved his head from one side of the panorama to the other. We stood in silence. He also seemed hypnotized by the beauty. "Tomorrow go to Vermont?" he asked.

"Yes, Tong, tomorrow you are going on the airplane to Vermont."

"Afraid," he said with a serious look.

"You're afraid?"

"Yes."

"Why are you afraid, Tong? It will all work out just fine."

"Ummmm, afraid Chicago."

"You're afraid of Chicago?"

"Yes."

"Oh, don't worry about it, Tong. A lady from the airlines. You know airplane?" He nodded his head. "Lady from airplane will help you in Chicago."

"Oh," he said.

"Lady very nice."

"Oh, no English," he pointed to his mouth.

"I know you don't know much English, Tong, but the lady will make sure you get on the right airplane. You have my telephone number, right?"

"Yes, in book."

"If you are afraid in Chicago, you call me. I will stay at home by the telephone. I will fly on an airplane to Chicago if you need me, O.K.?"

"You fly Chicago?"

"Only if lady does not help. If you are lost. Do you understand lost?"

"No. Lost?"

"Cannot find airplane?"

"Yes, cannot find airplane? Lady help."

"Yes, if lady will not help." I shook my head back and forth. "You call me and I will help."

"Yes," he nodded his head and shivered. "Very cold."

"Yes, very cold," I laughed. As Tong gazed out at the sky, I watched him being torn by the same forces I experienced—the warmth of the house and the beauty of the night.

"Tong, see the moon?" I pointed.

"Yes, moon?"

"Yes, moon. You have moon in Vietnam, too."

"Yes, moon in Vietnam."

"Tong, that moon, see? That moon is same moon your mother, father, and brothers see in Vietnam. You understand? Same moon."

"Same? Ummmm no understand."

"Ummmm identical? Ummmm not different?"

"Not different?"

"That moon is in Vietnam too."

"No," he chuckled. "Not in Vietnam, too," he shook his head.

"Yes. But daylight now in Vietnam. But when night comes, your family in Vietnam sees same moon as me in Boise and you in Vermont. Your mother, you, and I all see same moon," I said slowly.

"Nooo," he sighed.

"Yes, same moon. On map your mother in Vietnam, me in Boise, and you in Vermont all very far away. You understand?"

"Yes, Vietnam far away from Boise."

"Yes, and Boise far away from Vermont."

"Yes."

"Only far away on map. In our heart. You remember heart?" I put my hand over mine.

"Oh, yes, heart," he put his hand over his.

"On map Vietnam, Boise, Vermont, very far away. In heart, your mother in Vietnam, me," I pointed to my heart, "and you," I said pointing to his heart, "not far away. You understand?"

"Yes, my mother, Sandy, Tong heart not far away."

"Yes!" I exclaimed giving him a hug. "Yes. And Tong, when you look at the moon in Vermont, your mother in Vietnam, and I see the same moon. Not so far away."

"Oh yes, moon not far away."

"That's right Tong. When you miss your family. Understand miss?"

"Miss my family. Yes."

"When you miss your family, go outside at night and look at moon. Same moon in Vietnam. Not so far away."

"Yes," he smiled as his voice faded away.

"I love you, Tong," I put my hand on his head and kissed it.

"I love you, Sandy," he said laying his head on my shoulder.

I wanted to cry but knew I couldn't. There are some moments when the feelings are too strong to allow your body to let them escape in the form of tears: tears only serve to weaken the emotion by letting it escape, and I didn't want to lose any of the emotion that night.

"Cold," Tong broke the silence with a shiver.

"Yes, cold," I agreed. "We'd better go in or we'll turn into ice sculptures."

"Ice sculptures? No understand."

"Never mind, I'm not going to explain it to you tonight. I'm too tired. Let's go to bed."

Allen set the alarm for five o'clock to make sure we got everyone up and packed in time to catch the plane. I didn't have any problem falling asleep. I just had trouble staying asleep from about three o'clock on for fear of missing the alarm.

DAY 20: *The Parting and the Gift of Love*

I didn't wait for the alarm to go off. Instead I got out of bed at four thirty and put some coffee on. I decided to get myself ready before waking anyone else. Allen heard me fussing around in the bathroom and came stumbling in. He didn't say anything. He just staggered past me with his eyes three-quarters closed and got in the shower.

I got a cup of coffee, then knocked lightly on Khanh's door. There was no answer, so I opened it slowly. Khanh and Bo were both sound asleep, on top of the covers in their usual position. Bo had his parka and shoes on. Khanh opened her eyes, looked at me, and grinned. Before I could say anything, she sat up and shook Bo, telling him to wake up.

"Good morning!" I said, trying to sound wide awake.

Khanh nodded her head and smiled. "Bo, it's time to get up," I cheerfully said. "Why do you have your coat and shoes on?" I laughed.

He moaned and hid his head under the pillow. "We don't have much time, O.K.?" I told Khanh, pointing to my watch. I went upstairs to wake Tong. Nobody was in his bed so I looked down the hall and noticed the bathroom light was on. I knocked on the door and he opened it.

"Good morning, Tong," I greeted him.

"Good morning, Sandy," he cheerfully said.

"You're up early."

"Yes, wake up early."

Tong packed his toothbrush and comb in his backpack, then took his bag downstairs. Allen and

Tong loaded the boxes, backpacks, and bags in the van.

"I'll go wake the kids now. They can go to the airport in their pajamas," I said.

I went in and whispered to Jack. "Honey, it's time to take our refugees to the airport."

"Mom, can't I stay home? I'm too tired," he moaned.

"You don't want to see them off?"

"Mom, I can just tell them goodbye now. I want to go back to sleep," he whined.

"All right. You go downstairs and tell them goodbye then."

I went into Annie's room to wake her up, and she started crying because she was too tired. "I don't want to get up," she squealed.

"Do you want to stay home with Jack? He went downstairs to tell our refugees goodbye, and then he's going back to bed."

"Yeah, I want to do that too," she agreed. She stumbled out of bed and went downstairs. I went in and picked Benjamin up out of his baby crib, wrapping him in his blanket. He didn't even stir. We went downstairs where Jack and Annie were giving Khanh, Tong, and Bo hugs. Everyone except Tong was so tired I wasn't sure if they realized what was really going on.

"Come on, we have to go," Allen encouraged. "We're going to miss the plane if we don't hurry up."

"Jack, you have Grandma's phone number if you need anything, right?"

"Yup. Annie and I are going back to sleep now."

"All right. We'll be back in about an hour. You be sure and call Grandma if you need anything."

"O.K. Goodbye, Tong and Bo." Jack waved to them as he went down the hall.

"Goodbye Khanh and Tong and Bo," Annie said with a sad face. "We'll miss you."

"Goodbye, Jack and Annie," Tong waved and smiled.

Bo said goodbye to them in Vietnamese and waved.

It was silent most of the way to the airport until I said anxiously, "Do you have the tickets?"

"Yes, I have the tickets."

Allen dropped us off at the front door and hauled the boxes to the ticket counter. I stood in line while he went and parked the car.

When it was our turn to check in, the clerk looked at the tickets then glanced at me with a puzzled look and asked, "Are you the Trinhs?"

"Oh, no," I laughed. "They're over there." I pointed to Khanh, Tong, and Bo sitting on a bench.

"Oh, they look more like the Trinhs," she laughed.

"Do you have any special instructions on your computer?" I asked.

"Yes, it says that they don't speak English and need an escort to their connecting plane in Chicago."

"Good. Are you absolutely sure someone will be there?"

"Absolutely," she said firmly. She repeated their seat assignments and gave us the gate number. "They'll be loading in about ten minutes," she said pleasantly. "They should have a nice flight this morning."

"Thank you very much," I said and walked over to Khanh, Tong, and Bo. Allen had just come in with Benjamin, who peered at me with half-open eyes.

"Are we all set?" Allen asked.

"We're ready. She said they would start loading in about ten minutes."

Tong and Bo were carrying the teddy bears that we had given them when they arrived, and Khanh had her bag. As I walked behind them, I thought of how similar they looked to when they first arrived. Although they looked the same, in my heart they were completely different people. They were family. It wasn't possible that I'd only known them twenty days.

When we reached the gate, Khanh, Tong, and Bo sat down. I had a knot in my stomach. "Oh, Sweetheart, I feel awful sending them clear across the country on their own. What if nobody helps them in Chicago? They don't even speak English."

"They'll be just fine. There will be someone in Chicago to help them change planes. There's nothing to worry about. Remember, they managed to get all the way from Vietnam to Boise by themselves."

"I know. But I feel responsible for them now. I'd feel a lot better if they spoke English."

"Quit worrying, they'll be fine."

Suddenly, Bo jumped up and ran to the other side of the room giggling. He pointed to the balloon that Annie had accidentally lost the day our family arrived. It was still full of air.

"I better give them some money," I suddenly told Allen. "They might need some to call me in Chicago." I reached in my purse and found two ten dollar bills and three one dollar bills. I gave Khanh and Tong each ten dollars and Bo three dollars.

"Thank you," Tong said.

"Thank you," Khanh repeated. Bo just looked up at me and smiled.

"We will begin general boarding for flight number 463 to Chicago in a few minutes. We would like to begin pre-boarding now for anyone who needs special help or adults traveling with children."

"Oh, my God, that's us. It's already time to board!" I said, panicked. I wasn't ready. My head was spinning. I was sure I had forgotten something. I hadn't had time to tell them goodbye. I looked over at my refugees and saw Allen giving Bo a hug. I felt like a ghost watching the scene from another world. Then Allen gave Tong a hug and said, "Tong, you study hard at school." Tong smiled at Allen and answered, "Yes, study hard."

"Goodbye, Khanh," Allen said, giving her a big hug. She hugged him back, and I could see tears rolling down her cheeks. I stared at them as if in a trance.

"Aren't you going to tell them goodbye, Mom?" Allen asked.

"Yeah, I'll help them get on the plane to make sure they get in the right seats," I said, as the words stumbled out of my mouth. "Can you take Ben?" I asked Allen, suddenly realizing I was still holding him.

"Sure."

I walked with my refugees to the lady collecting the tickets at the top of the on-ramp. "Can I have your tickets?" she asked sharply.

"Oh, yes," I stammered, looking around to see who had the tickets. Khanh handed them calmly to the lady and walked with Tong and Bo down the ramp. "I'm going to help them on the plane to make sure they get in their proper seats," I said.

"No, you're not. You can't go on the plane unless

you have a ticket," the lady said in a snotty voice. Khanh, Tong, and Bo were almost to the end of the ramp, and I was stuck on the other end. The lady started taking tickets from the next passengers, and I noticed that a long line had formed behind us. What do I do? I was bewildered! Tears filled my eyes.

"Goodbye, Bo," I yelled and waved. "Goodbye, Tong," I cried. "Goodbye, Khanh." My voice faded. They turned around and waved, tears streaming down their faces. Soon they were lost in a long line of passengers waiting to board the plane. My first reaction was that I felt cheated. I hadn't gotten to really tell them goodbye the way I wanted to.

"Come on, Sweetheart. You're blocking the way for passengers to get on," I heard Allen say as he led me to the window. "Let's stand here so we can watch them take off."

"She wouldn't let me help them on the plane," I said, still in a state of shock.

"I know, but they'll do just fine."

"I know, but I didn't get to tell them goodbye," my voice drifted off. I stared at the airplane, hoping to catch a glimpse of them but the windows on the plane were too small. As I stared out the window, a feeling of relief swept over me. I had dreaded having to tell them goodbye, and through circumstance I had managed to avoid the dreadful parting. Somehow my heart felt light. I had escaped a tearful departure, which I knew would tear at my heart and fill me with mourning for at least the rest of the day and probably tomorrow—Christmas day. Now instead of feeling awful, I felt relieved I had escaped a sorrowful departure and felt at peace that my family was going to live with their cousins.

"Mommy, hold me," Ben whined with outstretched arms.

I looked at him with his big brown eyes longing for me to hold him. "Come here, Sweetheart," I whispered as my voice cracked. I put my arms around him and he laid his head on my shoulder. "I love you, Benjamin," I said softly, laying my head on top of his.

We watched the airplane slowly taxi onto the runway. Then it left our viewing range for a few minutes until we saw it speeding again in front of us. As the wheels left the ground, I breathed a sigh of relief. We watched as the plane steadily climbed into the sky. It was heading east where the sun would soon be rising. I looked over to the west and noticed that the moon was still in the sky, claiming dominion over its territory for one more hour.

* * * * * * *

On Christmas day, all of our family gathered together to celebrate and open presents. As I took part in our Christmas rituals—singing carols, enjoying a feast, and attending church—I felt like a part of our family was missing. I received many beautiful presents that year; however, the present I will cherish forever was our gift from Vietnam.

Epilogue

It has been almost five years since our refugees left for Vermont, and another Christmas approaches without Tong being reunited with his family. During this time Tong has regularly corresponded with his family, but until recently was unable to speak to them. Six months ago he received a call from his mother and father. He called me shortly afterwards to share the news. His mood was one of excitement, relief, and sadness.

Two years ago, I made airline reservations, secured a passport, and obtained his school's blessing for Tong to miss a month of classes so that he could fly to Vietnam with a friend of his cousins. At the last minute, Tong received a letter from his parents telling him not to come. Tong's parents had heard of numerous cases of Vietnamese children being accompanied by non-relatives to Vietnam, with the person stealing the child's passport and returning to America with one of his own relatives rather than the child.

I have watched Tong grow from a brave young boy to a proud seventeen-year-old man. During that time he has experienced the political and religious freedom which Americans value and has lived with the security of good housing, nutrition and health care. But I have learned that freedom and security are not a substitute for a family's love.

Tong has returned to Boise several times, for both Christmas and summer vacations. We have not seen Khanh or Bo since they left for Vermont, but we talk to them at least monthly on the telephone. Tong calls me weekly at my office to update me on his school work and other activities.

Tong is now in the ninth grade. He was able to skip the eighth grade because he worked hard to excel in school. Tong has already attended school longer than any one else in his family. He is determined to go to college and study engineering. He hopes one day to move back to Vietnam and support his family. Tong has enriched many lives since he arrived in America. He has a beautiful voice and sings Latin and Spanish solos in the school choir. He has won a number of awards for his fundraising efforts on behalf of the choir. He currently works as a tour guide in a museum. Bo is an eleven-year-old fourth-grader. The little boy I remember who would barely speak English at all now talks to me over the phone without even a trace of an accent.

Khanh's baby boy, Qui, is now four. Khanh's husband in the Philipine refugee camp committed suicide shortly after receiving pictures of Qui's second birthday party. I wonder how much more tragedy Khanh will have to suffer in her life.

Khanh works for a company that makes ski goggles. During the winter, after working all week, she brings goggles home for her, Tong, and Bo to assemble. The family lives in a one-bedroom apartment. Their cousins live in an apartment above them in the same building. Like most Vietnamese immigrants, Khanh and her family have worked hard to learn English, adapt to our culture and support themselves.

We have corresponded with Tong's family in Vietnam over the years. My hope is that one day we will go to Ho Chi Minh City and visit them. I also hope that an American businessman who reads this book might volunteer to accompany Tong to Vietnam and safely back to the United States.

Friends and previous readers of this book have often commented that our refugees were lucky to have us as their sponsors. However, I know that it is me and my family who are the lucky ones. In their short time with us, and in the days that have passed since, Khanh, Tong, and Bo have given us something that no amount of money can buy—a renewed appreciation of family, and a friendship based in love. What greater gift can one give?

About the Author

Sandy Dalton was born and raised in Idaho, currently living in Boise with her husband and three children. She attended Boise State University and graduated with a B.S. in accounting from Virginia Tech. She is a Vice President and million dollar producer with Merrill Lynch.

Sandy has been active in many nonprofit organizations, currently serving as Board President of Luther Heights Bible Camp in the Sawtooth Mountains, on the Board of Roadway Ministries, and on several committees.

She and her family enjoy basketball, baseball, swimming, skiing, fishing, and the beauty of the Idaho mountains.

The author welcomes comments and suggestions
for subsequent editions of
A Christmas Gift From Vietnam.
Please write c/o Four Sisters Press, LLP,
PO Box 1924, Boise, ID 83701.
Dalton@micron.net

Addditional copies of *A Christmas Gift From Vietnam*
can be found in fine bookstores nationwide or
directly from the publisher.

If ordering direct, please include a check for $18.95
(book @ $15.95 plus a shipping/handling charge of
$3.00). Idaho residents should send $19.75
(book @ $15.95, shipping/handling $3.00,
and Idaho tax $.80).

Send your name, address, and check to:

A Christmas Gift From Vietnam
Four Sisters Press, LLP
PO Box 1924
Boise, ID 83701

To place orders using MasterCard or Visa,
please call 1-800-448-8207

MANAGEMENT CENTER /APO 96309/ Viết tắt là (AMMC) – Giấy nhận Việc ngày 27 – 09 – 1968.

Chỉ huy trưởng tổ Vị là Anh Tá ORMAN.E HICK (COLOI ORMAN E. HICK COMANDANT). Đơn Vị đóng tại Sân bay TÂN SƠN NHẤT – Sài gòn. Ngày nghỉ việc: 28.3.1973

2/ Trần Sanh

Năm Sinh: 29 – 11 – 1940   Nơi Sinh: Sài gòn.

– Gia nhập Quân Lực Việt Nam Cộng Hòa, binh chủng Bộ binh, C Trung Sĩ I, Số Quân 60/142,148. Nơi làm Việc tại Quân y Viện Cộng Hòa – Sài gòn. Cư ngụ: 156/1 đ. Nhiêu Tứ, F07, Q. Phú n

3/ Trần tuấn Quốc

Sinh Năm: 18 – 07 – 1973   Nơi Sinh: tỉnh Gia định, Sài Gò

Nghề nghiệp: Đạp Xích Lô.

Cư ngụ: 156/1 tường nhiêu Tứ, F07, Quận Phú nhuận, TP. HCM

4/ Trần Quốc Bảo

Sinh năm: 13 – 12 – 1974   Nơi Sinh: tỉnh Giadịnh, Sài

Hiện Cư ngụ: 156/1 Nhiêu Tứ, đường 07, Q. Phú nhuận, Tp. Hơn

5/ Trần Bảo Minh

Sinh Năm: 29 – 12 – 1980   Nơi Sinh: tỉnh Gia định – Sài

Hiện Cư ngụ: 156/1 đ. Nhiêu Tứ, F07, Q. Phú nhuận, TP. HCM.

– Nếu Sau đây còn thiếu những loại giấy tờ gì hoặc nh tiêu kiện cần thiết khác, xin Ông Bà Vui lòng Báo cho chúng tô Chúng tôi Sẽ cố gắng Cung Cấp thêm để Ông bà được thuận Tiệ trong Việc lập hồ Sơ Bảo Lãnh.

Trong khi Chờ đợi, một lần nữa Chúng tôi Xin Gửi lời c inh Mến đến Ông Bà Và Xin nhận nơi đây lòng thành thật Bi n của Toàn thể gia đình Chúng tôi.

Chúng tôi rất mong Sự giúp đỡ và trả lời của Ông Bà)

Chào Ôi

Nguyễn thị Cẩm Lệ